AMERICA

AN ILLUSION OF FREEDOM

DR. RICHARD A. NIXON
B.S. PHYSICS
J.D. LAW

i

AMERICA - AN ILLUSION OF FREEDOM

Copyright © 2010 by Dr. Richard A. Nixon

Library of Congress Control Number 2011924640

First Printing December 2011

Second Printing April 2014

Third Printing June 2018

Fourth Printing November 2025

ISBN   978-0-615-45318-7

Published in the United States of America by

Dr. Richard A. Nixon

pres37th @ aol.com

Printed on recycled paper

IN RECOGNITION

Of those who signed a piece of paper called the Declaration
of Independence, but of those men . . .

Five were captured and executed by the British for treason;

Nine died fighting on the battlefield;

Twelve lost everything they had to the British fires;

Of those sage old men who authored the Constitution with
the intent of creating and limiting the federal government to only
those powers expressly granted to it and to retain or reserve all
other powers to the States and their respective People;

Of all others who fought and especially to those who were
injured and died to preserve and maintain those freedoms granted
by such Constitution;

Of those who unwittingly remained reticent while our
freedoms were being usurped, not by an enemy army but by our
own Supreme Court;

Of those who intend to reinstate those freedoms lost and
restore this nation to its status as envisioned by our Founding
Fathers . . . a very limited federal government and the vital
rebirth of the powerful 10th Amendment;

This Work has as its sole purpose this Renaissance . . .

IN GRATITUDE

To all my colleagues, friends and relatives who supported my

efforts and tolerated my incessant reference to "my book" . . .

and to the growing recognition that the body of law comprising

"constitutional law" only asymptotically approaches the actual text

of the Constitution and that such law resides entirely and

exclusively within the prolific, collective minds of the Justices...

CONTENTS

PROLOGUE

Once upon a time there was a convention. It was held in Philadelphia, Pennsylvania in 1787. This convention produced a document, the United States Constitution. This document in turn, created the federal government, defined its three separate branches, and defined and limited its functions, making it clear that all power not granted to the newly formed government was to remain resident in the states and the People. The convention attendees are sometimes referred to as the Founders.

The Founders of this country were men to whom we owe a great debt. Their generosity and benevolence was unique among men forming a government. Rather than taking all the power for themselves by forming a strong federal government, they chose to create a government based upon a compact or agreement with the People. It was agreed that the federal government would hold only certain enumerated powers. All other power was to remain in the respective States and the People.

Our Forefathers believed that ultimately the People should decide the laws and conditions under which they would live.

The agreement to which we refer is of course the United States Constitution. It guarantees that certain rights will not be taken from the People by the federal government. It is a remarkable document and one from which this country has considerably departed. This departure, which has cost the People of this country countless freedoms, is the subject of this Work.

This Work is written for the layperson. It requires no legal background to understand and is concerned with the most significant instances of the Supreme Court's misinterpreting and disrespecting the U.S. Constitution.

This Work is not intended to be an exhaustive treatise on the U.S. Constitution, but rather a highlight of numerous of the laws governing our everyday lives . . . laws not written by our elected representatives, but by judges, accountable only to themselves, in clear violation of the Constitution they purport to uphold.

It is anticipated that with a reading of this Work, the reader will come away with an enlightened determination to restore those freedoms lost ... by wresting them from the government and restoring them to the People.

The federal government has violated the agreement upon which this country was founded. It has breached the Constitution to the damage of all its citizens. The government must remedy the situation and restore these freedoms to the People - perhaps without an armed revolution ...

"The powers of the legislature are defined and limited; and that those limits may not be mistaken or forgotten, the constitution is written . . ."   Marbury v. Madison (1803)

CHAPTER 1

THE CONSPIRACY'S GENESIS

The Constitution was ratified in 1789 and the Supreme Court wasted little time, once the ink was dry, in improperly imposing its will upon the People; the People about whose liberty the Constitution was created to uphold.

Our Federal Government, in the guise of the Supreme Court, began its tour of tyranny by announcing in *Marbury v. Madison* (1803) that the judicial branch had the power of judicial review, i.e., power to declare acts or statutes enacted by Congress in violation of the Constitution and therefore void. *No such power is expressly granted to the Federal Courts by the Constitution..*

The U.S. Supreme Court, under the stewardship of Chief Justice Marshall *granted itself* the power of judicial review, thereby declaring itself the final arbiter of what the Constitution meant. Hence, subsequently, the federal courts could declare acts of the Congress unconstitutional, thereby erecting themselves superior to the other two branches of government and ultimately dictators to the People. Thus a judicial oligarchy was formed, as predicted and feared by none other than Thomas Jefferson.

The *Marbury* case:

U.S. SUPREME COURT
MARBURY v. MADISON
5 U.S. 137 (1803)

John Marshall was Secretary of State in the Adam's administration when he took office as Chief Justice on January 31,1801. He continued as acting Secretary of State until the last day of the Adam's administration, March 3,1801. William Marbury was one of a number of persons who had been appointed justices of the peace in the District of Columbia and who were confirmed by the Senate on March 3. His commission remained in Marshall's office undelivered when the new administration took over. President Jefferson directed his Secretary of State, James Madison, to withhold several commissions, including that of Marbury. Marbury then brought this suit against Madison, taking the unusual step of initiating the action in the Supreme Court, invoking its original jurisdiction.

The-then Chief Justice John Marshall held that the Supreme Court lacked jurisdiction to hear the matter but ignored its own finding and declared itself King, by holding:

"The s/b constitution vests the whole judicial power of the United States in one supreme court, and such inferior courts as congress shall, from time to time, ordain and establish.[Article III]

"In the distribution of this power it is declared that 'the supreme court shall have original jurisdiction in all cases affecting ambassadors, other public ministers and consuls, and those in which a state shall be a party. In all other cases, the supreme court shall have appellate jurisdiction . . .

"The powers of the legislature are defined and limited; and that those limits may not be mistaken or forgotten, the s/b constitution is written. To what purpose are powers limited, and to what purpose is that limitation committed to writing; if these limits may, at any time, be passed by those intended to be restrained? The distinction between a government with limited and unlimited powers is abolished, if those limits do not confine the persons on whom they are imposed, and if acts prohibited and acts allowed are of equal obligation. It is a proposition too plain to be contested, that the constitution controls any legislative act repugnant to it; or, that the legislature may alter the constitution by an ordinary act."

Brilliant words by Chief Justice Marshall, but, amazingly, applied only to the legislature and not to his own court. As stated earlier, the s/b Constitution did not grant the Supreme Court the power of judicial review. By his logic, since the power of judicial review was not written, it was not granted. If it was not granted, it therefore should not have been exercised by the Court. However, Marshall ignored this logic and brazenly went on to hold:

"It is emphatically the province and duty of the judicial department to say what the law is. Those who apply the rule to particular cases, must of necessity expound and interpret that rule. If two laws conflict with each other, the courts must decide on the operation of each. So if a law be in opposition to the constitution: if both the law and the constitution apply to a particular case, so that the court must either decide that case conformably to the law, disregarding the constitution; or conformably to the constitution, disregarding the law: the court must determine which of these conflicting rules governs the case. This is of the very essence of judicial duty."

Thus it began, the U.S. Supreme Court's voiding acts of Congress enacted by duly elected representatives of the People and setting the stage for future Supreme Court decisions to replace the actual words of the Constitution with doctrines and theories concocted by the Court and bearing no relation to the s/b Constitution.

Thus, laws were being made by a body of men, with life tenure, accountable to no one.

2.

In order to avoid autocracy, the powers of the federal government were to be distributed among three branches, the Legislative branch, defined in Article I; the Executive branch, found in Article II, and the Judiciary, found in Article III. This was to ensure that no one branch would be superior to any of the others.

However, as the country has developed and the U.S. Supreme Court has been called-upon to decide matters before it, the Court, beginning with the *Marbury* case, as stated above, assumed power not granted it by the Constitution. The Court continued its own expansion by literally rewriting the Constitution.

If in fact, the three branches of our federal government were intended to be equal, it does not comport with the concept of equality to permit one branch to essentially overrule the actions of another branch. It is submitted that said power assumed by the U.S. Supreme Court in fact creates an inherently unequal form of government with the U.S. Supreme Court's being the superior or supreme branch of the federal government.

Thomas Jefferson had a few things to say about the *Marbury* case in particular, and judicial review in general. The following are just a few:

Mr.Jefferson's thoughts:
"The question whether the judges are invested with exclusive authority to decide on the constitutionality of a law has been heretofore a subject of consideration with me in the exercise of official duties. Certainly there is not a word in the Constitution which has given that power to them more than to the Executive or Legislative branches." --Thomas Jefferson to W. H. Torrance, 1815.

"But the Chief Justice says, 'There must be an ultimate arbiter somewhere.' True, there must; but does that prove it is either party? The ultimate arbiter is the people of the Union, assembled by their deputies in convention, at the call of Congress or of two-thirds of the States. Let them decide to which they mean to give an authority claimed by two of their organs. And it has been the peculiar wisdom and felicity of our Constitution, to have provided this peaceable appeal, where that of other nations is at once to force." Thomas Jefferson to William Johnson, 1823.

"The Constitution... meant that its coordinate branches should be checks on each other. But the opinion which gives to the judges the right to decide what laws are constitutional and what not, not only for themselves in their own sphere of action but for the Legislature and Executive also in their spheres, would make the Judiciary a despotic branch." --Thomas Jefferson to Abigail Adams, 1804.

"To consider the judges as the ultimate arbiters of all constitutional questions [is] a very dangerous doctrine indeed, and one which would place us under the despotism of an oligarchy. Our judges are as honest as other men and not more so. They have with others the same passions for party, for power, and the privilege of their corps. Their maxim is *boni judicis est ampliare jurisdictionem* [good justice is broad jurisdiction], and their power the more dangerous as they are in office for life and not responsible, as the other functionaries are, to the elective control. The Constitution has erected no such single tribunal, knowing that to whatever hands confided, with the corruptions of time and party, its members would become despots. It has more wisely made all the departments co-equal and co-sovereign within themselves." --Thomas Jefferson to William C. Jarvis, 1820.

"In denying the right [the Supreme Court usurps] of exclusively explaining the Constitution, I go further than [others] do, if I understand rightly [this] quotation from the Federalist of an opinion that 'the judiciary is the last resort in relation to the other departments of the government, but not in relation to the rights of the parties to the compact under which the judiciary is derived.' If this opinion be sound, then indeed is our Constitution a complete *felo de se* [act of suicide]. For intending to establish three departments, coordinate and independent, that they might check and balance one another, it has given, according to this opinion, to one of them alone the right to prescribe rules for the government of the others, and to that one, too, which is unelected by and independent of the nation. For experience has already shown that the impeachment it has provided is not even a scare-crow... The Constitution on this hypothesis is a mere thing of wax in the hands of the judiciary, which they may twist and shape into any form they please." Jefferson to Spencer Roane, 1819.

"This member of the Government was at first considered as the most harmless and helpless of all its organs. But it has proved that the power of declaring what the law is, *ad libitum*, by sapping and mining slyly and without alarm the foundations of the Constitution, can do what open force would not dare to attempt." --Thomas Jefferson to Edward Livingston, 1825.

"My construction of the Constitution is... that each department is truly independent of the others and has an equal right to decide for itself what is the meaning of the Constitution in the cases submitted to its action; and especially where it is to act ultimately and without appeal." --Thomas Jefferson to Spencer Roane, 1819.

"Nothing in the Constitution has given [the judges] a right to decide for the Executive, more than to the Executive to decide for them. Both magistrates are equally independent in the sphere of action assigned to them." --Thomas Jefferson to Abigail Adams, 1804.

"Each of the three departments has equally the right to decide for itself what is its duty under the Constitution without regard to what the others may have decided for themselves under a similar question." --Thomas Jefferson to Spencer Roane, 1819.

"The judges certainly have more frequent occasion to act on constitutional questions, because the laws of *meum* and *tuum* and of criminal action, forming the great mass of the system of law, constitute their particular department. When the legislative or executive functionaries act unconstitutionally, they are responsible to the people in their elective capacity. The exemption of the judges from that is quite dangerous enough... The people themselves,... [with] their discretion [informed] by education, [are] the true corrective of abuses of constitutional power." --Thomas Jefferson to William C. Jarvis, 1820.

"[How] to check these unconstitutional invasions of... rights by the Federal judiciary? Not by impeachment in the first instance, but by a strong protestation of both houses of Congress that such and such doctrines advanced by the Supreme Court are contrary to the Constitution; and if afterwards they relapse into the same heresies, impeach and set the whole adrift. For what was the government divided into three branches, but that each should watch over the others and oppose their usurpations?" --Thomas Jefferson to Nathaniel Macon, 1821.

Hence, according to Jefferson, judicial review is clearly contrary to the framers of the Constitution. Thomas Jefferson argued that if the framers had intended such a formidable power to reside in the judiciary, it would clearly have been granted expressly. This power does not exist expressly in the U.S. Constitution.

Jefferson predicted what has indeed come to pass . . . the judiciary has become the most powerful and dangerous of the three federal branches as it alone enjoys life tenure and decides which law, federal or state, is or is not in compliance with the U.S. Constitution; and in exercising such power is accountable to no one.

Federalist Papers:

The Federalist Papers were written and published during the years 1787 and 1788 in several New York State newspapers to persuade New York voters to ratify the proposed constitution.

In total, the Federalist Papers consist of 85 essays outlining how this new government would operate and why this type of government was the best choice for the United States of America. All of the essays were signed "PUBLIUS" and the actual authors of some are under dispute, but the general consensus is that Alexander Hamilton wrote 52, James Madison wrote 28, and John Jay contributed the remaining five.

In Federalist no.48, Madison states that it is evident that none of the three branches of government "...ought to possess, directly or indirectly, an overruling influence over the others, in the administration of their respective powers..."

Hence, Marshall did precisely what was prohibited by the constitution he was purporting to interpret. He grabbed this power for the federal courts and neither We the People, nor our representatives, have yet to demand its return to its proper owners- the legislature and the People..

Some argue that the Constitution is a living, breathing document that must be interpreted by the court's using current values, not those of the 18th century.

The Constitution addresses this issue . . . Article V of the Constitution provides the exclusive manner by which the Constitution is to be amended. This method includes the People and their duly-elected representatives. It includes neither the Supreme Court nor any other court...and this method has been employed some 27 times throughout our American history. It is neither necessary nor proper for the Supreme Court to amend the Constitution. *In fact, it's unconstitutional for it to do so!* But they do so unabashed and unchecked...the Supreme Court has become our "mastah." *We are all on the plantation.*

Marbury can also be criticized on the grounds that it was improper for the Court to consider any issues beyond jurisdiction. After concluding that the Court lacked jurisdiction in the case, the further review regarding the substantive issues presented was improper.

Further, Chief Justice Marshall should have recused himself on the grounds that he was still acting Secretary of State at the time the commissions were to be delivered and it was his brother, James Marshall, who was charged with delivering a number of the commissions.

In conclusion, as of 1803, the Supreme Court ignored the fact that the three branches of the federal government were to be co-equal and instead declared itself superior to the other two by granting to itself the power of judicial review; a power not granted it by the Constitution.

What's more, since the Justices of the Supreme Court are appointed for life, by the President, they are accountable to no one and their decisions are final; they are a collective King . . . unless the solution to this dilemma, as offered by this Work, is adopted.

As stated by Marshall in his opinion,

"The constitution vests the whole judicial power of the United States in one supreme court, and such inferior courts as congress shall, from time to time, ordain and establish. [Article III]."

One might ask why Congress failed to react to the *Marbury* decision, which essentially emasculated Congress and rendered it subservient to the Supreme Court. Congress refrained from reining-in the Supreme Court via Article III, although Congress had and has the power to do so.

Article III, § 2.2 states, in pertinent part: " In all cases... [where] the supreme Court [has] appellate jurisdiction, both as to Law and Fact, [such jurisdiction is] with such Exceptions, and under such Regulations as the Congress shall make."

The answer to this question is the subject of Chapter 2, wherein the Supreme Court returns the favor to Congress for their reticence, by rewriting the "necessary and proper" clause of Article I, section 8 of the U.S. Constitution and thereby forever expanding the role of their co-conspirator, Congress, in our daily lives.

6.

" That the judicial power of the United States will lean strongly in favor of the general government, and will give such an explanation to the Constitution as will favor an extension of its jurisdiction, is very evident from a variety of considerations..." Brutus (1788)

CHAPTER 2

CONSUMMATION OF THE GRAND CONSPIRACY

This chapter concerns itself with two cases, *McCulloch*, 1819, and its modern-day counterpart, *Kelo*, of 2005. In both instances, the court substituted its own words for the actual text of the Constitution. Thus the rewriting has spanned just less than two hundred years, unabated, with very few exceptions.

The Supreme Court delivered the second of the one-two punch to the body of the American People by handing down the *McCulloch v. Maryland* case in 1819. In this case, Congress had gone well beyond the confines of their defined authority as clearly stated in the "enumerated powers" clause of the Constitution. Congress created a national bank and the Supreme Court rewrote the "necessary and proper" clause of the Constitution permitting Congress to so do and to enact any law "appropriate" to its purpose.

As noted earlier, the only powers granted to congress by the Constitution are those explicitly enumerated in Article I, Section 8 of the Constitution. Authority to incorporate a national bank is not explicitly stated, therefore Congress neither had, nor has, such power.

In the *McCulloch* case, Chief Justice Marshall feigned humility by asserting "...On the Supreme Court of the United States has the constitution of our country devolved this important duty..." Hence, Marshall claims authority in the Supreme Court in *McCulloch* which he himself granted previously to the Supreme Court in *Marbury*, and then subsequently and disingenuously, claims that this authority simply "devolved" from the Constitution; a classic case of begging-the-question.

In *McCulloch*, Chief Justice Marshall correctly and actually admits that the government of the United States is limited in it's powers, i.e., that Congress can exercise only those powers granted to it. This is referred to as the doctrine of "enumerated powers." Chief Justice Marshall goes on to correctly state that where the United States government enacts laws pursuant to the Constitution, this is the supreme law of the land "...anything in the constitution or laws of any state to the contrary notwithstanding."

Article I, § 8, clause 18 states that congress has the power to enact that which is "necessary and proper" to the execution of the previous enumerated powers explicitly stated.

Chief Justice Marshall went on to redefine the word "necessary" as "appropriate", and by so doing he rewrote the Constitution, that is, even though the "necessary and proper" clause was intended to limit the method by which congress could enact the foregoing enumerated powers, Chief Justice Marshall, by redefining the word "necessary" actually expanded the power of Congress beyond that intended by the original framers of the Constitution.

The Founders intended, by enumerating the powers granted to the federal government, to reserve most power to the States and the People. This is explicitly stated in the 10th Amendment.

The 10th amendment states, "The powers not delegated to the United States by the Constitution, nor prohibited by it to the States, are reserved to the States respectively, or to the people."

In any event, after these two cases, *Marbury vs. Madison* and *McCulloch vs. Maryland*, the former giving total power to the Supreme Court to interpret the Constitution and to void acts of congress determined to be repugnant to the Constitution and the latter, granting expansive powers to Congress to enact any law convenient, rather than necessary and proper, to the functioning of the federal government, put the United States government in the position to expand their role in our lives. Congress has wasted no time in doing so, with the approval of their co-conspirator, the United States Supreme Court.

It is indeed hypocritical that Chief Justice Marshall, in the midst of rewriting the Constitution, or legislating from the bench, actually states that if they, the Supreme Court, were to define "necessary" to mean "necessary" and not merely "convenient" or "appropriate," would be to tread on legislative ground and concludes the thought by stating "...This court disclaims all pretensions to such a power".

In fact, Chief Justice Marshall strained to interpret the constitution to grant the United States government authority that it did not, and does not, possess.

The method of re-empowering the People, as originally intended, is to shift the power back *to* the states and indirectly *to* the People as the People have more impact on their local and state representatives than on their federal counterparts..

Unfortunately, Congress and the Supreme Court, since 1803, have taken power *from* the People. Their mutual intent was to shift power *from* the states and the people *to* the federal government by grossly misinterpreting the grandest of all documents, the United States Constitution.

Their disdain and disrespect for the Constitution has been nothing short of solemn mockery.

Here now, excerpts from the *McCulloch* case:

SUPREME COURT OF THE UNITED STATES
McCULLOCH v. MARYLAND
17 U.S 316 (1819)
MARSHALL, Chief Justice, delivered the opinion of the Court...

"The ...question is– has Congress the power to incorporate a bank?

"This Government is acknowledged by all to be one of enumerated powers. The principle that it can exercise only the powers granted to it would seem too apparent to have required to be enforced by all those arguments which its enlightened friends, while it was depending before the people, found it necessary to urge; that principle is now universally admitted. But the question respecting the extent of the powers actually granted is perpetually arising, and will probably continue to arise so long as our system shall exist. In discussing these questions, the conflicting powers of the General and State Governments must be brought into view, and the supremacy of their respective laws, when they are in opposition, must be settled.

"If any one proposition could command the universal assent of mankind, we might expect it would be this -- that the Government of the Union, though limited in its powers, is supreme within its sphere of action... The Government of the United States, then, though limited in its powers, is supreme, and its laws, when made in pursuance of the Constitution, form the supreme law of the land,'anything in the Constitution or laws of any State to the contrary notwithstanding.

"Among the enumerated powers, we do not find that of establishing a bank or creating a corporation. But there is no phrase in the instrument which, like the Articles of Confederation, excludes incidental or implied powers and which requires that everything granted shall be expressly and minutely described. Even the 10th Amendment, which was framed for the purpose of quieting the excessive jealousies which had been excited, omits the word "expressly," and declares only that the powers "not delegated to the United States, nor prohibited to the States, are reserved to the States or to the people," thus leaving the question whether the particular power which may become the subject of contest has been delegated to the one Government, or prohibited to the other, to depend on a fair construction of the whole instrument.

"The men who drew and adopted this amendment had experienced the embarrassments resulting from the insertion of this word in the Articles ...of Confederation, and probably omitted it to avoid those embarrassments. A Constitution, to contain an accurate detail of all the subdivisions of which its great powers will admit, and of all the means by which they may be carried into execution, would partake of the prolixity of a legal code, and could scarcely be embraced by the human mind. It would probably never be understood by the public.

"Its nature, therefore, requires that only its great outlines should be marked, its important objects designated, and the minor ingredients which compose those objects be deduced from the nature of the objects themselves. That this idea was entertained by the framers of the American Constitution is not only to be inferred from the nature of the instrument, but from the language. Why else were some of the limitations found in the 9th section of the 1st article introduced? It is also in some degree warranted by their having omitted to use any restrictive term which might prevent its receiving a fair and just interpretation. In considering this question, then, we must never forget that it is a Constitution we are expounding.

"Although, among the enumerated powers of Government, we do not find the word 'bank' or 'incorporation,' we find the great powers, to lay and collect taxes; to borrow money; to regulate commerce; to declare and conduct a war; and to raise and support armies and navies. The sword and the purse, all the external relations, and no inconsiderable portion of the industry of the nation are intrusted to its Government. It can never be pretended...that these vast powers draw after them others of inferior importance merely because they are inferior. Such an idea can never be advanced. But it may with great reason be contended that a Government intrusted with such ample powers, on the due execution of which the happiness and prosperity of the Nation so vitally depends, must also be intrusted with ample means for their execution.

"The power being given, it is the interest of the Nation to facilitate its execution. It can never be their interest, and cannot be presumed to have been their intention, to clog and embarrass its execution by withholding the most appropriate means. Throughout this vast republic, from the St. Croix to the Gulf of Mexico, from the Atlantic to the Pacific, revenue is to be collected and expended, armies are to be marched and supported. The exigencies of the Nation may require that the treasure raised in the north should be transported to the south that raised in the east, conveyed to the west, or that this order should be reversed. Is that construction of the Constitution to be preferred which would render these operations difficult, hazardous and expensive? Can we adopt that construction (unless the words imperiously require it) which would impute to the framers of that instrument, when granting these powers for the public good, the intention of impeding their exercise, by withholding a choice of means? If, indeed, such be the mandate of the Constitution, we have only to obey; but that instrument does not profess to enumerate the means by which the powers it confers may be executed; nor does it prohibit the creation of a corporation,...if the existence of such a being be essential, to the beneficial exercise of those powers. It is, then, the subject of fair inquiry how far such means may be employed.

"It is not denied that the powers given to the Government imply the ordinary means of execution. That, for example, of raising revenue and applying it to national purposes is admitted to imply the power of conveying money from place to place as the exigencies of the Nation may require, and of employing the usual means of conveyance. But it is denied that the Government has its choice of means, or that it may employ the most convenient means if, to employ them, it be necessary to erect a corporation. On what foundation does this argument rest?

On this alone: the power of creating a corporation is one appertaining to sovereignty, and is not expressly conferred on Congress.

"This is true. But all legislative powers appertain to sovereignty. The original power of giving the law on any subject whatever is a sovereign power, and if the Government of the Union is restrained from creating a corporation as a means for performing its functions, on the single reason that the creation of a corporation is an act of sovereignty, if the sufficiency of this reason be acknowledged, there would be some difficulty in sustaining the authority of Congress to pass other laws for the accomplishment of the same objects. The Government which has a right to do an act and has imposed on it the duty of performing that act must, according to the dictates of reason, be allowed to select the means, and those who contend that it may not select any appropriate means that one particular mode of effecting the object is excepted take upon themselves the burden of establishing that exception...

"But the Constitution of the United States has not left the right of Congress to employ the necessary means for the execution of the powers conferred on the Government to general reasoning. To its enumeration of powers is added that of making laws which shall be necessary and proper for carrying into execution the foregoing powers, and all other powers vested by this Constitution in the Government of the United States or in any department thereof....

"But the argument on which most reliance is placed is drawn from that peculiar language of this clause. Congress is not empowered by it to make all laws which may have relation to the powers conferred on the Government, but such only as may be "necessary and proper" for carrying them into execution. The word "necessary" is considered as controlling the whole sentence, and as limiting the right to pass laws for the execution of the granted powers to such as are indispensable, and without which the power would be nugatory. That it excludes the choice of means, and leaves to Congress in each case that only which is most direct and simple...

"To have prescribed the means by which Government should, in all future time, execute its powers would have been to change entirely the character of the instrument and give it the properties of a legal code. It would have been an unwise attempt to provide by immutable rules for exigencies which, if foreseen at all, must have been seen dimly, and which can be best provided for as they occur. To have declared that the best means shall not be used, but those alone without which the power given would be nugatory, would have been to deprive the legislature of the capacity to avail itself of experience, to exercise its reason, and to accommodate its legislation to circumstances."

Justice Marshall ignores the fact that the federal government was intended to be one of limited powers. Hence their powers were and are to be construed narrowly, not broadly. His remarks/arguments would more aptly apply to state

11.

governments, not to the federal government. To allow Congress to do that which is best is to put no limit at all on Congress . . . .

Justice Marshall was a federalist, a group of individuals who believed in a strong federal government and relatively weak state powers. He was not an objective observer or arbiter as to what the Constitution meant. Hence, neither Marbury nor McCulloch came as a surprise.

Marshall knew damn-well that the powers enumerated in Article I, § 8 were to be interpreted narrowly, granting the federal government only those powers expressly stated and only those implied powers as were necessary to carry out those expressly granted.

In rewriting the "necessary and proper" clause to mean that which was "appropriate" or "convenient" makes a mockery of the Constitution and the drafters of the document.

Marshall continues:

"In ascertaining the sense in which the word 'necessary' is used in this clause of the Constitution, we may derive some aid from that with which it it is associated. Congress shall have power 'to make all laws which shall be necessary and proper to carry into execution' the powers of the Government. If the word 'necessary' was used in that strict and rigorous sense for which the counsel for the State of Maryland contend, it would be an extraordinary departure from the usual course of the human mind, as exhibited in composition, to add a word the only possible effect of which is to qualify that strict and rigorous meaning, to present to the mind the idea of some choice of means of legislation not strained and compressed within the narrow limits for which gentlemen contend.

"But the argument which most conclusively demonstrates the error of the construction contended for by the counsel for the State of Maryland is founded on the intention of the convention as manifested in the whole clause. To waste time and argument in proving that, without it, Congress might carry its powers into execution would be not much less idle than to hold a lighted taper to the sun. As little can it be required to prove that, in the absence of this clause, Congress would have some choice of means. That it might employ those which, in its judgment, would most advantageously effect the object to be accomplished. That any means adapted to the end, any means which tended directly to the execution of the Constitutional powers of the Government, were in themselves Constitutional. This clause, as construed by the State of Maryland, would abridge, and almost annihilate, this useful and necessary right of the legislature to select its means. That this could not be intended is, we should think, had it not been already controverted, too apparent for controversy.

"We think so for the following reasons:

"1st. The clause is placed among the powers of Congress, not among the limitations on those powers...

"2d. Its terms purport to enlarge, not to diminish, the powers vested in the Government. It purports to be an additional power, not a restriction on those already granted. No reason has been or can be assigned for thus concealing an intention to narrow the discretion of the National Legislature under words which purport to enlarge it. The framers of the Constitution wished its adoption, and well knew that it would be endangered by its strength, not by its weakness. Had they been capable of using language which would convey to the eye one idea and, after deep reflection, impress on the mind another, they would rather have disguised the grant of power than its limitation. If, then, their intention had been, by this clause, to restrain the free use of means which might otherwise have been implied, that intention would have been inserted in another place, and would have been expressed in terms resembling these. "In carrying into execution the foregoing powers, and all others," &c., "no laws shall be passed but such as are necessary and proper." Had the intention been to make this clause restrictive, it would unquestionably have been so in form, as well as in effect.

"The result of the most careful and attentive consideration bestowed upon this clause is that, if it does not enlarge, it cannot be construed to restrain, the powers of Congress, or to impair the right of the legislature to exercise its best judgment in the selection of measures to carry into execution the Constitutional powers of the Government. If no other motive for its insertion can be suggested, a sufficient one is found in the desire to remove all doubts respecting ...the right to legislate on that vast mass of incidental powers which must be involved in the Constitution if that instrument be not a splendid bauble.

"We admit, as all must admit, that the powers of the Government are limited, and that its limits are not to be transcended. But we think the sound construction of the Constitution must allow to the national legislature that discretion with respect to the means by which the powers it confers are to be carried into execution which will enable that body to perform the high duties assigned to it in the manner most beneficial to the people. *Let the end be legitimate, let it be within the scope of the Constitution, and all means which are appropriate, which are plainly adapted to that end, which are not prohibited, but consist with the letter and spirit of the Constitution, are Constitutional.*

"And this Court, proceeding to render such judgment as the said Court of Appeals should have rendered, it is further adjudged and ordered that the judgment of the said Baltimore County Court be reversed and annulled, and that judgment be entered in the said Baltimore County Court for the said James W. McCulloch."

JEFFERSON'S RESPONSE to the *McCulloch* case:

"I consider the foundation of the Constitution as laid on this ground . That "all powers not delegated to the United States, by the Constitution, nor prohibited by it to the States, are reserved to the States or to the people."... To take a single step beyond the boundaries thus specially drawn around the powers of Congress, is to take possession of a boundless field of power, no longer susceptible of any definition.

The incorporation of a bank, and the powers assumed by this bill, have not, in my opinion, been delegated to the United States, by the Constitution.

I. They are not among the powers specially enumerated. . .

II. Nor are they within either of the general phrases, which are the two following: -

"1.To lay taxes to provide for the general welfare of the United States, that is to say, "to lay taxes for the purpose of providing for the general welfare." For the laying taxes is the power, and the general welfare the purpose for which the power is to be exercised. They are not to lay taxes ad libitum for any purpose they please; but only to pay the debts or provide for the welfare of the Union. In like manner, they are not to do anything they please to provide for the general welfare, but only to lay taxes for that purpose. To consider the latter phrase, not as describing the purpose of the first, but as giving a distinct and independent power to do any act they please, which might be for the good of the Union, would render all the preceding and subsequent enumerations of power completely useless.

"It would reduce the whole instrument to a single phrase, that of instituting a Congress with power to do whatever would be for the good of the United States; and, as they would be the sole judges of the good or evil, it would be also a power to do whatever evil they please....

"....It is known that the very power now proposed as a means was rejected as an end by the Convention which formed the Constitution. A proposition was made to them to authorize Congress to open canals, and an amendatory one to empower them to incorporate. But the whole was rejected, and one of the reasons for rejection urged in debate was, that then they would have a power to erect a bank, which would render the great cities, where there were prejudices and jealousies on the subject, adverse to the reception of the Constitution.

"2. The second general phrase is, "to make all laws necessary and proper for carrying into execution the enumerated powers." But they can all be carried into execution without a bank. A bank therefore is not necessary, and consequently not authorized by this phrase.

"It has been urged that a bank will give great facility or convenience in the collection of taxes. Suppose this were true: yet the Constitution allows only the means which are "necessary," not those which are merely "convenient" for effecting the enumerated powers. If such a latitude of construction be allowed to this phrase as to give any non-enumerated power it will go to every one, for there is not one which ingenuity may not torture into a convenience in some instance or other, to some one of so long a list of enumerated powers. It would swallow up all the delegated powers, and reduce the whole to one power, as before observed. Therefore it was that the Constitution restrained them to the necessary

14.

means, that is to say, to those means without which the grant of power would be nugatory...

"Can it be thought that the Constitution intended that for a shade or two of convenience, more or less, Congress should be authorized to break down the most ancient and fundamental laws of the several States; such as those inst Mortmain, the laws of Alienage, the rules of descent, the acts of distribution, the laws of escheat and forfeiture, the laws of monopoly? Nothing but a necessity invincible by any other means, can justify such a prostitution of laws, which constitute the pillars of our whole system of jurisprudence."

So, as has been shown, with the *Marbury* case of 1803 and the *McCulloch* case of 1819, respectively, the Supreme Court granted itself the right to declare acts of congress void, thus elevating itself above the other two branches of government and then, in the spirit of rewarding Congress for remaining reticent, granted immense power to the Congress by allowing Congress to enact laws that clearly went beyond the confines set down for it in the "necessary and proper" clause of the Constitution.

The 10th Amendment states very clearly: "The powers not delegated to the United States by the Constitution, nor prohibited to the States, are reserved to the States respectively, or to the people."

As stated above, the expansion of congressional power began with the *McCulloch* case and , as will be shown herein, the expansion continues to the present.

The cases that follow in the succeeding chapters will illustrate the extent to which the courts have asserted their authority over the lives of the American People by rewriting the constitution to suit the then-Court's agenda. The Court literally invents doctrines and theories while ignoring the text of our Constitution. In determining the meaning of a phrase of the Constitution, one must first determine what the Founding Fathers intended by such phrase in the Constitution. If then, the People, through congress, disagree with the state of the law, the Founding Fathers provided a vehicle by which the People could express such dissatisfaction. This is exclusively and properly done by amending the Constitution via Article V.

Article 1, § 1, states: "All legislative powers herein granted shall be vested in a Congress of the United States."

Hence, the Constitution does not grant lawmaking power to the Courts. This power is expressly and exclusively granted to the legislature or Congress. The Court's rewriting the constitution is unconstitutional, in and of itself.

Again, as of 1819, the Supreme Court had granted itself the power to determine the meaning of the Constitution and to declare acts of congress unconstitutional via the 1803 case of *Marbury v. Madison*..Then, with this assumed, not granted, power, the Supreme Court began its tour to rewrite and disrespect the Constitution. In the 1819 case of *McCulloch v. Maryland*, the

Court ignored the "necessary and proper" clause of Article I, § 8, clause 18, of the Constitution and substituted its own words of "convenient" or "appropriate" for the actual words of "necessary and proper."

By so doing, the court expanded the power of Congress and specifically permitted the formation of a national bank, which is not authorized by the constitution, as admitted by Chief Justice Marshall, and also thereby expanded the role of Congress in our everyday lives.

Hence, congress was rewarded for remaining reticent and taking no action in response to the *Marbury* case whereby the court set itself up as King. Now, the King had an ally... Congress ....

A more recent example of the Court's rewriting the literal words of the constitution is the following *Kelo* case. In this case, the Court rewrote a part of the 5th Amendment, which states, "... nor shall private property be taken for public use without just compensation."

The Court simply substituted "purpose" for "use" in this amendment and as a result, the property of *Kelo* and others was taken for the benefit of other private entities...contrary to the clear intent of the 5th Amendment...

Here now, excerpts from *Kelo:*

U.S. SUPREME COURT
KELO v. CITY OF NEW LONDON
545 U.S. 469 (2005)

Stevens, J., delivered the opinion of the Court, in which Kennedy, Souter, Ginsburg, and Breyer, JJ., joined. Kennedy, J., filed a concurring opinion. O'Connor, J., filed a dissenting opinion, in which Rehnquist, C. J.,and Scalia and Thomas, JJ., joined. Thomas, J., filed a dissenting opinion.

The following excerpts are of Justice Stevens' majority opinion:

"In 2000, the City of New London approved a development plan that, in the words of the Supreme Court of Connecticut, was 'projected to create in excess of 1,000 jobs, to increase tax and other revenues, and to revitalize an economically distressed city, including its downtown and waterfront areas.' In assembling the land needed for this project, the city's development agent has purchased property from willing sellers and proposes to use the power of eminent domain to acquire the remainder of the property from unwilling owners in exchange for just compensation. The question presented is whether the city's proposed disposition of this property qualifies as a 'public use' within the meaning of the Takings Clause of the Fifth Amendment to the Constitution.

"We granted certiorari to determine whether a city's decision to take property for the purpose of economic development satisfies the 'public use' requirement of the Fifth Amendment. Two polar propositions are perfectly clear. On the one hand, it has long been accepted that the sovereign may not take the property of A for the sole purpose of transferring it to another private party B, even though A is paid just compensation. On the other hand, it is equally clear that a State may transfer property from one private party to another if future 'use by the public' is the purpose of the taking; the condemnation of land for a railroad with common-carrier duties is a familiar example. Neither of these propositions, however, determines the disposition of this case.

"As for the first proposition, the City would no doubt be forbidden from taking petitioners' land for the purpose of conferring a private benefit on a particular private party. 'A purely private taking could not withstand the scrutiny of the public use requirement; it would serve no legitimate purpose of government and would thus be void'. Nor would the City be allowed to take property under the mere pretext of a public purpose, when its actual purpose was to bestow a private benefit. The takings before us, however, would be executed pursuant to a 'carefully considered' development plan.

"On the other hand, this is not a case in which the City is planning to open the condemned land--at least not in its entirety--to use by the general public. Nor will the private lessees of the land in any sense be required to operate like common carriers, making their services available to all comers. But although such a projected use would be sufficient to satisfy the public use requirement, this 'Court long ago rejected any literal requirement that condemned property be put into use for the general public.'

"Indeed, while many state courts in the mid-19th century endorsed "use by the public" as the proper definition of public use, that narrow view steadily eroded over time. Not only was the 'use by the public' test difficult to administer (e.g., what proportion of the public need have access to the property? at what price?) but it proved to be impractical given the diverse and always evolving needs of society. Accordingly, when this Court began applying the Fifth Amendment to the States at the close of the 19th century, it embraced the broader and more natural interpretation of public use as 'public purpose.' Thus, in a case upholding a mining company's use of an aerial bucket line to transport ore over property it did not own, Justice Holmes' opinion for the Court stressed 'the inadequacy of use by the general public as a universal test.' We have repeatedly and consistently rejected that narrow test ever since.

So, the Court adopted a previous rewrite of the Constitution, i.e., that public use, as in the text of the Constitution, is to be interpreted as public purpose. The rest of the Stevens' opinion is simply shoring-up a decision already made.

"The disposition of this case therefore turns on the question whether the City's development plan serves a 'public purpose.' Without exception, our cases have defined that concept broadly, reflecting our longstanding policy of deference to legislative judgments in this field.

Again, the Court defines public use broadly and equates it to public purpose and then defines public purpose broadly to grant great deference to the legislature. All the while moving further and further away from the text of the Constitution. Thus rewriting the document they have sworn to uphold.

"In *Berman v. Parker*, (1954), this Court upheld a redevelopment plan targeting a blighted area of Washington, D. C., in which most of the housing for the area's 5,000 inhabitants was beyond repair. Under the plan, the area would be condemned and part of it utilized for the construction of streets, schools, and other public facilities. The remainder of the land would be leased or sold to private parties for the purpose of redevelopment, including the construction of low-cost housing.

"The owner of a department store located in the area challenged the condemnation, pointing out that his store was not itself blighted and arguing that the creation of a 'better balanced, more attractive community' was not a valid public use. Writing for a unanimous Court, Justice Douglas refused to evaluate this claim in isolation, deferring instead to the legislative and agency judgment that the area 'must be planned as a whole' for the plan to be successful. The Court explained that 'community redevelopment programs need not, by force of the Constitution, be on a piecemeal basis--lot by lot, building by building.' The public use underlying the taking was unequivocally affirmed:

"We do not sit to determine whether a particular housing project is or is not desirable. The concept of the public welfare is broad and inclusive... . The values it represents are spiritual as well as physical, aesthetic as well as monetary. It is within the power of the legislature to determine that the community should be beautiful as well as healthy, spacious as well as clean, well-balanced as well as carefully patrolled. In the present case, the Congress and its authorized agencies have made determinations that take into account a wide variety of values. It is not for us to reappraise them.

"If those who govern the District of Columbia decide that the Nation's Capital should be beautiful as well as sanitary, there is nothing in the Fifth Amendment that stands in the way.

"In *Hawaii Housing Authority v. Midkiff* (1984), the Court considered a Hawaii statute whereby fee title was taken from lessors and transferred to lessees (for just compensation) in order to reduce the concentration of land ownership. We unanimously upheld the statute and rejected the Ninth Circuit's view that it was "a naked attempt on the part of the state of Hawaii to take the property of A and transfer it to B solely for B's private use and benefit.' Reaffirming *Berman's* deferential approach to legislative judgments in this field, we concluded that the State's purpose of eliminating the 'social and economic evils of a land oligopoly' qualified as a valid public use. Our opinion also rejected the contention that the mere fact that the State immediately transferred the properties to private individuals upon condemnation somehow diminished the public character of the taking.

"[I]t is only the taking's purpose, and not its mechanics," we explained, that matters in determining public use. Viewed as a whole, our jurisprudence has recognized that the needs of society have varied between different parts of the Nation, just as they have evolved over time in response to changed circumstances. Our earliest cases in particular embodied a strong theme of federalism, emphasizing the 'great respect' that we owe to state legislatures and state courts in discerning local public needs... For more than a century, our public use jurisprudence has wisely eschewed rigid formulas and intrusive scrutiny in favor of affording legislatures broad latitude in determining what public needs justify the use of the takings power.

Here the Court notes that "[their] jurisprudence has recognized that the needs of society, etc....", ignoring all the while that it is the Constitution that they are interpreting, not their previous decisions having ignored its text.

"Those who govern the City were not confronted with the need to remove blight in the Fort Trumbull area, but their determination that the area was sufficiently distressed to justify a program of economic rejuvenation is entitled to our deference. The City has carefully formulated an economic development plan that it believes will provide appreciable benefits to the community, including--but by no means limited to--new jobs and increased tax revenue. As with other exercises in urban planning and development, the City is endeavoring to coordinate a variety of commercial, residential, and recreational uses of land, with the hope that they will form a whole greater than the sum of its parts. To effectuate this plan, the City has invoked a state statute that specifically authorizes the use of eminent domain to promote economic development.

"Given the comprehensive character of the plan, the thorough deliberation that preceded its adoption, and the limited scope of our review, it is appropriate for us, as it was in *Berman*, to resolve the challenges of the individual owners, not on a piecemeal basis, but rather in light of the entire plan. Because that plan unquestionably serves a public purpose, the takings challenged here satisfy the public use requirement of the Fifth Amendment.

Here now, excerpts from Justice O'Connor's more reasoned approach:

"Over two centuries ago, just after the Bill of Rights was ratified, Justice Chase wrote:

"An act of the Legislature (for I cannot call it a law) contrary to the great first principles of the social compact, cannot be considered a rightful exercise of legislative authority ... A few instances will suffice to explain what I mean... . [A] law that takes property from A. and gives it to B: It is against all reason and justice, for a people to entrust a Legislature with such powers; and, therefore, it cannot be presumed that they have done it, *Calder v. Bull* (1798).

"Today the Court abandons this long-held, basic limitation on government power. Under the banner of economic development, all private property is now vulnerable to being taken and transferred to another private owner, so long as it might be upgraded--i.e., given to an owner who will use it in a way that the legislature deems more beneficial to the public--in the process. To reason, as the Court does, that the incidental public benefits resulting from the subsequent ordinary use of private property render economic development takings 'for public use' is to wash out any distinction between private and public use of property--and thereby effectively to delete the words 'for public use' from the Takings Clause of the Fifth Amendment. Accordingly I respectfully dissent.

"To save their homes, petitioners sued New London and the NLDC, to whom New London has delegated eminent domain power. Petitioners maintain that the Fifth Amendment prohibits the NLDC from condemning their properties for the sake of an economic development plan. Petitioners are not hold-outs; they do not seek increased compensation, and none is opposed to new development in the area. Theirs is an objection in principle: They claim that the NLDC's proposed use for their confiscated property is not a 'public' one for purposes of the Fifth Amendment. While the government may take their homes to build a road or a railroad or to eliminate a property use that harms the public, say petitioners, it cannot take their property for the private use of other owners simply because the new owners may make more productive use of the property.

"The Fifth Amendment to the Constitution, made applicable to the States by the Fourteenth Amendment, provides that 'private property [shall not] be taken for public use, without just compensation.' When interpreting the Constitution, we begin with the unremarkable presumption that every word in the document has independent meaning, 'that no word was unnecessarily used, or needlessly added.' In keeping with that presumption, we have read the Fifth Amendment's language to impose two distinct conditions on the exercise of eminent domain: 'the taking must be for a 'public use' and 'just compensation' must be paid to the owner.

The statement immediately above, in italics, i.e., 'The Fifth Amendment to the Constitution, made applicable to the States by the Fourteenth Amendment,' points up another problem, that of applying the Bill of Rights to the states. This will be discussed in Chapter 5, The Doctrine of Incorporation. In essence, this matter should not have been heard by the Supreme Court. The State of Connecticut and its citizens should have decided the contours of the state's eminent domain power, and if such power should exist in the first instance. Further, if Justice O'Connor had taken her own advice she would have recognized that the Constitution nowhere even remotely suggests that the 14th Amendment was ever intended to apply the Bill of Rights to the states.

Justice O'Connor continues:

"These two limitations serve to protect "the security of Property," which Alexander Hamilton described to the Philadelphia Convention as one of the "great obj[ects] of Gov[ernment]." Together they ensure stable property ownership by providing safeguards against excessive, unpredictable, or unfair use of the government's eminent domain power--particularly against those owners who, for whatever reasons, may be unable to protect themselves in the political process against the majority's will.

"While the Takings Clause presupposes that government can take private property without the owner's consent, the just compensation requirement spreads the cost of condemnations and thus 'prevents the public from loading upon one individual more than his just share of the burdens of government.' The public use requirement, in turn, imposes a more basic limitation, circumscribing the very scope of the eminent domain power: Government may compel an individual to forfeit her property for the public's use, but not for the benefit of another private person. This requirement promotes fairness as well as security.

"Where is the line between 'public' and 'private' property use? We give considerable deference to legislatures' determinations about what governmental activities will advantage the public. But were the political branches the sole arbiters of the public-private distinction, the Public Use Clause would amount to little more than hortatory fluff. An external, judicial check on how the public use requirement is interpreted, however limited, is necessary if this constraint on government power is to retain any meaning.

"Our cases have generally identified three categories of takings that comply with the public use requirement, though it is in the nature of things that the boundaries between these categories are not always firm. Two are relatively straightforward and uncontroversial. First, the sovereign may transfer private property to public ownership--such as for a road, a hospital, or a military base. Second, the sovereign may transfer private property to private parties, often common carriers, who make the property available for the public's use--such as with a railroad, a public utility, or a stadium. But 'public ownership' and 'use-by-the-public' are sometimes too constricting and impractical ways to define the scope of the Public Use Clause.

"Thus we have allowed that, in certain circumstances and to meet certain exigencies, takings that serve a public purpose also satisfy the Constitution even if the property is destined for subsequent private use.

This case returns us for the first time in over 20 years to the hard question of when a purportedly "public purpose" taking meets the public use requirement. It presents an issue of first impression: Are economic development takings constitutional? I would hold that they are not. We are guided by two precedents about the taking of real property by eminent domain.

"In *Berman*, we upheld takings within a blighted neighborhood of Washington, D. C. The neighborhood had so deteriorated that, for example, 64.3% of its dwellings were beyond repair. It had become burdened with 'overcrowding of dwellings,' 'lack of adequate streets and alleys,' and 'lack of light and air.' Congress had determined that the neighborhood had become 'injurious to the public health, safety, morals, and welfare' and that it was necessary to 'eliminat[e] all such injurious conditions by employing all means necessary and appropriate for the purpose,' including eminent domain. Mr. Berman's department store was not itself blighted. Having approved of Congress' decision to eliminate the harm to the public emanating from the blighted neighborhood, however, we did not second-guess its decision to treat the neighborhood as a whole rather than lot-by-lot.

"In *Midkiff*, we upheld a land condemnation scheme in Hawaii whereby title in real property was taken from lessors and transferred to lessees. At that time, the State and Federal Governments owned nearly 49% of the State's land, and another 47% was in the hands of only 72 private landowners. Concentration of land ownership was so dramatic that on the State's most urbanized island, Oahu, landowners owned 72.5% of the fee simple titles. The Hawaii Legislature had concluded that the oligopoly in land ownership was 'skewing the State's residential fee simple market, inflating land prices, and injuring the public tranquility and welfare,' and therefore enacted a condemnation scheme for redistributing title.

"In those decisions, we emphasized the importance of deferring to legislative judgments about public purpose. Because courts are ill-equipped to evaluate the efficacy of proposed legislative initiatives, we rejected as unworkable the idea of courts 'deciding on what is and is not a governmental function and ... invalidating legislation on the basis of their view on that question at the moment of decision, a practice which has proved impracticable in other fields.' The legislature, not the judiciary, is the main guardian of the public needs to be served by social legislation.

"Likewise, we recognized our inability to evaluate whether, in a given case, eminent domain is a necessary means by which to pursue the legislature's ends. Yet for all the emphasis on deference, *Berman* and *Midkiff* hewed to a bedrock principle without which our public use jurisprudence would collapse: 'A purely private taking could not withstand the scrutiny of the public use requirement; it would serve no legitimate purpose of government and would thus be void.'

"[T]he Court's cases have repeatedly stated that 'one person's property may not be taken for the benefit of another private person without a justifying public purpose, even though compensation be paid.' To protect that principle, those decisions reserved 'a role for courts to play in reviewing a legislature's judgment of what constitutes a public use' ... [though] the Court in *Berman* made clear that it is 'an extremely narrow' one.

"The Court's holdings in *Berman* and *Midkiff* were true to the principle underlying the Public Use Clause. In both those cases, the extraordinary, precondemnation use of the targeted property inflicted affirmative harm on society--in Berman through blight resulting from extreme poverty and in Midkiff through oligopoly resulting from extreme wealth. And in both cases, the relevant legislative body had found that eliminating the existing property use was necessary to remedy the harm. Thus a public purpose was realized when the harmful use was eliminated. Because each taking directly achieved a public benefit, it did not matter that the property was turned over to private use.

"Here, in contrast, New London does not claim that Susette Kelo's and Wilhelmina Dery's well-maintained homes are the source of any social harm. Indeed, it could not so claim without adopting the absurd argument that any single-family home that might be razed to make way for an apartment building, or any church that might be replaced with a retail store, or any small business that might be more lucrative if it were instead part of a national franchise, is inherently harmful to society and thus within the government's power to condemn.

"In moving away from our decisions sanctioning the condemnation of harmful property use, the Court today significantly expands the meaning of public use. It holds that the sovereign may take private property currently put to ordinary private use, and give it over for new, ordinary private use, so long as the new use is predicted to generate some secondary benefit for the public--such as increased tax revenue, more jobs, maybe even aesthetic pleasure. But nearly any lawful use of real private property can be said to generate some incidental benefit to the public. Thus, if predicted (or even guaranteed) positive side-effects are enough to render transfer from one private party to another constitutional, then the words 'for public use' do not realistically exclude any takings, and thus do not exert any constraint on the eminent domain power.

"There is a sense in which this troubling result follows from errant language in *Berman* and *Midkiff*. In discussing whether takings within a blighted neighborhood were for a public use, *Berman* began by observing: 'We deal, in other words, with what traditionally has been known as the police power.' From there it declared that '[o]nce the object is within the authority of Congress, the right to realize it through the exercise of eminent domain is clear. 'Following up, we said in *Midkiff* that '[t]he 'public use' requirement is coterminous with the scope of a sovereign's police powers.'

"This language was unnecessary to the specific holdings of those decisions. *Berman* and *Midkiff* simply did not put such language to the constitutional test, because the takings in those cases were within the police power but also for 'public use' for the reasons I have described. The case before us now demonstrates why, when deciding if a taking's purpose is constitutional, the police power and 'public use' cannot always be equated. The Court protests that it does not sanction the bare transfer from A to B for B's benefit. It suggests two limitations on what can be taken after today's decision. First, it maintains a role for courts in ferreting out takings whose sole purpose is to bestow a benefit on the private transferee--without detailing how courts are to conduct that complicated inquiry.

"For his part, Justice Kennedy suggests that courts may divine illicit purpose by a careful review of the record and the process by which a legislature arrived at the decision to take--without specifying what courts should look for in a case with different facts, how they will know if they have found it, and what to do if they do not. Whatever the details of Justice Kennedy's as-yet-undisclosed test, it is difficult to envision anyone but the 'stupid staff[er]' failing it. The trouble with economic development takings is that private benefit and incidental public benefit are, by definition, merged and mutually reinforcing. In this case, for example, any boon for Pfizer or the plan's developer is difficult to disaggregate from the promised public gains in taxes and jobs.

"Even if there were a practical way to isolate the motives behind a given taking, the gesture toward a purpose test is theoretically flawed. If it is true that incidental public benefits from new private use are enough to ensure the 'public purpose' in a taking, why should it matter, as far as the Fifth Amendment is concerned, what inspired the taking in the first place? How much the government does or does not desire to benefit a favored private party has no bearing on whether an economic development taking will or will not generate secondary benefit for the public. And whatever the reason for a given condemnation, the effect is the same from the constitutional perspective--private property is forcibly relinquished to new private ownership.

"A second proposed limitation is implicit in the Court's opinion. The logic of today's decision is that eminent domain may only be used to upgrade--not downgrade--property. At best this makes the Public Use Clause redundant with the Due Process Clause, which already prohibits irrational government action. The Court rightfully admits, however, that the judiciary cannot get bogged down in predictive judgments about whether the public will actually be better off after a property transfer. In any event, this constraint has no realistic import. For who among us can say she already makes the most productive or attractive possible use of her property? The specter of condemnation hangs over all property.

" Nothing is to prevent the State from replacing any Motel 6 with a Ritz-Carlton, any home with a shopping mall, or any farm with a factory. The Court also puts special emphasis on facts peculiar to this case: The NLDC's plan is the product of a relatively careful deliberative process; it proposes to use eminent domain for a multipart, integrated plan rather than for isolated property transfer; it promises an array of incidental benefits (even aesthetic ones), not just increased tax revenue; it comes on the heels of a legislative determination that New London is a depressed municipality. Justice Kennedy, too, takes great comfort in these facts. But none has legal significance to blunt the force of today's holding. If legislative prognostications about the secondary public

24.

benefits of a new use can legitimate a taking, there is nothing in the Court's rule or in Justice Kennedy's gloss on that rule to prohibit property transfers generated with less care, that are less comprehensive, that happen to result from less elaborate process, whose only projected advantage is the incidence of higher taxes, or that hope to transform an already prosperous city into an even more prosperous one.

"Finally, in a coda, the Court suggests that property owners should turn to the States, who may or may not choose to impose appropriate limits on economic development takings. This is an abdication of our responsibility. States play many important functions in our system of dual sovereignty, but compensating for our refusal to enforce properly the Federal Constitution (and a provision meant to curtail state action, no less) is not among them.

"It was possible after *Berman* and *Midkiff* to imagine unconstitutional transfers from A to B. Those decisions endorsed government intervention when private property use had veered to such an extreme that the public was suffering as a consequence. Today nearly all real property is susceptible to condemnation on the Court's theory. In the prescient words of a dissenter from the infamous decision in Poletown, '[n]ow that we have authorized local legislative bodies to decide that a different commercial or industrial use of property will produce greater public benefits than its present use, no homeowner's, merchant's or manufacturer's property, however productive or valuable to its owner, is immune from condemnation for the benefit of other private interests that will put it to a 'higher' use.'

"This is why economic development takings 'seriously jeopardiz[e] the security of all private property ownership.' Any property may now be taken for the benefit of another private party, but the fallout from this decision will not be random. The beneficiaries are likely to be those citizens with disproportionate influence and power in the political process, including large corporations and development firms. As for the victims, the government now has license to transfer property from those with fewer resources to those with more. The Founders cannot have intended this perverse result. '[T]hat alone is a just government,' wrote James Madison, 'which impartially secures to every man, whatever is his own.'

"I would hold that the takings are unconstitutional, reverse the judgment of the Supreme Court of Connecticut, and remand for further proceedings.

Justice Thomas dissenting:

"Long ago, William Blackstone wrote that 'the law of the land ... postpone[s] even public necessity to the sacred and inviolable rights of private property.' The Framers embodied that principle in the Constitution, allowing the government to take property not for 'public necessity,' but instead for 'public use.' Defying this understanding, the Court replaces the Public Use Clause with a ' [P]ublic [P]urpose', a restriction that is satisfied, the Court instructs, so long as the purpose is 'legitimate' and the means 'not irrational.' This deferential shift in phraseology enables the Court to hold, against all common sense, that a costly urban-renewal project whose stated purpose is a vague promise of new jobs and increased tax revenue, but which is also suspiciously agreeable to the Pfizer Corporation, is for a 'public use.'

"I cannot agree. If such 'economic development' takings are for a 'public use,' any taking is, and the Court has erased the Public Use Clause from our Constitution, as Justice O'Connor powerfully argues in dissent.

"I do not believe that this Court can eliminate liberties expressly enumerated in the Constitution and therefore join her dissenting opinion.

"Regrettably, however, the Court's error runs deeper than this. Today's decision is simply the latest in a string of our cases construing the Public Use Clause to be a virtual nullity, without the slightest nod to its original meaning. In my view, the Public Use Clause, originally understood, is a meaningful limit on the government's eminent domain power. Our cases have strayed from the Clause's original meaning, and I would reconsider them.

"The Fifth Amendment provides:

'No person shall be held to answer for a capital, or otherwise infamous crime, unless on a presentment or indictment of a Grand Jury, except in cases arising in the land or naval forces, or in the Militia,when in actual service in time of War or public danger; nor shall any person be subject for the same offence to be twice put in jeopardy of life or limb, nor shall be compelled in any criminal case to be a witness against himself, nor be deprived of life, liberty, or property, without due process, of law; nor shall private property be taken for public use, without just compensation.'

"It is the last of these liberties, the Takings Clause, that is at issue in this case. In my view, it is 'imperative that the Court maintain absolute fidelity to' the Clause's express limit on the power of the government over the individual, no less than with every other liberty expressly enumerated in the Fifth Amendment or the Bill of Rights more generally.

"Though one component of the protection provided by the Takings Clause is that the government can take private property only if it provides 'just compensation' for the taking, the Takings Clause also prohibits the government from taking property except 'for public use.' Were it otherwise, the Takings Clause would either be meaningless or empty.

"If the Public Use Clause served no function other than to state that the government may take property through its eminent domain power--for public or private uses--then it would be surplusage, *Marbury v. Madison*, (1803). 'It cannot be presumed that any clause in the constitution is intended to be without effect'.

"Alternatively, the Clause could distinguish those takings that require compensation from those that do not. That interpretation, however, 'would

26.

permit private property to be taken or appropriated for private use without any compensation whatever.' In other words, the Clause would require the government to compensate for takings done 'for public use,' leaving it free to take property for purely private uses without the payment of compensation. This would contradict a bedrock principle well established by the time of the founding: that all takings required the payment of compensation. The Public Use Clause, like the Just Compensation Clause, is therefore an express limit on the government's power of eminent domain.

"The most natural reading of the Clause is that it allows the government to take property only if the government owns, or the public has a legal right to use, the property, as opposed to taking it for any public purpose or necessity whatsoever. At the time of the founding, dictionaries primarily defined the noun 'use' as '[t]he act of employing any thing to any purpose.' The term 'use,' moreover, 'is from the Latin utor, which means 'to use, make use of, avail one's self of, employ, apply, enjoy, etc.' When the government takes property and gives it to a private individual, and the public has no right to use the property, it strains language to say that the public is 'employing' the property, regardless of the incidental benefits that might accrue to the public from the private use.

"The term 'public use,' then, means that either the government or its citizens as a whole must actually 'employ' the taken property. The Constitution's common-law background reinforces this understanding. The common law provided an express method of eliminating uses of land that adversely impacted the public welfare: nuisance law...When the public took property, in other words, it took it as an individual buying property from another typically would: for one's own use. The Public Use Clause, in short, embodied the Framers' understanding that property is a natural, fundamental right, prohibiting the government from 'tak[ing] property from A. and giv[ing] it to B,' Calder v. Bull (1798).

"The public purpose interpretation of the Public Use Clause also unnecessarily duplicates a similar inquiry required by the Necessary and Proper Clause. The Takings Clause is a prohibition, not a grant of power: The Constitution does not expressly grant the Federal Government the power to take property for any public purpose whatsoever. Instead, the Government may take property only when necessary and proper to the exercise of an expressly enumerated power... to take property 'needed for forts, armories, and arsenals, for navy-yards and light-houses, for custom-houses, post-offices, and court-houses, and for other public uses'.

"For a law to be within the Necessary and Proper Clause,..... it must bear an 'obvious, simple, and direct relation' to an exercise of Congress' enumerated powers, and it must not 'subvert basic principles of' constitutional design. In other words, a taking is permissible under the Necessary and Proper Clause only if it serves a valid public purpose. Interpreting the Public Use Clause likewise to limit the government to take property only for sufficiently public purposes replicates this inquiry. If this is all the Clause means, it is, once again, surplusage. The Clause is thus most naturally read to concern whether the property is used by the public or the government, not whether the purpose of the taking is legitimately public...Public Use Clause is most naturally read to authorize takings for public use only if the government or the public actually uses the taken property. Our current Public Use Clause jurisprudence, as the Court notes, has rejected this natural reading of the Clause. The Court adopted its modern reading blindly, with little discussion of the Clause's history and original meaning, in two distinct lines of cases: first, in cases adopting the 'public purpose' interpretation of the Clause, and second, in cases deferring to legislatures' judgments regarding what constitutes a valid public purpose.

"Those questionable cases converged in the boundlessly broad and deferential conception of 'public use' adopted by this Court in Berman v. Parker and Hawaii Housing Authority v. Midkiff, cases that take center stage in the Court's opinion. The weakness of those two lines of cases, and consequently Berman and Midkiff, fatally undermines the doctrinal foundations of the Court's decision. Today's questionable application of these cases is further proof that the "public purpose" standard is not susceptible of principled application.

"This Court's reliance by rote on this standard is ill-advised and should be reconsidered.Still worse, it is backwards to adopt a searching standard of constitutional review for nontraditional property interests, such as welfare benefits, while deferring to the legislature's determination as to what constitutes a public use when it exercises the power of eminent domain, and thereby invades individuals' traditional rights in real property. The Court has elsewhere recognized 'the overriding respect for the sanctity of the home that has been embedded in our traditions since the origins of the Republic', when the issue is only whether the government may search a home.

"Yet today the Court tells us that we are not to 'second-guess the City's considered judgments', when the issue is, instead, whether the government may take the infinitely more intrusive step of tearing down petitioners' homes. Something has gone seriously awry with this Court's interpretation of the Constitution. Though citizens are safe from the government in their homes, the homes themselves are not. Once one accepts, as the Court at least nominally does, that the Public Use Clause is a limit on the eminent domain power of the Federal Government and the States, there is no justification for the almost complete deference it grants to legislatures as to what satisfies it.

"These two misguided lines of precedent converged in Berman v. Parker and Hawaii Housing Authority v. Midkiff, Relying on those lines of cases, the Court in Berman and Midkiff upheld condemnations for the purposes of slum clearance and land redistribution, respectively. 'Subject to specific constitutional limitations,' Berman proclaimed, 'when the legislature has spoken, the public interest has been declared in terms well-nigh conclusive. In such cases the legislature, not the judiciary, is the main guardian of the public needs to be served by social legislation.'

"That reasoning was question begging, since the question to be decided was whether the 'specific constitutional limitation' of the Public Use Clause prevented the taking of the appellant's (concededly "nonblighted") department store. Berman also appeared to reason that any exercise by Congress of an enumerated power (in this case, its plenary power over the District of Columbia) was per se a 'public use' under the Fifth Amendment. But the very point of the Public Use Clause is to limit that power.

"The 'public purpose' test applied by *Berman* and *Midkiff* also cannot be applied in principled manner. "When we depart from the natural import of the term 'public use,' and substitute for the simple idea of a public possession and occupation, that of public utility, public interest, common benefit, general advantage or convenience ... we are afloat without any certain principle to guide us. Once one permits takings for public purposes in addition to public uses, no coherent principle limits what could constitute a valid public use-at least, none beyond Justice O'Connor's (entirely proper) appeal to the text of the Constitution itself.

"I share the Court's skepticism about a public use standard that requires courts to second-guess the policy wisdom of public works projects. The 'public purpose' standard this Court has adopted, however, demands the use of such judgment, for the Court concedes that the Public Use Clause would forbid a purely private taking. It is difficult to imagine how a court could find that a taking was purely private except by determining that the taking did not, in fact, rationally advance the public interest. The Court is therefore wrong to criticize the "actual use" test as 'difficult to administer.' It is far easier to analyze whether the government owns or the public has a legal right to use the taken property than to ask whether the taking has a 'purely private purpose' - unless the Court means to eliminate public use scrutiny of takings entirely. "Obliterating a provision of the Constitution, of course, guarantees that it will not be misapplied.

For all these reasons, I would revisit our Public Use Clause cases and consider returning to the original meaning of the Public Use Clause: that the government may take property only if it actually uses or gives the public a legal right to use the property.

"The consequences of today's decision are not difficult to predict, and promise to be harmful. So-called 'urban renewal' programs provide some compensation for the properties they take, but no compensation is possible for the subjective value of these lands to the individuals displaced and the indignity inflicted by uprooting them from their homes. Allowing the government to take property solely for public purposes is bad enough, but extending the concept of public purpose to encompass any economically beneficial goal guarantees that these losses will fall disproportionately on poor communities.

"Those communities are not only systematically less likely to put their lands to the highest and best social use, but are also the least politically powerful. If ever there were justification for intrusive judicial review of constitutional provisions that protect 'discrete and insular minorities,',surely that principle would apply with great force to the powerless groups and individuals the Public Use Clause protects. The deferential standard this Court has adopted for the Public Use Clause is therefore deeply perverse. It encourages 'those citizens with dis-proportionate influence and power in the political process, including large corporations and development firms' to victimize the weak.

"Those incentives have made the legacy of this Court's 'public purpose' test an unhappy one. In the 1950's, no doubt emboldened in part by the expansive understanding of 'public use' this Court adopted in *Berman,* cities 'rushed to draw plans' for downtown development. 'Of all the families displaced by urban renewal from 1949 through 1963, 63 percent of those whose race was known were nonwhite, and of these families, 56 percent of nonwhites and 38 percent of whites had incomes low enough to qualify for public housing, which, however, was seldom available to them.

"Public works projects in the 1950's and 1960's destroyed predominantly minority communities in St. Paul, Minnesota, and Baltimore, Maryland. In 1981, urban planners in Detroit, Michigan, uprooted the largely 'lower-income and elderly' Poletown neighborhood for the benefit of the General Motors Corporation. Urban renewal projects have long been associated with the displacement of blacks; '[i]n cities across the country, urban renewal came to be known as 'Negro removal.' Over 97 percent of the individuals forcibly removed from their homes by the 'slum-clearance' project upheld by this Court in *Berman* were black.

"Regrettably, the predictable consequence of the Court's decision will be to exacerbate these effects.

The Court relies almost exclusively on this Court's prior cases to derive today's far-reaching, and dangerous, result. But the principles this Court should employ to dispose of this case are found in the Public Use Clause itself, not in Justice Peckham's high opinion of reclamation laws.

"When faced with a clash of constitutional principle and a line of unreasoned cases wholly divorced from the text, history, and structure of our founding document, we should not hesitate to resolve the tension in favor of the Constitution's original meaning. For the reasons I have given, and for the reasons given in Justice O'Connor's dissent, the conflict of principle raised by this boundless use of the eminent domain power should be resolved in petitioners' favor. I would reverse the judgment of the Connecticut Supreme Court."

Justice Thomas' closing paragraph points out, with the accuracy of a laser, the egregious malfeasance of the Supreme Court's conduct too-often employed, i.e., choosing its former holdings, often unreasoned, over and above the actual text of the Constitution, all the while feigning to be interpreting the Constitution.

Justice Thomas' reasoning is excellent, of course. However, his position assumes that which is not actually correct, based on a true textual interpretation of the Constitution. *Justice Thomas has adopted the flawed conclusion that the 14th Amendment Due Process clause applies the Bill of Rights to the states. As a justice very attuned to the actual text of the constitution and an adherent of applying the original meaning of said document, Justice Thomas knows better.*

This concept will be discussed in chapter 5 of this work. There it will be shown that the original, intended application of the Bill of Rights was to the federal government only...it was never intended to apply to the states.

This case, therefore, should not have been brought before the Supreme Court. The state of Connecticut should have had the last word on the matter.

In all fairness, it must be admitted that there is a silver-lining in the holding of this case. By granting such deference to the state in this rather limited area, the court has shifted power back to the states at least to define the contours of eminent domain power within the state. Hence, as a result of this ruling, the states are now free to fashion their own limitations on eminent domain as it exists within their own particular state.

It is unfortunate that the Supreme Court does not grant such deference to more of the legislatures of this country regarding cases brought before it, thus allowing the states and their citizens to enact the laws under which they must live.

In 1788, in the New-York Journal and Weekly Register, under the name of Brutus, the following most-prescient article appeared:

" The judicial power will operate to effect, in the most certain but yet silent and imperceptible manner, what is evidently the tendency of the Constitution: I mean, an entire subversion of the legislative, executive and judicial powers of the individual states. Every adjudication of the Supreme Court on any question that may arise upon the nature and extent of the general government will affect the limits of the state jurisdiction. In proportion, as the former enlarge the exercise of their powers will that of the latter be restricted.

" That the judicial power of the United States will lean strongly in favor of the general government, and will give such an explanation to the Constitution as will favor an extension of its jurisdiction, is very evident from a variety of considerations..."

It is precisely because of this pervasive lack of deference to the state legislatures and the unwarranted extension of the power of the federal government that this work became essential. *This work may be necessary, but it is not sufficient. Sufficiency will be effected by action...action based on the sound principles elucidated herein.*

"If, in the opinion of the people, the distribution or modification of the constitutional powers be in any particular wrong, let it be corrected by amendment in the way which the constitution designates..."   George Washington, Farewell Address (1796)

CHAPTER 3

AMENDING OR REWRITING THE CONSTITUTION

The Constitution was intended to be amended as prescribed in Article V of the Constitution. Several methods were provided therein. Each method employs Congress and the state legislatures. In neither case, were the federal courts to take part in the amendment process. Hence, as stated in the previous chapter, the federal courts, including the Supreme Court, had and have, no authority to amend the Constitution. . . they do it anyway. . . .

Of course it's bad enough that the court violates the Constitution it swears to uphold but each time it amends the Constitution without utilizing Article V, We the People are denied the right to be heard on that subject to which the amendment is addressed. To exacerbate the matter even further, to whom do the People petition for a redress of their grievances? The first amendment of the constitution guarantees that We the People have the right to "...petition the government for a redress of grievances. . . . "

Once the Supreme Court speaks on a particular matter, that matter appears to be "over." Since our inception, the People, through their representatives, have done little about a Supreme Court decision with which they disagree.

The People *can* petition the Congress however, and it is for this reason that the Founding Fathers intended the Congress to write the laws and to amend the Constitution, *not* the courts.

Article V states, in pertinent part:

"The Congress, whenever two thirds of both houses shall deem it necessary, shall propose amendments to this Constitution, or, on the application of the legislatures of two thirds of the several States, shall call a convention for proposing amendments, which in either case shall be valid in all intents and purposes, as part of this Constitution when ratified by the legislatures of three fourth of the several States, or by conventions in three fourths thereof, as the one or the other mode of ratification may be proposed by the Congress . . . . "

Utilizing the proper method of amending the Constitution, i.e.,via Article V, the Constitution has been amended by the People, through their representatives, 27 times. Hence, it is clearly *not* necessary to involve the Courts in the amendment process.

Those 27 amendments are listed, of course, as part of the Constitution in Appendix A. In fact, each time the Supreme Court improperly rewrites the Constitution, thereby amending it *de facto*, the People are eliminated from the process.

The means by which the Constitution is amended is presented early in this work to indicate that there *is* a proper method by which to amend the Constitution. This necessarily precludes "amendment" by court decision.

The two previous chapters illustrated several cases by which the Constitution was rewritten. *Marbury, McCulloch,* and *Kelo* are examples of the inappropriate means of amending the Constitution. By court decree, *Marbury* gave the court itself power, not authorized by the Constitution, to determine what the Constitution meant and to declare acts of Congress unconstitutional.

In *McCulloch,* the Supreme Court returned the favor to Congress for their reticence in not objecting to the holding in *Marbury* which essentially emasculated Congress. Recall that Congress was given *carte blanche* to do as it pleased regarding laws which they enacted. There was no need to limit their legislation to that which was "necessary and proper", but that which was "convenient" or "appropriate" would suffice.

Kelo, in 2005, held that in the area of eminent domain, "public use" actually meant "public purpose". Justice Thomas' obviously correct and brilliant dissent, notwithstanding.

Having early-on granted itself expansive powers over the People, through *Marbury* and *McCulloch,* the Court then turned to devise methods by which they could utilize those powers to further enhance their powers. To do so, they employed several methods.

The first of these, discussed in Chapter 4, The Doctrine of Enumerated Powers, deals with Article I, § 8, which describes and defines the *only* powers granted to the legislative branch of the federal government, i.e.,Congress. These 18 powers, including the "necessary and proper" clause, were intended to be construed narrowly, as the states which granted these powers, intended to reserve all powers, not so granted, to the states and their citizens.

This is made abundantly clear in the 10th Amendment as it states:

"The powers not delegated to the United States by the Constitution, nor prohibited by it to the States, are reserved to the States respectively, or to the people."

The second of these concocted methods, by which the Peoples' freedoms have been taken, is the application of the Bill of Rights to the states through the 14th Amendment Due Process Clause. This is discussed in Chapter 5, The Doctrine of Incorporation. As will be shown, the Bill of Rights was intended to apply to, and thereby limit, the federal government *only.*

The third method, discussed in Chapter 6, is the Equal Protection Clause of the 14th Amendment. As will be shown, this method vastly exceeds the confines set-down by the drafters of this amendment.

Lest one think the Supreme Court has been lethargic in applying its *sui generis* power, the Court has found *federal* statutes 159 times and *state constitutions* and municipal codes 224 times, *un*constitutional, up through 2006.The complete list can be found on-line at "onecle.com" and "wiki.answers.com."

Hence, the constitution has been amended *properly* only 27 times and *improperly* a total of 383 times.

George Washington, in 1796, in his farewell address had a few words to say about *properly* amending the Constitution:

"It is important, likewise, that the habits of thinking in a free country should inspire caution in those entrusted with its administration to confine themselves within their respective constitutional spheres, avoiding in the exercise of the powers of one department to encroach upon another. The spirit of encroachment tends to consolidate the powers of all the departments in one and thus to create, whatever the form of government, a real despotism. A just estimate of that love of power and proneness to abuse it which predominates in the human heart is sufficient to satisfy us of the truth of this position.

"The necessity of reciprocal checks in the exercise of political power, by dividing and distributing it into different depositories, and constituting each the guardian of the public weal against invasions by the others, has been evinced by experiments ancient and modern, some of them in our country and under our own eyes. To preserve them must be as necessary as to institute them. *If, in the opinion of the people, the distribution or modification of the constitutional powers be in any particular wrong, let it be corrected by amendment in the way which the Constitution designates. . . . "*

It is submitted that the Supreme Court has been, and is, acting in defiance of our First President's admonition ... and instead has become King George III ... reincarnated.

". . . Within the scope of its powers, as enumerated and defined, it is supreme and above the states, but beyond it has no existence. . ." U.S. v. Cruikshank (1875)

CHAPTER 4

DOCTRINE OF ENUMERATED POWERS OR UNLIMITED FEDERAL GOVERNMENT

Upon formation of the Constitution, it was intended, indeed it was a material basis of the bargain, that the Federal government would exercise *only* those powers specifically granted to it. In addition, it was agreed that the Fed eral government would be further restricted by enacting the Bill of Rights.

Those powers explicitly granted to the legislative branch of the federal government, i.e., Congress, appear as Article I, § 8, of the U..S. Constitution. There, are listed 17 express powers and an 18th, the "necessary and proper" clause. This clause was improperly disposed of by Justice Marshall in *McCulloch* as discussed in Chapter 2.

Legislative power is fundamentally the power to make laws, but also includes the power to investigate, hear and consider matters upon which legislation may be enacted, and do all other things "necessary and proper" to the enactment of legislation.

Article I ,§1 provides: *"All legislative powers herein granted shall be vested in a Congress of the United States..."*

Article I, §8, provides, *inter alia*, for such important powers as those to lay and collect taxes, to borrow money on the credit of the U. S., to regulate commerce with foreign nations and among the several states, to declare war, to raise and support armies, to provide and maintain a navy, etc..

The 10th Amendment provides that *"The powers not delegated to the United States by the Constitution, nor prohibited by it to the States, are reserved to the States respectively, or to the people."*

As a result of the enumeration of powers in Article I, §8, and the 10th Amendment reservation to the states, it is clear that the federal government was to be one of "enumerated" or "delegated" powers, and that the powers not expressly delegated were "reserved" to, or to remain within, the states. *U.S. v. Cruikshank,* (1875) held:

"The government thus established and defined is to some extent a government of the States in their political capacity. It is also, for certain purposes, a government of the pepole.{sic} Its powers are limited in number, but not in degree. *Within the scope of its powers, as enumerated and defined, it is supreme and above the States; but beyond, it has no existence.* It was erected for special purposes, and endowed with all the powers necessary for its own preservation and the accomplishment of the ends its people had in view. It can neither grant nor secure to its citizens any right or privilege not expressly or by implication placed under its jurisdiction."

Cruikshank continues:

"The government of the United States is one of delegated powers alone. Its authority is defined and limited by the Constitution. All powers not granted to it by that instrument are reserved to the States or the people. No rights can be acquired under the constitution or laws of the United States, except such as the government of the United States has the authority to grant or secure. All that cannot be so granted or secured are left under the protection of the States."

Hence, it is without dispute that as of 1875, the Supreme Court recognized that the power of the federal government was expressly limited to that which was granted it in the U.S. Constitution.

Although this chapter is titled ,"Doctrine of Enumerated Powers," it will include more than the Commerce Clause and the Tax and Spend Clause. The 14th Amendment, Due Process clause will be introduced as well.

The Commerce Clause, Article I, § 8, clause 3, states:

"Congress shall have the power to regulate commerce with foreign nations, and among the several states, and with the Indian tribes." Article I, § 8, clause 3.

James Madison, often referred to as the Father of the Constitution, had this to say about the Commerce Clause:

"... it is very certain that it [the Commerce clause] grew out of the abuse of the power by the importing States in taxing the nonimporting, and was intended as a negative and preventive provision against injustice among the States themselves, *rather than as a power to be used for the positive purposes of the General Government*, in which alone, however, the remedial power could be lodged." - Letter to Cabell, February 13, 1829.

Notwithstanding Madison's definition, and admonishing its use "... for positive purposes of the General Government", the Supreme Court has upheld Congress's power to regulate virtually every aspect of business pursuant to the Commerce Clause.

Using essentially the same rationale as used in *Wickard v. Filburn*, discussed below, i.e., even though the activity is *conducted entirely within a state*, the activity *might* have *an impact* on interstate commerce, hence it can be regulated by Big Brother, the federal government.

Far from granting Congress the power to create the massive regulatory, central economic planning, nearly limitless federal government in existence today, *the Commerce Clause was intended to be a restriction on States, not a positive grant of power to Congress*. It was intended that the federal government have the power to resolve trade disputes among the states and essentially provide for free trade among the states. Perhaps no clause in the Constitution has been so perverted as the commerce clause.

In the case of *Gibbons v. Ogden* (1824), a case involving the "commerce clause," the Supreme Court held:

"Congress shall have the power to regulate commerce with foreign nations, and among the several states, and with the Indian tribes."

"The genius and character of the whole gov't seem to be, that its action seem to be applied to all the external concerns of the nation and to those internal concerns which affect the states generally; but not to those which are completely within a particular state, which do not affect the other states, and within which it is not necessary to interfere for the purpose of executing some of the general powers of the government. *The completely internal commerce of a state...may be considered as reserved for the state itself."*

Numerous cases over the years further confirmed the "enumerated powers" doctrine such as *Schechter Poultry Corp v. US* (1935), which held that sales after interstate travel was not considered commerce and therefore not subject to control by the federal government, and *Carter v. Carter Coal Co.* (1936), which held that regulation of production within a state was *not* commerce and *not* subject to federal government regulation.

In *US v. Butler* (1937), the Court interpreted both the commerce clause and the "spending clause."

The *Butler* Court held that a tax enacted by the federal government for the purpose of reducing farm production of certain goods and payment of benefits for compliance, was unconstitutional because not authorized by said "spending clause."

The *Butler* Court continued:

"From the accepted doctrine that the United States is a government of delegated powers, it follows that those not expressly granted, or reasonably to be implied from such as are conferred, are reserved to the states, or to the people. To forestall any suggestion to the contrary, the Tenth Amendment was adopted. The same proposition, otherwise stated, is that powers not granted are prohibited. None to regulate agricultural production is given, and therefore legislation by Congress for that purpose is forbidden.

"It is an established principle that the attainment of a prohibited end may not be accomplished under the pretext of the exertion of powers which are granted.

"Congress cannot, under the pretext of executing delegated power, pass laws for the accomplishment of objects not entrusted to the Federal Government. And we accept as established doctrine that any provision of an act of Congress ostensibly enacted under power granted by the Constitution, not naturally and reasonably adapted to the effective exercise of such power but solely to the achievement of something plainly within power reserved to the States, is invalid and cannot be enforced...

"These principles are as applicable to the power to lay taxes as to any other federal power....

"Congress is not empowered to tax for those purposes which are within the exclusive province of the States. . . ."

Hence, *Butler* correctly held that farm production was *not* commerce as it was within the exclusive province of the states and Congress was *not* permitted to tax to regulate such farm production.

In an attempt to further the power of the federal government over the economy and therefore the states and ultimately the people, the Court began to rethink their self-imposed and constitutionally-correct decisions as indicated above, and held the following:

In *NLRB v. Jones and Laughlin Steel* (1937), the Court held that a manufacturing company, *even where all production was done within a state,* having nationwide sales, could have an "appreciable affect" upon interstate commerce, and could therefore be regulated by the federal government.

This marked the beginning of the end as far the states' power to regulate their own "homegrown" companies and has culminated in *Wickard v. Filburn* (1942), where the Court actually held *that even where farm production was intended wholly for consumption on the farm*, it is subject to federal regulation since the consumption *might* reduce the demand for other commodities which *might* have an effect on interstate commerce.

Note that the court said that because consumption on the farm *might* reduce the demand for other commodities which in turn *might* have an effect on interstate commerce, Big Brother will regulate farm production.

It appears that between 1937 and 1995, the Supreme Court upheld virtually every regulation of business enacted by Congress. Then in 1995 in *United States v. Lopez*, the Court held as invalid a federal statute barring possession of a gun in a school zone because such an act would be a criminal act, not related to economics, and therefore not a proper subject for the commerce clause.

Again in 2000, in *United States v. Morrison*, the court held invalid the Violence Against Women Act which was intended to protect women against gender-based violence, because it did not involve interstate commerce. The Court also held that the Constitution distinguishes between national and local matters, and that the police power, i.e., the general power to regulate health, safety, morals and welfare belongs to the states.

Hence the Commerce Clause is one of the most potent vehicles by which the federal government has amassed power far in excess of what the framers of the Constitution envisioned and far in excess of what the decisions virtually contemporaneous with the Constitution itself had held.

The Spending Clause, Article I, § 8, clause 1:

"The Congress shall have the power to lay and collect taxes, duties, imposts and excises to pay the debts and provide for the common defense and general welfare of the United States. . . ."

40.

Thomas Jefferson's excerpted discussion of the "tax and spend" clause follows:

"I consider the foundation of the constitution as laid on this ground . That "all powers not delegated to the united states, by the constitution, nor prohibited by it to the states, are reserved to the states or to the people. . . " *To take a single step beyond the boundaries thus specially drawn around the powers of congress, is to take possession of a boundless field of power, no longer susceptible of any definition....*

"1.To lay taxes [is]to provide for the general welfare of the United States, that is to say, "to lay taxes for the purpose of providing for the general welfare." For the laying of taxes is the power, and the general welfare the purpose for which the power is to be exercised. They are not to lay taxes *ad libitum* for any purpose they please; but only to pay the debts or provide for the welfare of the Union. In like manner, they are not to do anything they please to provide for the general welfare, but only to lay taxes for that purpose. *To consider the latter phrase, not as describing the purpose of the first, but as giving a distinct and independent power to do any act they please, which might be for the good of the Union, would render all the preceding and subsequent enumerations of power completely useless.*

"It would reduce the whole instrument to a single phrase, that of instituting a Congress with power to do whatever would be for the good of the United States; and, as they would be the sole judges of the good or evil, it would be also a power to do whatever evil they please....

More recently in *King v. Burwell* (2015) the Supreme Court did it again, i.e., it utilized Orwellian logic to arrive at the decision it decided it wanted. The issue before the Court was whether a particular assessment, within the Affordable Care Act, by the federal government, was a tax or a penalty. In order to retain jurisdiction to hear the matter, it was necessary to describe it as a penalty. This was necessary as were it a tax, proof of having paid such "tax" was necessary in order to oppose it. The tax was not yet due and hence had not been paid, hence it necessarily was determined to be a penalty.

Now, having retained jurisdiction for purposes of adjudication, it was then determined to be a tax for purposes of Article I, Section 8, clause 1 of the U.S. Constitution. Hence, having decided previously that a tax is appropriate for any purpose deemed appropriate by Congress, the tax was necessarily appropriate and hence Constitutional.

Although this reasoning by Chief Justice Roberts is questionable, his "justification" for such reasoning was presented in his conclusion, to wit:

" In a democracy, the power to make the law rests with those chosen by the people. Our role is more confined - to say what the law is, *Marbury v. Madison,* 1 Cranch 137, 177 (1803). That is easier in some case than in others. But in every case we must respect the role of the Legislature, and take care not to undo

41.

what it has done. A fair reading of legislation demands a fair understanding of the legislative plan.

"Congress passed the Affordable Care Act to improve health insurance markets, not to destroy them. If at all possible, we must interpret the Act in a way that is consistent with the former, and avoids the latter. Section 36B can fairly be read consistent with what we see as Congress's plan, and that is the reading we adopt.

"The judgment of the United States Court of Appeal for the Fourth Circuit is Affirmed."

Again, notwithstanding the sage advice of Mr. Jefferson, and the *Butler* decision, the following cases upheld Congress's exceeding both its "commerce" power and its "tax and spend" power.

Thus in *Mulford v. Smith* (1939), the Court upheld a federal penalty tax for "excess" tobacco production even though such production was entirely within the state and therefore a state function.

According to *United States v. Gerlach Live Stock Co.,* (1950) Congress's power to spend must be exercised for the "general welfare."

However, under *Helvering v. Davis*, (1937), what constitutes "general welfare" is left entirely to Congress.

A more recent case permitting Congress to amass power onto itself is *South Dakota v. Dole* (1987), in which the court held that even though the federal government may be prohibited from enacting certain legislation, perhaps because such power resides within the state, such as the minimum drinking age, the federal government may condition its federal spending on the state's enacting laws which are consistent with the federal government's position. This of course permits an end-run around limitations the enumerated powers were intended to ensure.

Hence, the Supreme Court, by casting aside obviously correct decisions, i.e., decisions comporting with the true intent of the drafters of the Constitution, and instead opting for amassing to themselves the power to create a country in their own image, have intruded into almost every aspect of American life.

As a result, the people are left with fewer decisions which they can make regarding their own lives ... Big Brother increasingly does it for us ...

Hence, the bottom line is if Congress can regulate it, Congress can tax it. Since, under *Wickard v Filburn*, discussed above, Congress can regulate, *ad infinitum,* provided their wilful co-conspirator, the Supreme Court, accedes, it would appear that Congress can also tax within the same limitless contours.

On the subject of taxation, George Mason, in 1788, in a speech to the Virginia Ratifying Convention, in opposition to ratification of the proposed Constitution, stated:

... "*The power [to tax] is calculated to annihilate totally the state governments. Will the people of this great community submit to being individually taxed by two different and distinct powers? Will they suffer themselves to be doubly harassed? These two concurrent powers cannot exist long together; the one will destroy the other: the general government being paramount to and in every respect more powerful than the state governments, the latter must give way to the former."*

Congress has passed legislation, i.e., the Affordable Care Act, essentially forcing the People to purchase health insurance and assessing penalties for not doing so. The Constitution does not authorize Congress to legislate in this area. It is therefore unconstitutional.

However, as seen above, the Court ignored the reasoning of Mason, Madison and Jefferson as employed in *Butler,* and permitted Congress to legislate in areas not authorized by the Constitution.

Stated another way, since the purchase, or non-purchase, of health insurance is not one of the enumerated powers in Article I, § 8, the federal government cannot regulate it and further since the federal government cannot regulate it, it cannot tax it. Hence, the federal government has no power to force the People to purchase health insurance and/or to tax us for this purpose.

In summary, thus far this work has concerned itself with the means by which the Supreme Court has amassed great power to itself and its coconspirator, Congress. This of course expanded the power of the federal government over our lives and necessarily reduced the powers of the states and their respective citizens. *It would not be long before the Court realized that to complete its task of reigning-over the People, it would be necessary to directly and specifically check the power of the respective states.*

The next two chapters present two means by which the Supreme Court, *via* concocted devices, has rendered *state* legislation and *state* constitutions subject to the unauthorized scrutiny of the Supreme Court, resulting in a vast number of state laws and state constitutional provisions being held unconstitutional.

A fairly recent example of the Court's redefining the text of the U.S. Constitution is *Obergefell v. Hodges* (2015). Therein the Court ignored 800 years of history and defined the term "liberty" in the 14th Amendment, Due Process clause to include the right to same-sex marriage. This is in violation of the oath taken by all members of the Supreme Court to "support this Constitution." As suggested by Thomas Jefferson, in 1821, to impeach and set the whole adrift is the appropriate and only remedy.

CHAPTER 5

DOCTRINE OF INCORPORATION OR EMASCULATION OF THE STATES

The doctrine of incorporation can best be described as perhaps the most ingenious, deceptive act of legerdemain perpetrated by the Supreme Court to emasculate the states and the People, thereby depriving them of their freedoms, as ever existed in American history, ". . . all with the stated purpose of extending to all the people of the nation the complete protection of the bill of rights. . ."

This court-made doctrine continues to clarify which of the first eight amendments, also referred to as the Bill of Rights, applies to the States through the 14th Amendment Due Process clause, with the result that the States and People are *stripped* of freedoms on a continuing basis.

The extent to which the 14th Amendment incorporates the Bill of Rights, i.e., to what extent it constrains the state as well as the federal government by applying the first eight amendments to the states is the subject of this chapter.

Our discussion of this doctrine necessarily involves a discussion of some of the first eight amendments. Amendments are stated in their entirety in Appendix A.

For example, the First Amendment states:

"Congress shall make no law respecting an establishment of religion, or prohibiting the free exercise thereof; or abridging the freedom of speech, or of the press; or the right of the people peaceably to assemble, and to petition the Government for a redress of grievances."

It must be noted that the very first word of this amendment is "Congress." Hence, as will be seen, there is no question that the Bill of Rights was originally intended to apply to the federal government *only* and *not* to the states.

It is critical to realize that the Bill of Rights was *not* a list of freedoms given *to* the states and the People *by* the newly formed federal government, but was instead a list of rights assuring that the federal government would not take these then-existing rights *from* the states and the People. *Stated another way, the Bill of Rights was a limitation on the power of the new federal government, not a limitation on the states.*

As for the first eight amendments, it was early confirmed that they, as originally enacted, protected the individual and the state *from actions of the federal government only* and that the Bill of Rights *did not apply to the States* and therefore were not limitations on the states, *Barron v. Baltimore,* (1833).

Barron's suit revolved around the 5th Amendment, which states in part:

"...No person shall...be deprived of life, liberty, or property, without due process of law; nor shall private property be taken for public use, without just compensation."

Barron brought an action against the City of Baltimore claiming that since the city had diverted the flow of streams so that they deposited silt in front of his wharf making the water too shallow, vessels could no longer reach *Barron's* wharf. *Barron* claimed that the Fifth Amendment to the Constitution guaranteed that the State Court had to protect Barron from this loss of property. The court held unequivocally that the Fifth Amendment applied *only* to the Federal Government and *not* to the state governments. This was of course correct as it was beyond dispute that the Bill of Rights were a list of rights in which the newly created federal government promised not to interfere with, in exchange for the states and the people creating the federal government.

Now comes the 14th Amendment, *Due Process* clause, ratified in 1868. It states in pertinent part:

"...Nor shall any State deprive any person of life, liberty or property without *due process* of law..."

As previously stated, the extent to which the 14th Amendment incorporates the Bill of Rights, i.e., to what extent it constrains the state as well as the federal government, by applying the first eight amendments to the states, is the subject of this chapter.

To state the doctrine is to call attention to its absurdity. There is nothing on the face of the due process clause, as written, that suggests its meaning to be anything other than what is clearly stated, i.e., that before the State can deprive a *person*, as opposed to a *citizen*, of life, liberty or property, there must be some process by which this is done. It says nothing about the Bill of Rights or any other portion of the then-existing Constitution.

In 1873 it was held, consistent with the above reasoning, that the Due Process clause of the 14th Amendment was *not* intended to apply the Bill of Rights to the states, *Slaughterhouse Cases*, 1873, which follows:

"The Louisiana legislature chartered a corporation and granted to it, for twenty-five years, an exclusive right to operate facilities in New Orleans for the landing, keeping and slaughter of livestock. All competing plants were required to cease operation, and independent butchers were given a right to slaughter at the corporation's plant on paying maximum charges which were fixed by statute. New Orleans butchers sued in the state courts to have the act declared invalid as a violation of both the 13th and 14th amendments."

The statute was upheld by the Louisiana Supreme Court.

Referring to the Due Process clause of the 14th Amendment, the *Slaughterhouse* court stated:

" ...The first of these paragraphs [the due process clause] has been in the Constitution since the adoption of the fifth amendment, as a restraint upon the Federal power. It is also to be found in some form of expression in the constitutions of nearly all the States, as a restraint upon the power of the States. This law then, has practically been the same as it now is during the existence of the government, except so far as the present amendment may place the restraining power over the States in this matter in the hands of the Federal government.

" We are not without judicial interpretation, therefore, both State and National, of the meaning of this clause. And it is sufficient to say that under no construction of that provision that we have ever seen, or any that we deem admissible, can the restraint imposed by the State of Louisiana upon the exercise of their trade by the butchers of New Orleans be held to be a deprivation of property within the meaning of the[14th Amendment due-process clause]"

So, as of 1873, the matter was closed. . . . the Due Process clause of the 14th Amendment did *not* apply the Bill of Rights to the States.

Then in 1937, in *the Palko v.Connecticut* case, which involved the *state's* right to appeal after the defendant had been found guilty of second degree murder. Defendant claimed the 5th amendment, double-jeopardy clause applied to the states through the 14th Amendment, Due Process clause and that defendant therefore could not be tried again.

The 5th amendment states, in pertinent part, "...No person shall be...subject for the same offense to be twice put in jeopardy of life or limb."

In the *Palko* case, Justice Cordozo held that ". . . there is no such general rule that..."Whatever would be a violation of the original bill of rights [Amendments 1 to 8] if done by the federal government is now equally unlawful by force of the Fourteenth Amendment if done by a state."

Hence he found that the 5th amendment double-jeopardy clause did *not* apply to the states through the 14th Amendment Due process clause. However he further stated that the 14th Amendment Due Process Clause incorporates:

"...those principles implicit in the concept of ordered liberty"... *Palko v. Connecticut* (1937);

"...the principles of liberty and justice which lie at the base of all our civil and political institutions..." *Herbert v. Louisiana* (1926);

"...The principles of justice so rooted in the traditions and conscience of our people as to be ranked fundamental..." Snyder v. Massachusetts (1934).

It is submitted that these formulae are completely unworkable except as they permit each justice to decide for himself (or herself, lest we be politically incorrect) what they mean. By allowing this subjective adjudication, the justices are bound by nothing and are free to fashion a next flowery phrase every bit as confounding as those preceding it.

In general, the trend continues to be to apply the Bill of Rights to the states in a piecemeal fashion depending on the collective agenda of the nine Justices of the Supreme Court. Of course the only factually and contextually correct response to the query re the extent to which the Due Process clause of the 14th Amendment applies or incorporates the Bill of Rights to the states, is that the Bill of Rights *were never intended to apply to the states.*

Instead, the court has opted for an open-ended approach, i.e., the 14th Amendment Due Process clause incorporates only those amendments whose rights are deemed *fundamental* by the court. *In other words, the incorporation doctrine includes only those amendments the Court determines it should include.* The absurdity of the Court's flailing about to define the proper theory by which the States and therefore the People can be ruled by the "nine lawyers in robes"will be illustrated by the *Adamson* case which follows.

Of course the reason the Court cannot come up with an objective test to determine which of the Bill of Rights the framers of the 14th Amendment Due Process clause meant to be applied to the states is that the framers of the 14th Amendment had no such intent.

Applying the Bill of Rights to the states simply permits the Supreme Court to emasculate the states and limit what the states may legislate, thereby limiting what the people of each state may choose to do for themselves. So what started out to be a limitation on the federal government *only*, as an inducement for the colonies to agree to the formation of said federal government, which they feared, has now been reversed and applied to the states; their worst fear recognized.

Perhaps the most pertinent and illuminating case is the 1947 case of *Adamson* which follows. Therein the case contains the various arguments, including the *Palko* rationale, used to invent another doctrine or theory upon which to justify applying the Bill of Rights to the states. As will be seen, some argued that the Due Process clause of the 14th Amendment incorporated *all* of the first 8 amendments and applied them to the states. Others argued that the power of the federal government was *not* limited by any particular clause in the Constitution, but that the federal government has *no actual limitation of power*. Others argued that the first eight amendments were applied *piecemeal* to the states *via* the *Due Process* clause of the 14th amendment.

What is pathetically obvious is that the Court had made up its collective mind to control the States by *some* means even though the Constitution clearly dictated otherwise. The *Adamson* case shows the various " lawyers in robes" flailing-about and vying for dominance as to the method by which the States, and their People, would be controlled.

Excerpts from the *Adamson* case:

U.S. SUPREME COURT
ADAMSON V. PEOPLE OF STATE OF CALIFORNIA
332 U.S. 46 (1947)

Mr. Justice REED delivered the opinion of the Court:

"The appellant, Adamson, a citizen of the United States, was convicted, ...by a jury in a Superior Court of the State of California of murder in the first degree. After considering the same objections to the conviction that are pressed here, the sentence of death was affirmed by the Supreme Court of the state...The provisions of California law which were challenged in the state proceedings as invalid under the Fourteenth Amendment to the Federal Constitution are those of the state constitution and penal code.

"They permit the failure of a defendant to explain or to deny evidence against him to be commented upon by court and by counsel and to be considered by court and jury. The defendant did not testify. As the trial court gave its instructions and the District Attorney argued the case in accordance with the constitutional and statutory provisions just referred to, we have for decision the question of their constitutionality in these circumstances under the limitations of the Fourteenth Amendment.

Justice Reed, writing for the majority, held:

"The due process clause of the Fourteenth Amendment, ... does not draw all the rights of the federal Bill of Rights under its protection... Nothing has been called to our attention that either the framers of the Fourteenth Amendment or the states that adopted [it] intended its due process clause to draw within its scope the earlier amendments to the Constitution..."

The 5th amendment states in its entirety:

" No person shall be held to answer for a capital, or otherwise infamous crime, unless on a presentment or indictment of a Grand Jury, except in cases arising in the land or naval forces, or in the Militia, when in actual service in time of War or public danger; nor shall any person be subject for the same offense to be twice put in jeopardy of life or limb; nor shall be compelled in any criminal case to be a witness against himself, nor be deprived of life, liberty, or property, without due process of law; nor shall private property be taken for public use, without just compensation."

The portion of the 5th amendment involved here is as follows:

"...No person... shall be compelled in any criminal case to be a witness against himself, nor be deprived of life, liberty, or property, without due process of law..."

The Court affirmed the conviction.

"Mr. Justice Frankfurter (concurring, and referring to the 6th Amendment).

"In Suits at common law, where the value in controversy shall exceed twenty dollars, the right of trial by jury shall be preserved, and no fact tried by a jury, shall be otherwise re-examined in any Court of the United States, than according to the rules of the common law."

"The short answer to the suggestion that the provision of the Fourteenth Amendment, which ordains 'nor shall any State deprive any person of life, liberty, or property, without due process of law,' was a way of saying that every State must thereafter initiate prosecutions through indictment by a grand jury, must have a trial by a jury of 12 in criminal cases, and must have trial by such a jury in common law suits where the amount in controversy exceeds $20, is *that it is a strange way of saying it. It would be extraordinarily strange for a Constitution to convey such specific commands in such a roundabout and inexplicit way.*

"After all, an amendment to the Constitution should be read in a 'sense most obvious to the common understanding at the time of its adoption... For it was for public adoption that it was proposed....' Those reading the English language with the meaning which it ordinarily conveys, those conversant with the political and legal history of the concept of due process, those sensitive to the relations of the States to the central government as well as the relation of some of the provisions of the Bill of Rights to the process of justice, *would hardly recognize the Fourteenth Amendment as a cover for the various explicit provisions of the first eight Amendments.*

"Some of these are enduring reflections of experience with human nature, while some express the restricted views of Eighteenth-Century England regarding the best methods for the ascertainment of facts.

"The notion that the Fourteenth Amendment was a covert way of imposing upon the States all the rules which it seemed important to Eighteenth Century statesmen to write into the Federal Amendments, was rejected by judges who were themselves witnesses of the process by which the Fourteenth Amendment became part of the Constitution. Arguments that may now be adduced to prove that the first eight Amendments were concealed within the historic phrasing of the Fourteenth Amendment were not unknown at the time of its adoption. A surer estimate of their bearing was possible for judges at the time than distorting distance is likely to vouchsafe. Any evidence of design or purpose not contemporaneously known could hardly have influenced those who ratified the Amendment. Remarks of a particular proponent of the Amendment, no matter

50.

how influential, are not to be deemed part of the Amendment. What was submitted for ratification was his proposal, not his speech.

"Thus, at the time of the ratification of the Fourteenth Amendment the constitutions of nearly half of the ratifying States did not have the rigorous requirements of the Fifth Amendment for instituting criminal proceedings through a grand jury. It could hardly have occurred to these States that by ratifying the Amendment they uprooted their established methods for prosecuting crime and fastened upon themselves a new prosecutorial system."

Discussion of the 6th amendment, repeated here, states:

"In Suits at common law, where the value in controversy shall exceed twenty dollars, the right of trial by jury shall be preserved, and no fact tried by a jury, shall be otherwise re-examined in any Court of the United States, than according to the rules of the common law."

"Indeed, the suggestion that the Fourteenth Amendment incorporates the first eight Amendments as such is not unambiguously urged. Even the boldest innovator would shrink from suggesting to more than half the States that they may no longer initiate prosecutions without indictment by grand jury, or that thereafter all the States of the Union must furnish a jury of 12 for every case involving a claim above $20.

"There is suggested merely a selective incorporation of the first eight Amendments into the Fourteenth Amendment. Some are in and some are out, but we are left in the dark as to which are in and which are out. Nor are we given the calculus for determining which go in and which stay out. If the basis of selection is merely that those provisions of the first eight Amendments are incorporated which commend themselves to individual justices as indispensable to the dignity and happiness of a free man, we are thrown back to a merely subjective test.

"The protection against unreasonable search and seizure might have primacy for one judge, while trial by a jury of 12 for every claim above $20 might appear to another as an ultimate need in a free society. In the history of thought 'natural law' has a much longer and much better founded meaning and justification than such subjective selection of the first eight Amendments for incorporation into the Fourteenth. If all that is meant is that due process contains within itself certain minimal standards which are *'of the very essence of a scheme of ordered liberty,'* *Palko v. Connecticut*, putting upon this Court the duty of applying these standards from time to time, then we have merely arrived at the insight which our predecessors long ago expressed.

"We are called upon to apply to the difficult issues of our own day the wisdom afforded by the great opinions in this field,... This guidance bids us to be duly mindful of the heritage of the past, with its great lessons of how liberties are won and how they are lost. As judges charged with the delicate task of subjecting the government of a continent to the Rule of Law we must be particularly mindful that it is 'a constitution we are expounding,' so that it should not be imprisoned in what are merely legal forms even though they have the sanction of the Eighteenth Century.

"And so, when, as in a case like the present, a conviction in a State court is here for review under a claim that a right protected by the Due Process Clause of the Fourteenth Amendment has been denied, the issue is *not* whether an infraction of one of the specific provisions of the first eight Amendments is disclosed by the record. The relevant question *is* whether the criminal proceedings which resulted in conviction deprived the accused of the due process of law to which the United States Constitution entitled him. Judicial review of that guaranty of the Fourteenth Amendment inescapably imposes upon this Court an exercise of judgment upon the whole course of the proceedings in order to ascertain whether they offend those canons of decency and fairness which express the notions of justice of English-speaking peoples even toward those charged with the most heinous offenses. These standards of justice are not authoritatively formulated anywhere as though they were prescriptions in a pharmacopoeia.

"But neither does the application of the Due Process Clause imply that judges are wholly at large. The judicial judgment in applying the Due Process Clause must move within the limits of accepted notions of justice and is not to be based upon the idiosyncrasies of a merely personal judgment. The fact that judges among themselves may differ whether in a particular case a trial offends accepted notions of justice is not disproof that general rather than idiosyncratic standards are applied. An important safeguard against such merely individual judgment is an alert deference to the judgment of the State court under review.

Hence, what began as a cogent, concurring opinion eventually descended into simply another form of subjective adjudication.

Mr. Justice BLACK, dissenting.

"This decision reasserts a constitutional theory that this Court is endowed by the Constitution with boundless power under 'natural law' periodically to expand and contract constitutional standards to conform to the Court's conception of what at a particular time constitutes 'civilized decency' and 'fundamental principles of liberty and justice. Invoking this...rule, the Court concludes that although comment upon testimony in a federal court would violate the Fifth Amendment, identical comment in a state court does not violate today's fashion in civilized decency and fundamentals and is therefore not prohibited by the Federal Constitution as amended.

52.

"I think the 'natural law' theory of the Constitution, degrades the constitutional safeguards of the Bill of Rights and simultaneously appropriates for this Court a broad power which we are not authorized by the Constitution to exercise.

"And I further contend that the 'natural law' formula which the Court uses to reach its conclusion in this case should be abandoned as an incongruous excrescence on our Constitution. I believe that formula to be itself a violation of our Constitution, in that it subtly conveys to courts, at the expense of legislatures, ultimate power over public policies in fields where no specific provision of the Constitution limits legislative power.

"I cannot consider the Bill of Rights to be an outworn 18th Century 'strait jacket'. Its provisions may be thought outdated abstractions by some. And it is true that they were designed to meet ancient evils. But they are the same kind of human evils that have emerged from century to century wherever excessive power is sought by the few at the expense of the many. In my judgment the people of no nation can lose their liberty so long as a Bill of Rights like ours survives and its basic purposes are conscientiously interpreted, enforced and respected so as to afford continuous protection against old, as well as new, devices and practices which might thwart those purposes. I fear to see the consequences of the Court's practice of substituting its own concepts of decency and fundamental justice for the language of the Bill of Rights as its point of departure in interpreting and enforcing that Bill of Rights.

" If the choice must be between the selective process of the Palko decision applying some of the Bill of Rights to the States, or the ... rule applying none of them, I would choose the *Palko* selective process.

" *But rather than accept either of these choices. I would follow what I believe was the original purpose of the Fourteenth Amendment-to extend to all the people of the nation the complete protection of the Bill of Rights.* To hold that this Court can determine what, if any, provisions of the Bill of Rights will be enforced, and if so to what degree, is to frustrate the great design of a written Constitution.

"Conceding the possibility that this Court is now wise enough to improve on the Bill of Rights by substituting natural law concepts for the Bill of Rights. I think the possibility is entirely too speculative to agree to take that course. I would therefore hold in this case that the full protection of the Fifth Amendment's proscription against compelled testimony must be afforded by California. This I would do because of reliance upon the original purpose of the Fourteenth Amendment...

"But this formula also has been used in the past and can be used in the future, to license this Court, in considering regulatory legislation, to roam at large in the broad expanses of policy and morals and to trespass, all too freely, on the legislative domain of the States as well as the Federal Government.

"Since *Marbury v. Madison*, 1803, was decided, the practice has been firmly established for better or worse, that courts can strike down legislative enactments which violate the Constitution. This process, of course, involves interpretation, and since words can have many meanings, interpretation obviously may result in contraction or extension of the original purpose of a constitutional provision thereby affecting policy.

"But to pass upon the constitutionality of statutes by looking to the particular standards enumerated in the Bill of Rights and other parts of the Constitution is one thing; to invalidate statutes because of application of 'natural law' deemed to be above and undefined by the Constitution is another. *'In the one instance, courts proceeding within clearly marked constitutional boundaries seek to execute policies written into the Constitution; in the other they roam at will in the limitless area of their own beliefs as to reasonableness and actually select policies, a responsibility which the Constitution entrusts to the legislative representatives of the people.*

"Mr. Justice DOUGLAS joins in this opinion.

"Mr. Justice MURPHY, with whom Mr. Justice RUTLEDGE concurs, dissenting.

"While in substantial agreement with the views of Mr. Justice BLACK, I have one reservation and one addition to make. I agree that the specific guarantees of the Bill of Rights should be carried over intact into the first section of the Fourteenth Amendment. *But I am not prepared to say that the latter is entirely and necessarily limited by the Bill of Rights.* Occasions may arise where a proceeding falls so far short of conforming to fundamental standards of procedure as to warrant constitutional condemnation in terms of a lack of due process despite the absence of a specific provision in the Bill of Rights."

To summarize the respective Justice's holdings:

Justice Reed, writing for the majority, held that the California law was not unconstitutional as "The due process clause of the Fourteenth Amendment, ... does not draw all the rights of the federal Bill of Rights under its protection... Nothing has been called to our attention that either the framers of the Fourteenth Amendment or the states that adopted [it] intended its due process clause to draw within its scope the earlier amendments to the Constitution..."

Of course, Justice Reed was precisely correct.

Justice Frankfurter, concurring in the decision, also argued that the due process clause of the 14th amendment did *not* incorporate the first eight amendments and apply them to the states, but then argued that the Court should apply the 'natural law' doctrine which is itself a 'subjective adjudication', and stated that the Court had no limitation on ruling on the States' statutes!

Justice Murphy joined by Justice Rutledge dissented and argued that the due process clause *does* incorporate the Bill of Rights and applies them to the states but that the power of the federal government to control the actions of the states may exceed, under the proper circumstances, the Bill of Rights.

Justice Black, joined by Justice Douglas, argued that the *entire Bill of Rights* were incorporated by the Due Process clause of the 14th amendment and applied to the states.

So, in the *Adamson* case, the court revealed its internal thinking and discussed the various theories or doctrines resident in their fertile minds with the result that some entirely invented concoction would be the decision of the court which purports to inform the world of the meaning of our U.S. Constitution. This is an example of the most egregious of judicial activism, often with the result that the court actually rewrites the U.S. Constitution . . . an act of which they should be embarrassed . . . instead of which they appear to be proud.

As if it wasn't enough for the Court to perpetuate this myth re incorporation, the Court went even further in *Griswold v. Connecticut*, 1965, by holding that the 14th amendment Due Process clause limited states as to their ability to legislate regarding married persons using contraceptive devices. Some on the Court "justified" this result by finding a right which does not exist in the Constitution, i.e., the *right to privacy*, thereby going beyond the Bill of Rights in controlling the States and their People.

Others claimed it was justified because of the 9th amendment which states in pertinent part, " the enumeration of certain rights shall not be construed to deny or disparage others retained by the people."

Still other justices found justification for this result in the Due Process clause of the 14th Amendment.

So in *Griswold*, the Supreme Court expanded their role in our lives and control of the states by liberating themselves from the self-imposed Bill of Rights and natural law limitations and simply declared a new "right" heretofore unknown and conceived from body parts of various of the Bill of Rights, much in the fashion of Mary Shelley and the Frankenstein monster, then applied this new right to the states through the 14th Amendment Due Process Clause... another egregious act of legerdemain . . . .

Griswold is presented as a precursor to the landmark case of *Roe v. Wade* This is the case from which the legal fiction of the "right of privacy" was given birth and thereafter stood as "authority" for *Roe* and the "Constitutional right" to an abortion.

U.S. SUPREME COURT
GRISWOLD V. CONNECTICUT
381 U.S. 479 (1965)

MR. JUSTICE DOUGLAS delivered the opinion of the Court. ...

"We do not sit as a super-legislature to determine the wisdom, need, and propriety of laws that touch economic problems, business affairs, or social conditions. This law, however, operates directly on an intimate relation of husband and wife and their physician's role in one aspect of that relation."

Justice Douglas apparently admits that they *do* sit as a super-legislature in this case involving intimacy between husband and wife.

"The association of people is not mentioned in the Constitution nor in the Bill of Rights. The right to educate a child in a school of the parents' choice - whether public or private or parochial - is also not mentioned. Nor is the right to study any particular subject or any foreign language. Yet the First Amendment has been construed to include certain of those rights.

"Previous cases suggest that specific guarantees in the Bill of Rights have penumbras, formed by emanations from those guarantees that help give them life and substance...Various guarantees create zones of privacy. The right of association contained in the penumbra of the First Amendment is one, as we have seen. The Third Amendment in its prohibition against the quartering of soldiers 'in any house' in time of peace without the consent of the owner is another facet of that privacy. The Fourth Amendment explicitly affirms the 'right of the people to be secure in their persons, houses, papers, and effects, against unreasonable searches and seizures.' The Fifth Amendment in its Self-Incrimination Clause enables the citizen to create a zone of privacy which government may not force him to surrender to his detriment. The Ninth Amendment provides: 'The enumeration in the Constitution, of certain rights, shall not be construed to deny or disparage others retained by the people.'

"The Fourth and Fifth Amendments were described... as protection against all governmental invasions 'of the sanctity of a man's home and the privacies of life.' We recently referred to the Fourth Amendment as creating a 'right to privacy, no less important than any other right carefully and particularly reserved to the people.'

"We have had many controversies over these penumbral rights of 'privacy and repose'....the right of privacy which presses for recognition here is a legitimate one. The present case, then, concerns a relationship lying within the zone of privacy created by several fundamental constitutional guarantees. And it concerns a law which, in forbidding the use of contraceptives rather than regulating their manufacture or sale, seeks to achieve its goals by means having a maximum destructive impact upon that relationship. Such a law cannot stand in light of the familiar principle, so often applied by this Court, that a 'governmental purpose to control or prevent activities constitutionally subject to state regulation may not be achieved by means which sweep unnecessarily broadly and thereby invade the area of protected freedoms.' NAACP v. Alabama... Would we allow the police to search the sacred precincts of marital bedrooms for telltale signs of the use of contraceptives? The very idea is repulsive to the notions of privacy surrounding the marriage relationship.

"We deal with a right of privacy older than the Bill of Rights - older than our political parties, older than our school system. Marriage is a coming together for better or for worse, hopefully enduring, and intimate to the degree of being sacred. It is an association that promotes a way of life, not causes; a harmony in living, not political faiths; a bilateral loyalty, not commercial or social projects. Yet it is an association for as noble a purpose as any involved in our prior decisions. Reversed.

MR. JUSTICE GOLDBERG, whom THE CHIEF JUSTICE and MR. JUSTICE BRENNAN join, concurring.

"I agree with the Court that Connecticut's birth-control law unconstitutionally intrudes upon the right of marital privacy, and I join in its opinion and judgment. Although I have not accepted the view that "due process" as used in the Fourteenth Amendment incorporates all of the first eight Amendments (see my concurring opinion in Pointer v. Texas, I do agree that the concept of liberty protects those personal rights that are fundamental, and is not confined to the specific terms of the Bill of Rights.

"My conclusion that the concept of liberty is not so restricted and that it embraces the right of marital privacy though that right is not mentioned explicitly in the Constitution is supported both by numerous decisions of this Court, referred to in the Court's opinion, and by the language and history of the Ninth Amendment. In reaching the conclusion that the right of marital privacy is protected, as being within the protected penumbra of specific guarantees of the Bill of Rights, the Court refers to the Ninth Amendment. I add these words to emphasize the relevance of that Amendment to the Court's holding.

"The Court stated many years ago that the Due Process Clause protects those liberties that are 'so rooted in the traditions and conscience of our people as to be ranked as fundamental.' *Snyder v. Massachusetts.*

"This Court, in a series of decisions, has held that the Fourteenth Amendment absorbs and applies to the States those specifics of the first eight amendments which express fundamental personal rights. The language and history of the Ninth Amendment reveal that the Framers of the Constitution believed that there are additional fundamental rights, protected from governmental infringement, which exist alongside those fundamental rights specifically mentioned in the first eight constitutional amendments.

"The Ninth Amendment reads, 'The enumeration in the Constitution, of certain rights, shall not be construed to deny or disparage others retained by the people.' The Amendment is almost entirely the work of James Madison. It was introduced in Congress by him and passed the House and Senate with little or no debate and virtually no change in language. It was proffered to quiet expressed fears that a bill of specifically enumerated rights could not be sufficiently broad to cover all essential rights and that the specific mention of certain rights would be interpreted as a denial that others were protected.

In presenting the proposed Amendment, Madison said:

'It has been objected also against a bill of rights, that, by enumerating particular exceptions to the grant of power, it would disparage those rights which were not placed in that enumeration; and it might follow by implication, that those rights which were not singled out, were intended to be assigned into the hands of the General Government, and were consequently insecure. This is one of the most plausible arguments I have ever heard urged against the admission of a bill of rights into this system; but, I conceive, that it may be guarded against. I have attempted it, as gentlemen may see by turning to the last clause of the fourth resolution [the Ninth Amendment].'...

"Mr. Justice Story, in 1891, wrote of this argument against a bill of rights and the meaning of the Ninth Amendment:

'In regard to . . . [a] suggestion, that the affirmance of certain rights might disparage others, or might lead to argumentative implications in favor of other powers, it might be sufficient to say that such a course of reasoning could never be sustained upon any solid basis . . . . But a conclusive answer is, that such an attempt may be interdicted (as it has been) by a positive declaration in such a bill of rights that the enumeration of certain rights shall not be construed to deny or disparage others retained by the people.'

"These statements of Madison and Story make clear that the Framers did not intend that the first eight amendments be construed to exhaust the basic and fundamental rights which the Constitution guaranteed to the people. While this Court has had little occasion to interpret the Ninth Amendment, '[i]t cannot be presumed that any clause in the constitution is intended to be without effect.' *Marbury v. Madison*, 1803.

"In interpreting the Constitution, 'real effect should be given to all the words it uses.' ... The Ninth Amendment to the Constitution may be regarded by some as a recent discovery and may be forgotten by others, but since 1791 it has been a basic part of the Constitution which we are sworn to uphold. To hold that a right so basic and fundamental and so deep-rooted in our society as the right of privacy in marriage may be infringed because that right is not guaranteed in so many words by the first eight amendments to the Constitution is to ignore the Ninth Amendment and to give it no effect whatsoever. Moreover, a judicial construction that this fundamental right is not protected by the Constitution because it is not mentioned in explicit terms by one of the first eight amendments or elsewhere in the Constitution would violate the Ninth Amendment, which specifically states that ' [t]he enumeration in the Constitution, of certain rights, shall not be construed to deny or disparage others retained by the people.'

"A dissenting opinion suggests that my interpretation of the Ninth Amendment somehow 'broaden[s] the powers of this Court.' With all due respect, I believe

58.

that it misses the import of what I am saying. I do not take the position of my Brother BLACK in his dissent in Adamson v. California, that the entire Bill of Rights is incorporated in the Fourteenth Amendment, and I do not mean to imply that the Ninth Amendment is applied against the States by the Fourteenth. Nor do I mean to state that the Ninth Amendment constitutes an independent source of rights protected from infringement by either the States or the Federal Government.

Rather, the Ninth Amendment shows a belief of the Constitution's authors that fundamental rights exist that are not expressly enumerated in the first eight amendments and an intent that the list of rights included there not be deemed exhaustive. As any student of this Court's opinions knows, this Court has held, often unanimously, that the Fifth and Fourteenth Amendments protect certain fundamental personal liberties from abridgment by the Federal Government or the States...

"The Ninth Amendment simply shows the intent of the Constitution's authors that other fundamental personal rights should not be denied such protection or disparaged in any other way simply because they are not specifically listed in the first eight constitutional amendments. I do not see how this broadens the authority of the Court; rather it serves to support what this Court has been doing in protecting fundamental rights.

"Nor am I turning somersaults with history in arguing that the Ninth Amendment is relevant in a case dealing with a State's infringement of a fundamental right. While the Ninth Amendment - and indeed the entire Bill of Rights - originally concerned restrictions upon federal power, the subsequently enacted Fourteenth Amendment prohibits the States as well from abridging fundamental personal liberties. And, the Ninth Amendment, in indicating that not all such liberties are specifically mentioned in the first eight amendments, is surely relevant in showing the existence of other fundamental personal rights, now protected from state, as well as federal, infringement.

"In sum, the Ninth Amendment simply lends strong support to the view that the "liberty" protected by the Fifth and Fourteenth Amendments from infringement by the Federal Government or the States is not restricted to rights specifically mentioned in the first eight amendments.

"In determining which rights are fundamental, judges are not left at large to decide cases in light of their personal and private notions. Rather, they must look to the 'traditions and [collective] conscience of our people' to determine whether a principle is 'so rooted [there] . . . as to be ranked as fundamental', *Snyder v. Massachusetts.*

"The entire fabric of the Constitution and the purposes that clearly underlie its specific guarantees demonstrate that the rights to marital privacy and to marry and raise a family are of similar order and magnitude as the fundamental rights specifically protected.

"Although the Constitution does not speak in so many words of the right of privacy in marriage, I cannot believe that it offers these fundamental rights no protection. The fact that no particular provision of the Constitution explicitly forbids the State from disrupting the traditional relation of the family - a relation as old and as fundamental as our entire civilization - surely does not show that the Government was meant to have the power to do so. Rather, as the Ninth Amendment expressly recognizes, there are fundamental personal rights such as this one, which are protected from abridgment by the Government though not specifically mentioned in the Constitution.

"My Brother STEWART, while characterizing the Connecticut birth control law as 'an uncommonly silly law,'would nevertheless let it stand on the ground that it is not for the courts to `substitute their social and economic beliefs for the judgment of legislative bodies, who are elected to pass laws.' Elsewhere, I have stated that '[w]hile I quite agree with Mr. Justice Brandeis that . . . `a . . . State may . . . serve as a laboratory; and try novel social and economic experiments,' I do not believe that this includes the power to experiment with the fundamental liberties of citizens . . . .' The vice of the dissenters' views is that it would permit such experimentation by the States in the area of the fundamental personal rights of its citizens. I cannot agree that the Constitution grants such power either to the States or to the Federal Government.

"The logic of the dissents would sanction federal or state legislation that seems to me even more plainly unconstitutional than the statute before us. Surely the Government, absent a showing of a compelling subordinating state interest, could not decree that all husbands and wives must be sterilized after two children have been born to them. Yet by their reasoning such an invasion of marital privacy would not be subject to constitutional challenge because, while it might be 'silly,' no provision of the Constitution specifically prevents the Government from curtailing the marital right to bear children and raise a family. While it may shock some of my Brethren that the Court today holds that the Constitution protects the right of marital privacy, in my view it is far more shocking to believe that the personal liberty guaranteed by the Constitution does not include protection against such totalitarian limitation of family size, which is at complete variance with our constitutional concepts. Yet, if upon a showing of a slender basis of rationality, a law outlawing voluntary birth control by married persons is valid, then, by the same reasoning, a law requiring compulsory birth control also would seem to be valid. In my view, however, both types of law would unjustifiably intrude upon rights of marital privacy which are constitutionally protected.

"In sum, I believe that the right of privacy in the marital relation is fundamental and basic - a personal right 'retained by the people' within the meaning of the Ninth Amendment. Connecticut cannot constitutionally abridge this fundamental right, which is protected by the Fourteenth Amendment from infringement by the States. I agree with the Court that petitioners' convictions must therefore be reversed.

MR. JUSTICE HARLAN, concurring in the judgment.

"I fully agree with the judgment of reversal, but find myself unable to join the Court's opinion. The reason is that it seems to me to evince an approach to this case very much like that taken by my Brothers BLACK and STEWART in dissent, namely: the Due Process Clause of the Fourteenth Amendment does not touch this Connecticut statute unless the enactment is found to violate some right assured by the letter or penumbra of the Bill of Rights.

"In other words, what I find implicit in the Court's opinion is that the "incorporation" doctrine may be used to restrict the reach of Fourteenth Amendment Due Process. For me this is just as unacceptable constitutional doctrine as is the use of the "incorporation" approach to impose upon the States all the requirements of the Bill of Rights as found in the provisions of the first eight amendments and in the decisions of this Court interpreting them...

"In my view, the proper constitutional inquiry in this case is whether this Connecticut statute infringes the Due Process Clause of the Fourteenth Amendment because the enactment violates basic values 'implicit in the concept of ordered liberty,' *Palko v. Connecticut*. I believe that it does. While the relevant inquiry may be aided by resort to one or more of the provisions of the Bill of Rights, it is not dependent on them or any of their radiations. The Due Process Clause of the Fourteenth Amendment stands, in my opinion, on its own bottom.

"A further observation seems in order respecting the justification of my Brothers BLACK and STEWART for their "incorporation" approach to this case. Their approach does not rest on historical reasons, which are of course wholly lacking, but on the thesis that by limiting the content of the Due Process Clause of the Fourteenth Amendment to the protection of rights which can be found elsewhere in the Constitution, in this instance in the Bill of Rights, judges will thus be confined to "interpretation" of specific constitutional provisions, and will thereby be restrained from introducing their own notions of constitutional right and wrong into the 'vague contours of the Due Process Clause.'

"While I could not more heartily agree that judicial 'self restraint' is an indispensable ingredient of sound constitutional adjudication, I do submit that the formula suggested for achieving it is more hollow than real. 'Specific' provisions of the Constitution, no less than 'due process,' lend themselves as readily to 'personal' interpretations by judges whose constitutional outlook is simply to keep the Constitution in supposed 'tune with the times.'

"Judicial self-restraint will not, I suggest, be brought about in the 'due process' area by the historically unfounded incorporation formula long advanced by my Brother BLACK, and now in part espoused by my Brother STEWART.

61.

"It will be achieved in this area, as in other constitutional areas, only by continual insistence upon respect for the teachings of history, solid recognition of the basic values that underlie our society, and wise appreciation of the great roles that the doctrines of federalism and separation of powers have played in establishing and preserving American freedoms.

"Adherence to these principles will not, of course, obviate all constitutional differences of opinion among judges, nor should it. Their continued recognition will, however, go farther toward keeping most judges from roaming at large in the constitutional field than will the interpolation into the Constitution of an artificial and largely illusory restriction on the content of the Due Process Clause...

MR. JUSTICE BLACK, with whom MR. JUSTICE STEWART joins, dissenting.

"I agree with my Brother STEWART'S dissenting opinion. And like him I do not to any extent whatever base my view that this Connecticut law is constitutional on a belief that the law is wise or that its policy is a good one. In order that there may be no room at all to doubt why I vote as I do, I feel constrained to add that the law is every bit as offensive to me as it is to my Brethren of the majority, who, reciting reasons why it is offensive to them, hold it unconstitutional. There is no single one of the graphic and eloquent strictures and criticisms fired at the policy of this Connecticut law either by the Court's opinion or by those of my concurring Brethren to which I cannot subscribe - *except their conclusion that the evil qualities they see in the law make it unconstitutional.*

"Had the doctor defendant here, or even the nondoctor defendant, been convicted for doing nothing more than expressing opinions to persons coming to the clinic that certain contraceptive devices, medicines or practices would do them good and would be desirable, or for telling people how devices could be used, I can think of no reasons at this time why their expressions of views would not be protected by the First and Fourteenth Amendments, which guarantee freedom of speech.

"The two defendants here were active participants in an organization which gave physical examinations to women, advised them what kind of contraceptive devices or medicines would most likely be satisfactory for them, and then supplied the devices themselves, all for a graduated scale of fees, based on the family income. Thus these defendants admittedly engaged with others in a planned course of conduct to help people violate the Connecticut law.

"Merely because some speech was used in carrying on that conduct - just as in ordinary life some speech accompanies most kinds of conduct - we are not in my view justified in holding that the First Amendment forbids the State to punish their conduct. Strongly as I desire to protect all First Amendment freedoms, I am unable to stretch the Amendment so as to afford protection to the conduct of these defendants in violating the Connecticut law. What would be the constitutional fate of the law if hereafter applied to punish nothing but speech is, as I have said, quite another matter.

"The Court talks about a constitutional 'right of privacy' as though there is some constitutional provision or provisions forbidding any law ever to be passed which might abridge the 'privacy' of individuals. But there is not. There are, of course, guarantees in certain specific constitutional provisions which are designed in part to protect privacy at certain times and places with respect to certain activities. Such, for example, is the Fourth Amendment's guarantee against 'unreasonable searches and seizures.'

"But I think it belittles that Amendment to talk about it as though it protects nothing but 'privacy.' To treat it that way is to give it a niggardly interpretation, not the kind of liberal reading I think any Bill of Rights provision should be given. The average man would very likely not have his feelings soothed any more by having his property seized openly than by having it seized privately and by stealth. He simply wants his property left alone. And a person can be just as much, if not more, irritated, annoyed and injured by an unceremonious public arrest by a policeman as he is by a seizure in the privacy of his office or home.

"One of the most effective ways of diluting or expanding a constitutionally guaranteed right is to substitute for the crucial word or words of a constitutional guarantee another word or words, more or less flexible and more or less restricted in meaning. This fact is well illustrated by the use of the term 'right of privacy' as a comprehensive substitute for the Fourth Amendment's guarantee against "unreasonable searches and seizures.'

"'Privacy'" is a broad, abstract and ambiguous concept which can easily be shrunken in meaning but which can also, on the other hand, easily be interpreted as a constitutional ban against many things other than searches and seizures. I have expressed the view many times that First Amendment freedoms, for example, have suffered from a failure of the courts to stick to the simple language of the First Amendment in construing it, instead of invoking multitudes of words substituted for those the Framers used.

"For these reasons I get nowhere in this case by talk about a constitutional 'right of privacy' as an emanation from one or more constitutional provisions. I like my privacy as well as the next one, but I am nevertheless compelled to admit that government has a right to invade it unless prohibited by some specific constitutional provision. For these reasons I cannot agree with the Court's judgment and the reasons it gives for holding this Connecticut law unconstitutional.

"This brings me to the arguments made by my Brothers HARLAN, WHITE and GOLDBERG for invalidating the Connecticut law. Brothers HARLAN and WHITE would invalidate it by reliance on the Due Process Clause of the Fourteenth Amendment, but Brother GOLDBERG, while agreeing with Brother

HARLAN, relies also on the Ninth Amendment. I have no doubt that the Connecticut law could be applied in such a way as to abridge freedom of speech and press and therefore violate the First and Fourteenth Amendments. My disagreement with the Court's opinion holding that there is such a violation here is a narrow one, relating to the application of the First Amendment to the facts and circumstances of this particular case.

"But my disagreement with Brothers HARLAN, WHITE and GOLDBERG is more basic. I think that if properly construed neither the Due Process Clause nor the Ninth Amendment, nor both together, could under any circumstances be a proper basis for invalidating the Connecticut law. I discuss the due process and Ninth Amendment arguments together because on analysis they turn out to be the same thing - merely using different words to claim for this Court and the federal judiciary power to invalidate any legislative act which the judges find irrational, unreasonable or offensive.

"*The due process argument which my Brothers HARLAN and WHITE adopt here is based, as their opinions indicate, on the premise that this Court is vested with power to invalidate all state laws that it considers to be arbitrary, capricious, unreasonable, or oppressive, or on this Court's belief that a particular state law under scrutiny has no "rational or justifying" purpose, or is offensive to a "sense of fairness and justice." If these formulas based on "natural justice," or others which mean the same thing, are to prevail, they require judges to determine what is or is not constitutional on the basis of their own appraisal of what laws are unwise or unnecessary.*

"*The power to make such decisions is of course that of a legislative body.* Surely it has to be admitted that no provision of the Constitution specifically gives such blanket power to courts to exercise such a supervisory veto over the wisdom and value of legislative policies and to hold unconstitutional those laws which they believe unwise or dangerous. I readily admit that no legislative body, state or national, should pass laws that can justly be given any of the invidious labels invoked as constitutional excuses to strike down state laws. But perhaps it is not too much to say that no legislative body ever does pass laws without believing that they will accomplish a sane, rational, wise and justifiable purpose.

"While I completely subscribe to the holding of *Marbury v. Madison*, 1803, and subsequent cases, that our Court has constitutional power to strike down statutes, state or federal, that violate commands of the Federal Constitution, I do not believe that we are granted power by the Due Process Clause or any other constitutional provision or provisions to measure constitutionality by our belief that legislation is arbitrary, capricious or unreasonable, or accomplishes no justifiable purpose, or is offensive to our own notions of 'civilized standards of conduct.' Such an appraisal of the wisdom of legislation is an attribute of the power to make laws, not of the power to interpret them.

64.

"The use by federal courts of such a formula or doctrine or whatnot to veto federal or state laws simply takes away from Congress and States the power to make laws based on their own judgment of fairness and wisdom and transfers that power to this Court for ultimate determination - a power which was specifically denied to federal courts by the convention that framed the Constitution.

"My Brother GOLDBERG has adopted the recent discovery that the Ninth Amendment as well as the Due Process Clause can be used by this Court as authority to strike down all state legislation which this Court thinks violates 'fundamental principles of liberty and justice,' or is contrary to the 'traditions and [collective] conscience of our people.' He also states, without proof satisfactory to me, that in making decisions on this basis judges will not consider 'their personal and private notions.' One may ask how they can avoid considering them. Our Court certainly has no machinery with which to take a Gallup Poll. And the scientific miracles of this age have not yet produced a gadget which the Court can use to determine what traditions are rooted in the '[collective] conscience of our people.'

"Moreover, one would certainly have to look far beyond the language of the Ninth Amendment to find that the Framers vested in this Court any such awesome veto powers over lawmaking, either by the States or by the Congress. Nor does anything in the history of the Amendment offer any support for such a shocking doctrine. The whole history of the adoption of the Constitution and Bill of Rights points the other way, and the very material quoted by my Bother GOLDBERG shows that the Ninth Amendment was intended to protect against the idea that 'by enumerating particular exceptions to the grant of power' to the Federal Government, 'those rights which were not singled out, were intended to be assigned into the hands of the General Government [the United States], and were consequently insecure.'

"That Amendment was passed, not to broaden the powers of this Court or any other department of 'the General Government,' but, as every student of history knows, to assure the people that the Constitution in all its provisions was intended to limit the Federal Government to the powers granted expressly or by necessary implication.

"If any broad, unlimited power to hold laws unconstitutional because they offend what this Court conceives to be the '[collective] conscience of our people' is vested in this Court by the Ninth Amendment, the Fourteenth Amendment, or any other provision of the Constitution, it was not given by the Framers, but rather has been bestowed on the Court by the Court.

"This fact is perhaps responsible for the peculiar phenomenon that for a period of a century and a half no serious suggestion was ever made that the Ninth Amendment, enacted to protect state powers against federal invasion, could be used as a weapon of federal power to prevent state legislatures from passing laws they consider appropriate to govern local affairs. *Use of any such broad, unbounded judicial authority would make of this Court's members a day-to-day constitutional convention.*

"I repeat so as not to be misunderstood that this Court does have power, which it should exercise, to hold laws unconstitutional where they are forbidden by the Federal Constitution. My point is that there is no provision of the Constitution which either expressly or impliedly vests power in this Court to sit as a supervisory agency over acts of duly constituted legislative bodies and set aside their laws because of the Court's belief that the legislative policies adopted are unreasonable, unwise, arbitrary, capricious or irrational. The adoption of such a loose, flexible, uncontrolled standard for holding laws unconstitutional, if ever it is finally achieved, will amount to a great unconstitutional shift of power to the courts which I believe and am constrained to say will be bad for the courts and worse for the country. Subjecting federal and state laws to such an unrestrained and unrestrainable judicial control as to the wisdom of legislative enactments would, I fear, jeopardize the separation of governmental powers that the Framers set up and at the same time threaten to take away much of the power of States to govern themselves which the Constitution plainly intended them to have.

"I realize that many good and able men have eloquently spoken and written, sometimes in rhapsodical strains, about the duty of this Court to keep the Constitution in tune with the times. The idea is that the Constitution must be changed from time to time and that this Court is charged with a duty to make those changes. For myself, I must with all deference reject that philosophy. The Constitution makers knew the need for change and provided for it. Amendments suggested by the people's elected representatives can be submitted to the people or their selected agents for ratification. That method of change was good for our Fathers, and being somewhat old-fashioned I must add it is good enough for me. And so, I cannot rely on the Due Process Clause or the Ninth Amendment or any mysterious and uncertain natural law concept as a reason for striking down this state law.

"Since *Marbury v. Madison*, 1803, was decided, the practice has been firmly established, for better or worse, that courts can strike down legislative enactments which violate the Constitution. This process, of course, involves interpretation, and since words can have many meanings, interpretation obviously may result in contraction or extension of the original purpose of a constitutional provision, thereby affecting policy. But to pass upon the constitutionality of statutes by looking to the particular standards enumerated in the Bill of Rights and other parts of the Constitution is one thing; to invalidate statutes because of application of `natural law' deemed to be above and undefined by the Constitution is another.

"In the one instance, courts proceeding within clearly marked constitutional boundaries seek to execute policies written into the Constitution; in the other, they roam at will in the limitless area of their own beliefs as to reasonableness and actually select policies, a responsibility which the Constitution entrusts to the legislative representatives of the people.

"The late Judge Learned Hand, after emphasizing his view that judges should not use the due process formula suggested in the concurring opinions today or any other formula like it to invalidate legislation offensive to their "personal preferences," made the statement, with which I fully agree, that:

'For myself it would be most irksome to be ruled by a bevy of Platonic Guardians, even if I knew how to choose them, which I assuredly do not.'

"So far as I am concerned, Connecticut's law as applied here is not forbidden by any provision of the Federal Constitution as that Constitution was written, and I would therefore affirm.

"MR. JUSTICE STEWART, whom MR. JUSTICE BLACK joins, dissenting.

"Since 1879 Connecticut has had on its books a law which forbids the use of contraceptives by anyone. I think this is an uncommonly silly law. As a practical matter, the law is obviously unenforceable, except in the oblique context of the present case. As a philosophical matter, I believe the use of contraceptives in the relationship of marriage should be left to personal and private choice, based upon each individual's moral, ethical, and religious beliefs. As a matter of social policy, I think professional counsel about methods of birth control should be available to all, so that each individual's choice can be meaningfully made. But we are not asked in this case to say whether we think this law is unwise, or even asinine. We are asked to hold that it violates the United States Constitution. And that I cannot do.

"In the course of its opinion the Court refers to no less than six Amendments to the Constitution: the First, the Third, the Fourth, the Fifth, the Ninth, and the Fourteenth. But the Court does not say which of these Amendments, if any, it thinks is infringed by this Connecticut law...

As to the First, Third, Fourth, and Fifth Amendments, I can find nothing in any of them to invalidate this Connecticut law, even assuming that all those Amendments are fully applicable against the States... and surely, unless the solemn process of constitutional adjudication is to descend to the level of a play on words, there is not involved here any abridgment of 'the freedom of speech, or of the press; or the right of the people peaceably to assemble, and to petition the Government for a redress of grievances.' No soldier has been quartered in any house. There has been no search, and no seizure. Nobody has been compelled to be a witness against himself.

"The Court also quotes the Ninth Amendment, and my Brother GOLDBERG'S concurring opinion relies heavily upon it. But to say that the Ninth Amendment has anything to do with this case is to turn somersaults with history. The Ninth Amendment, like its companion the Tenth, which this Court held 'states but a truism that all is retained which has not been surrendered,' was framed by James

Madison and adopted by the States simply to make clear that the adoption of the Bill of Rights did not alter the plan that the Federal Government was to be a government of express and limited powers, and that all rights and powers not delegated to it were retained by the people and the individual States. Until today no member of this Court has ever suggested that the Ninth Amendment meant anything else, and the idea that a federal court could ever use the Ninth Amendment to annual [sic] passed by the elected representatives of the people of the State of Connecticut would have caused James Madison no little wonder.

"What provision of the Constitution, then, does make this state law invalid? The Court says it is the right of privacy 'created by several fundamental constitutional guarantees.' With all deference, I can find no such general right of privacy in the Bill of Rights, in any other part of the Constitution, or in any case ever before decided by this Court.

"At the oral argument in this case we were told that the Connecticut law does not 'conform to current community standards.' But it is not the function of this Court to decide cases on the basis of community standards. We are here to decide cases 'agreeably to the Constitution and laws of the United States.' It is the essence of judicial duty to subordinate our own personal views, our own ideas of what legislation is wise and what is not. *If, as I should surely hope, the law before us does not reflect the standards of the people of Connecticut, the people of Connecticut can freely exercise their true Ninth and Tenth Amendment rights to persuade their elected representatives to repeal it. That is the constitutional way to take this law off the books.*

A fair reading of the above case requires very little comment. The dissents of Black and Stewart point out the objectionable (mis)conduct which has become all too typical of the Supreme Court. Correcting this misconduct requires action by the People through their representatives in Congress.

The reason for the Court's finding another freedom enjoyed by the People via the 9th Amendment, is *not* to expand the rights and liberties of the People, *but to expand the power of the Supreme Court over the respective state legislatures and their citizens.*

Based on the 9th and 10th Amendments, all power, i.e., all power, not specifically granted to the federal government, by the Constitution, belongs to the states and the People.

Hence, the states have the power to pass any law they see fit, provided it does not violate their own state constitution. It was at no time intended that the states laws were to pass through the Supreme Court acting as gate-keeper to determine whether such law was permitted. Madison would most certainly recoil at the suggestion that the federal government would presume to dictate to the states regarding matters clearly outside the federal government's enumerated, limited powers.

Comes now another true and profound violation of the Justices'oath to uphold the Constitution ... by rewriting it *again*, based on the most egregious foundation of the previous case of *Griswold.*

Having created a *new* "constitutional right," the right of privacy, the Court was now prepared to engraft upon the Constitution a *newer* right, i.e., the right to an abortion.

Here now, *Roe v Wade*:

U.S. SUPREME COURT

ROE v. WADE 410
U.S. 113 (1973)

A pregnant single woman *(Roe)* brought a class action challenging the constitutionality of the Texas criminal abortion laws, which proscribe procuring or attempting to procure an abortion except on medical advice for the purpose of saving the mother's life...The court held:

"(a) For the stage prior to approximately the end of the first trimester, the abortion decision and its effectuation must be left to the medical judgment of the pregnant woman's attending physician.

"(b) For the stage subsequent to approximately the end of the first trimester, the State, in promoting its interest in the health of the mother, may, if it chooses, regulate the abortion procedure in ways that are reasonably related to maternal health.

"(c) For the stage subsequent to viability the State, in promoting its interest in the potentiality of human life, may, if it chooses, regulate, and even proscribe, abortion except where necessary, in appropriate medical judgment, for the preservation of the life or health of the mother.

MR. JUSTICE BLACKMUN delivered the opinion of the Court.

"This Texas federal appeal and its Georgia companion, *Doe v. Bolton*, present constitutional challenges to state criminal abortion legislation. The Texas statutes under attack here are typical of those that have been in effect in many States for approximately a century. The Georgia statutes, in contrast, have a modern cast and are a legislative product that, to an extent at least, obviously reflects the influences of recent attitudinal change, of advancing medical knowledge and techniques, and of new thinking about an old issue.

"We forthwith acknowledge our awareness of the sensitive and emotional nature of the abortion controversy, of the vigorous opposing views, even among physicians, and of the deep and seemingly absolute convictions that the subject inspires. One's philosophy, one's experiences, one's exposure to the raw edges of human existence, one's religious training, one's attitudes toward life and family and their values, and the moral standards one establishes and seeks to observe, are all likely to influence and to color one's thinking and conclusions about abortion.

"In addition, population growth, pollution, poverty, and racial overtones tend to complicate and not to simplify the problem.

"Our task, of course, is to resolve the issue by constitutional measurement, free of emotion and of predilection. We seek earnestly to do this, and, because we do, we have inquired into, and in this opinion place some emphasis upon, medical and medical-legal history and what that history reveals about man's attitudes toward the abortion procedure over the centuries. We bear in mind, too, Mr. Justice Holmes' admonition in his now-vindicated dissent in *Lochner v. New York*.

"The Constitution is made for people of fundamentally differing views, and the accident of our finding certain opinions natural and familiar or novel and even shocking ought not to conclude our judgment upon the question whether statutes embodying them conflict with the Constitution of the United States.

"The Texas statutes that concern us here make it a crime to 'procure an abortion,' as therein defined, or to attempt one, except with respect to 'an abortion procured or attempted by medical advice for the purpose of saving the life of the mother.' Similar statutes are in existence in a majority of the states.

"The principal thrust of appellant's attack on the Texas statutes is that they improperly invade a right, said to be possessed by the pregnant woman, to choose to terminate her pregnancy. Appellant would discover this right in the concept of personal 'liberty' embodied in the Fourteenth Amendment's Due Process Clause; or in personal, marital, familial, and sexual privacy said to be protected by the Bill of Rights or its penumbras, or among those rights reserved to the people by the Ninth Amendment.

"This right of privacy, whether it be founded in the Fourteenth Amendment's concept of personal liberty and restrictions upon state action, as we feel it is, or, as the District Court determined, in the Ninth Amendment's reservation of rights to the people, is broad enough to encompass a woman's decision whether or not to terminate her pregnancy. The detriment that the State would impose upon the pregnant woman by denying this choice altogether is apparent. Specific and direct harm medically diagnosable even in early pregnancy may be involved. Maternity, or additional offspring, may force upon the woman a distressful life and future. Psychological harm may be imminent. Mental and physical health may be taxed by child care.There is also the distress, for all concerned, associated with the unwanted child, and there is the problem of bringing a child into a family already unable, psychologically and otherwise, to care for it. In other cases, as in this one, the additional difficulties and continuing stigma of unwed motherhood may be involved. All these are factors the woman and her responsible physician necessarily will consider in consultation.

"On the basis of elements such as these, appellant and some amici argue that the woman's right is absolute and that she is entitled to terminate her pregnancy at whatever time, in whatever way, and for whatever reason she alone chooses.

70.

With this we do not agree. Appellant's arguments that Texas either has no valid interest at all in regulating the abortion decision, or no interest strong enough to support any limitation upon the woman's sole determination, are unpersuasive. The Court's decisions recognizing a right of privacy also acknowledge that some state regulation in areas protected by that right is appropriate. As noted above, a State may properly assert important interests in safeguarding health, in maintaining medical standards, and in protecting potential life. At some point in pregnancy, these respective interests become sufficiently compelling to sustain regulation of the factors that govern the abortion decision. The privacy right involved, therefore, cannot be said to be absolute. In fact, it is not clear to us that the claim asserted by some amici that one has an unlimited right to do with one's body as one pleases bears a close relationship to the right of privacy previously articulated in the Court's decisions. The Court has refused to recognize an unlimited right of this kind in the past.

"*We, therefore, conclude that the right of personal privacy includes the abortion decision, but that this right is not unqualified and must be considered against important state interests in regulation.*

"We note that those federal and state courts that have recently considered abortion law challenges have reached the same conclusion. A majority, in addition to the District Court in the present case, have held state laws unconstitutional, at least in part, because of vagueness or because of overbreadth and abridgment of rights. . . .

"Although the results are divided, most of these courts have agreed that the right of privacy, however based, is broad enough to cover the abortion decision; that the right, nonetheless, is not absolute and is subject to some limitations; and that at some point the state interests as to protection of health, medical standards, and prenatal life, become dominant. We agree with this approach.

"The appellee and certain amici argue that the fetus is a 'person' within the language and meaning of the Fourteenth Amendment. In support of this, they outline at length and in detail the well-known facts of fetal development. If this suggestion of personhood is established, the appellant's case, of course, collapses, for the fetus' right to life would then be guaranteed specifically by the Amendment. The appellant conceded as much on reargument. On the other hand, the appellee conceded on reargument that no case could be cited that holds that a fetus is a person within the meaning of the Fourteenth Amendment.

"The Constitution does not define 'person' in so many words. Section 1 of the Fourteenth Amendment contains three references to 'person.' The first, in defining 'citizens,' speaks of 'persons born or naturalized in the United States.' The word also appears both in the Due Process Clause and in the Equal Protection Clause. 'Person' is used in other places in the Constitution: in the listing of qualifications for Representatives and Senators, Art. I, 2, cl. 2, and 3, cl. 3; in the Apportionment Clause, Art. I, 2, cl. 3; 53 in the Migration and

71.

Importation provision, Art. I, 9, cl. 1; in the Emolument Clause, Art. I, 9, cl. 8; in the Electors provisions, Art. II, 1, cl. 2, and the superseded cl. 3; in the provision outlining qualifications for the office of President, Art. II, 1, cl. 5; in the Extradition provisions, Art. IV, 2, cl. 2, and the superseded Fugitive Slave Clause 3; and in the Fifth, Twelfth, and Twenty-second Amendments, as well as in 2 and 3 of the Fourteenth Amendment. But in nearly all these instances, the use of the word is such that it has application only postnatally. None indicates, with any assurance, that it has any possible pre-natal application.

"All this, together with our observation, supra, that throughout the major portion of the 19th century prevailing legal abortion practices were far freer than they are today, persuades us that the word "person," as used in the Fourteenth Amendment, does not include the unborn. This is in accord with the results reached in those few cases where the issue has been squarely presented...

This conclusion, however, does not of itself fully answer the contentions raised by Texas, and we pass on to other considerations.

"The pregnant woman cannot be isolated in her privacy. She carries an embryo and, later, a fetus, if one accepts the medical definitions of the developing young in the human uterus. The situation therefore is inherently different from marital intimacy, or bedroom possession of obscene material, or marriage, or procreation, or education, with which Eisenstadt and Griswold, Stanley, Loving, Skinner, and Pierce and Meyer were respectively concerned. As we have intimated above, it is reasonable and appropriate for a State to decide that at some point in time another interest, that of health of the mother or that of potential human life, becomes significantly involved. The woman's privacy is no longer sole and any right of privacy she possesses must be measured accordingly.

"Texas urges that, apart from the Fourteenth Amendment, life begins at conception and is present throughout pregnancy, and that, therefore, the State has a compelling interest in protecting that life from and after conception. We need not resolve the difficult question of when life begins. When those trained in the respective disciplines of medicine, philosophy, and theology are unable to arrive at any consensus, the judiciary, at this point in the development of man's knowledge, is not in a position to speculate as to the answer."

The Court admits that it cannot determine when life begins. At this point, prudence should have dictated that the Court abstain from making a ruling which would necessarily involve a matter about which they are admittedly ignorant. If, by permitting an abortion during the first trimester, it should subsequently be determined that life begins at conception, the Court will have authorized the taking of an innocent life.

"It should be sufficient to note briefly the wide divergence of thinking on this most sensitive and difficult question. There has always been strong support for the view that life does not begin until live birth. This was the belief of the Stoics. It appears to be the predominant, though not the unanimous, attitude of the Jewish faith. It may be taken to represent also the position of a large segment of the Protestant community, insofar as that can be ascertained; organized groups that have taken a formal position on the abortion issue have generally regarded abortion as a matter for the conscience of the individual and her family.

"As we have noted, the common law found greater significance in quickening. Physicians and their scientific colleagues have regarded that event with less interest and have tended to focus either upon conception, upon live birth, or upon the interim point at which the fetus becomes 'viable,' that is, potentially able to live outside the mother's womb, albeit with artificial aid. Viability is usually placed at about seven months (28 weeks) but may occur earlier, even at 24 weeks. The Aristotelian theory of 'mediate animation,' that held sway throughout the Middle Ages and the Renaissance in Europe, continued to be official Roman Catholic dogma until the 19th century, despite opposition to this 'ensoulment' theory from those in the Church who would recognize the existence of life from the moment of conception.

"The latter is now, of course, the official belief of the Catholic Church. As one brief amicus discloses, this is a view strongly held by many non-Catholics as well, and by many physicians. Substantial problems for precise definition of this view are posed, however, by new embryological data that purport to indicate that conception is a 'process' over time, rather than an event, and by new medical techniques such as menstrual extraction, the 'morning-after' pill, implantation of embryos, artificial insemination, and even artificial wombs.

"*In areas other than criminal abortion*, the law has been reluctant to endorse any theory that life, as we recognize it, begins before live birth or to accord legal rights to the unborn except in narrowly defined situations and except when the rights are contingent upon live birth. For example, the traditional rule of tort law denied recovery for prenatal injuries even though the child was born alive. "That rule has been changed in almost every jurisdiction. In most States, recovery is said to be permitted only if the fetus was viable, or at least quick, when the injuries were sustained, though few courts have squarely so held. In a recent development, generally opposed by the commentators, some States permit the parents of a stillborn child to maintain an action for wrongful death because of prenatal injuries. Such an action, however, would appear to be one to vindicate the parents' interest and is thus consistent with the view that the fetus, at most, represents only the potentiality of life. Similarly, unborn children have been recognized as acquiring rights or interests by way of inheritance or other devolution of property, and have been represented by guardians ad litem. Perfection of the interests involved, again, has generally been contingent upon

73.

live birth. In short, the unborn have never been recognized in the law as persons in the whole sense.

"In view of all this, we do not agree that, by adopting one theory of life, Texas may override the rights of the pregnant woman that are at stake.We repeat, however, that the State does have an important and legitimate interest in preserving and protecting the health of the pregnant woman, whether she be a resident of the State or a nonresident who seeks medical consultation and treatment there, and that it has still another important and legitimate interest in protecting the potentiality of human life. These interests are separate and distinct. Each grows in substantiality as the woman approaches term and, at a point during pregnancy, each becomes 'compelling.'

"With respect to the State's important and legitimate interest in the health of the mother, the 'compelling' point, in the light of present medical knowledge, is at approximately the end of the first trimester. This is so because of the now-established medical fact, that until the end of the first trimester mortality in abortion may be less than mortality in normal childbirth. It follows that, from and after this point, a State may regulate the abortion procedure to the extent that the regulation reasonably relates to the preservation and protection of maternal health. Examples of permissible state regulation in this area are requirements as to the qualifications of the person who is to perform the abortion; as to the licensure of that person; as to the facility in which the procedure is to be performed, that is, whether it must be a hospital or may be a clinic or some other place of less-than-hospital status; as to the licensing of the facility; and the like.

"If that decision is reached, the judgment may be effectuated by an abortion free of interference by the State.

"With respect to the State's important and legitimate interest in potential life, the 'compelling' point is at viability. This is so because the fetus then presumably has the capability of meaningful life outside the mother's womb. State regulation protective of fetal life after viability thus has both logical and biological justifications. If the State is interested in protecting fetal life after viability, it may go so far as to proscribe abortion during that period, except when it is necessary to preserve the life or health of the mother.

"Measured against these standards, the Texas Penal Code, in restricting legal abortions to those 'procured or attempted by medical advice for the purpose of saving the life of the mother,' sweeps broadly. The statute makes no distinction between abortions performed early in pregnancy and those performed later, and it limits to a single reason, 'saving' the mother's life, the legal justification for the procedure. The statute, therefore, cannot survive the constitutional attack made upon it here.

MR. JUSTICE REHNQUIST, dissenting.

"The Court's opinion brings to the decision of this troubling question both extensive historical fact and a wealth of legal scholarship. While the opinion

74.

thus commands my respect, I find myself nonetheless in fundamental disagreement with those parts of it that invalidate the Texas statute in question, and therefore dissent. . . .

"The Court's opinion decides that a State may impose virtually no restriction on the performance of abortions during the first trimester of pregnancy. Our previous decisions indicate that a necessary predicate for such an opinion is a plaintiff who was in her first trimester of pregnancy at some time during the pendency of her law-suit. While a party may vindicate his own constitutional rights, he may not seek vindication for the rights of others. The Court's statement of facts in this case makes clear, however, that the record in no way indicates the presence of such a plaintiff. We know only that plaintiff Roe at the time of filing her complaint was a pregnant woman; for aught that appears in this record, she may have been in her last trimester of pregnancy as of the date the complaint was filed.

"Nothing in the Court's opinion indicates that Texas might not constitutionally apply its proscription of abortion as written to a woman in that stage of pregnancy. Nonetheless, the Court uses her complaint against the Texas statute as a fulcrum for deciding that States may impose virtually no restrictions on medical abortions performed during the first trimester of pregnancy. In deciding such a hypothetical lawsuit, the Court departs from the longstanding admonition that it should never 'formulate a rule of constitutional law broader than is required by the precise facts to which it is to be applied.'

"Even if there were a plaintiff in this case capable of litigating the issue which the Court decides, I would reach a conclusion opposite to that reached by the Court. I have difficulty in concluding, as the Court does, that the right of 'privacy' is involved in this case. Texas, by the statute here challenged, bars the performance of a medical abortion by a licensed physician on a plaintiff such as *Roe.*

"A transaction resulting in an operation such as this is not 'private' in the ordinary usage of that word. Nor is the 'privacy' that the Court finds here even a distant relative of the freedom from searches and seizures protected by the Fourth Amendment to the Constitution, which the Court has referred to as embodying a right to privacy.

"If the Court means by the term 'privacy' no more than that the claim of a person to be free from unwanted state regulation of consensual transactions may be a form of 'liberty' protected by the Fourteenth Amendment, there is no doubt that similar claims have been upheld in our earlier decisions on the basis of that liberty. I agree with the statement of MR. JUSTICE STEWART in his concurring opinion that the 'liberty,' against deprivation of which without due process the Fourteenth Amendment protects, embraces more than the rights found in the Bill of Rights. *But that liberty is not guaranteed absolutely against deprivation, only against deprivation without due process of law.*

"The test traditionally applied in the area of social and economic legislation is whether or not a law such as that challenged has a rational relation to a valid state objective. The Due Process Clause of the Fourteenth Amendment undoubtedly does place a limit, albeit a broad one, on legislative power to enact laws such as this. If the Texas statute were to prohibit an abortion even where the mother's life is in jeopardy, I have little doubt that such a statute would lack a rational relation to a valid state objective under the test stated in Williamson, supra. But the Court's sweeping invalidation of any restrictions on abortion during the first trimester is impossible to justify under that standard, and the conscious weighing of competing factors that the Court's opinion apparently substitutes for the established test is far more appropriate to a legislative judgment than to a judicial one.

"The Court eschews the history of the Fourteenth Amendment in its reliance on the 'compelling state interest' test. But the Court adds a new wrinkle to this test by transposing it from the legal considerations associated with the Equal Protection Clause of the Fourteenth Amendment to this case arising under the Due Process Clause of the Fourteenth Amendment. Unless I misapprehend the consequences of this transplanting of the 'compelling state interest test,' the Court's opinion will accomplish the seemingly impossible feat of leaving this area of the law more confused than it found it.

"The decision here to break pregnancy into three distinct terms and to outline the permissible restrictions the State may impose in each one, for example, partakes more of judicial legislation than it does of a determination of the intent of the drafters of the Fourteenth Amendment.

"The fact that a majority of the States reflecting, after all, the majority sentiment in those States, have had restrictions on abortions for at least a century is a strong indication, it seems to me, that the asserted right to an abortion is not 'so rooted in the traditions and conscience of our people as to be ranked as fundamental,' *Snyder v. Massachusetts*. Even today, when society's views on abortion are changing, the very existence of the debate is evidence that the 'right' to an abortion is not so universally accepted as the appellant would have us believe.

"To reach its result, the Court necessarily has had to find within the scope of the Fourteenth Amendment a right that was apparently completely unknown to the drafters of the Amendment. As early as 1821, the first state law dealing directly with abortion was enacted by the Connecticut Legislature... By the time of the adoption of the Fourteenth Amendment in 1868, there were at least 36 laws enacted by state or territorial legislatures limiting abortion. While many States have amended or updated their laws, 21 of the laws on the books in 1868 remain in effect today. Indeed, the Texas statute struck down today was, as the majority notes, first enacted in 1857 and 'has remained substantially unchanged to the present time.'

76.

"There apparently was no question concerning the validity of this provision or of any of the other state statutes when the Fourteenth Amendment was adopted. The only conclusion possible from this history is that the drafters did not intend to have the Fourteenth Amendment withdraw from the States the power to legislate with respect to this matter.

"Even if one were to agree that the case that the Court decides were here, and that the enunciation of the substantive constitutional law in the Court's opinion were proper, the actual disposition of the case by the Court is still difficult to justify. The Texas statute is struck down in toto, even though the Court apparently concedes that at later periods of pregnancy Texas might impose these selfsame statutory limitations on abortion. My understanding of past practice is that a statute found to be invalid as applied to a particular plaintiff, but not unconstitutional as a whole, is not simply "struck down" but is, instead, declared unconstitutional as applied to the fact situation before the Court. For all of the foregoing reasons, I respectfully dissent."

In review, what started out to be an obviously correct series of cases, *Barron* and the *Slaughterhouse* cases, holding that the states were *not* bound by the first eight amendments of the U.S. Constitution, were eventually turned on their respective heads. The Supreme Court looked for a way to further expand federal influence and hence domination over the states and its people. The method was found and expounded upon in the 1937 *Palko* case, wherein the theory was first floated-out as a test balloon. It has since been adopted piecemeal, i.e., just a bit at a time lest the people become alarmed and informed as to what our Supreme Court has done and continues to do.

That most-devious method was of course the use of the 14th Amendment, Due Process Clause to apply the Bill of Rights *to the states*. These rights were at all times intended to apply to the federal government *only*, but were suddenly applied to and thereby limited the *states* and their laws and their people.

Further, the portion of the Bill of Rights applicable to the states was to be determined by the Supreme Court based on its then-agenda. Hence, the Court simply rewrote the Constitution as its then-makeup determined.

Of course this is the antithesis of what the drafters intended, i.e., the words and text of the Constitution were to be respected and applied *as written*. The Constitution was not to be disrespected and defiled by ignoring its text and substituting other words for its text.

Dobbs v. Jackson (2022) states the Constitution does not confer a right to abortion and the issue of abortion is returned to the people and their elected representatives. In *Obergefell v. Hodges* (2015), the Supreme Court held, in error, that the right to same-sex marriage was a constitutional right.

Here now, excerpts from *Miranda:*

U.S. SUPREME COURT
MIRANDA v. ARIZONA
384 U.S. 436 (1966)

The Court in *Miranda* was applying or interpreting the 5th Amendment of the Constitution to a conviction in state court. Of course, this was improper from the beginning, as the 5th Amendment was at no time intended to apply to the states. The 5th Amendment states, in pertinent part,

"No person...shall be compelled in any criminal case to be a witness against himself...".

However, the Court held:

"In the absence of other effective measures the following procedures to safeguard the Fifth Amendment privilege must be observed: (1) the person in custody must, prior to interrogation, be clearly informed that he has the right to remain silent, and (2) that anything he says will be used against him in court; (3) he must be clearly informed that he has the right to consult with a lawyer and (4) to have the lawyer with him during interrogation, and (5) that, if he is indigent, a lawyer will be appointed to represent him.

Comparing this holding to the actual text of the 5th Amendment, leads, without hesitation, to the conclusion that the Court rewrote the 5th Amendment and *again* ignored the actual words of the document they were sworn to uphold. Of this there can be no reasonable doubt.

The Court held:

"We reverse. From the testimony of the officers and by the admission of respondent, it is clear that Miranda was not in any way apprised of his right to consult with an attorney and to have one present during the interrogation, nor was his right not to be compelled to incriminate himself effectively protected in any other manner. Without these warnings the statements were inadmissible. The mere fact that he signed a statement which contained a typed-in clause stating that he had 'full knowledge' of his 'legal rights' does not approach the knowing and intelligent waiver required to relinquish constitutional rights....

Excerpts from Justice Clark's dissent affirms our conclusion by stating:

"The *ipse dixit* [unproved assertion] of the majority has no support in our cases. Indeed, the Court admits that 'we might not find the defendants' statements [here] to have been involuntary in traditional terms.' In short, the Court has added more to the requirements that the accused is entitled to consult with his lawyer and that he must be given the traditional warning that he may remain silent and that anything that he says may be used against him.

"Now, the Court fashions a constitutional rule that the police may engage in no custodial interrogation without additionally advising the accused that he has a right under the Fifth Amendment to the presence of counsel during interrogation and that, if he is without funds, counsel will be furnished him. When at any point during an interrogation the accused seeks affirmatively or impliedly to invoke his rights to silence or counsel, interrogation must be forgone or postponed. The Court further holds that failure to follow the new procedures requires inexorably the exclusion of any statement by the accused, as well as the fruits thereof. Such a strict constitutional specific inserted at the nerve center of crime detection may well kill the patient. Since there is at this time a paucity of information and an almost total lack of empirical knowledge on the practical operation of requirements truly comparable to those announced by the majority, I would be more restrained lest we go too far too fast.

"Custodial interrogation has long been recognized as 'undoubtedly an essential tool in effective law enforcement.'Recognition of this fact should put us on guard against the promulgation of doctrinaire rules. Indeed, the Court never hinted that an affirmative 'waiver' was a prerequisite to questioning; that the burden of proof as to waiver was on the prosecution; that the presence of counsel - absent a waiver - during interrogation was required; that a waiver can be withdrawn at the will of the accused; that counsel must be furnished during an accusatory stage to those unable to pay; nor that admissions and exculpatory statements are 'confessions.'To require all those things at one gulp should cause the Court to choke....

"The rule prior to today... depended upon 'a totality of circumstances evidencing an involuntary . . . admission of guilt.'

"Of course, detection and solution of crime is, at best, a difficult and arduous task requiring determination and persistence on the part of all responsible officers charged with the duty of law enforcement. And, certainly, we do not mean to suggest that all interrogation of witnesses and suspects is impermissible. Such questioning is undoubtedly an essential tool in effective law enforcement. The line between proper and permissible police conduct and techniques and methods offensive to due process is, at best, a difficult one to draw, particularly in cases such as this where it is necessary to make fine judgments as to the effect of psychologically coercive pressures and inducements on the mind and will of an accused. . . . We are here impelled to the conclusion, from all of the facts presented, that the bounds of due process have been exceeded.'

"I would continue to follow that rule. Under the 'totality of circumstances' rule of which my Brother Goldberg spoke in Haynes, I would consider in each case whether the police officer prior to custodial interrogation added warning the suspect might have counsel present at the interrogation and, further, that a court would appoint one at his request if he was too poor to employ counsel. In absence of warnings, the burden would be on the State to prove that counsel was knowingly and intelligently waived or that in the totality of the circumstances, including the failure to give the necessary warnings, the confession was clearly voluntary.

"Rather than employing the arbitrary Fifth Amendment rule which the Court lays down I would follow the more pliable dictates of Due Process Clauses of the Fifth and Fourteenth Amendments which we are accustomed to administering and which we know from our cases are effective instruments in protecting persons in police custody. In this way we would not be acting in the dark nor in one full sweep changing the traditional rules of custodial interrogation which this Court has for so long recognized as a justifiable and proper tool in balancing individual rights against the rights of society. It will be soon enough to go further when we are able to appraise with somewhat better accuracy the effect of such a holding. I would affirm the convictions.

MR. JUSTICE HARLAN, whom MR. JUSTICE STEWART and MR. JUSTICE WHITE join, dissenting:

"I believe the decision of the Court represents poor constitutional law and entails harmful consequences for the country at large. How serious these consequences may prove to be only time can tell. But the basic flaws in the Court's justification seem to me readily apparent now once all sides of the problem are considered.

"At the outset, it is well to note exactly what is required by the Court's new constitutional code of rules for confessions. The foremost requirement, upon which later admissibility of a confession depends, is that a fourfold warning be given to a person in custody before he is questioned, namely, that he has a right to remain silent, that anything he says may be used against him, that he has a right to have present an attorney during the questioning, and that if indigent he has a right to a lawyer without charge. To forgo these rights, some affirmative statement of rejection is seemingly required, and threats, tricks, or cajolings to obtain this waiver are forbidden. If before or during questioning the suspect seeks to invoke his right to remain silent, interrogation must be forgone or cease; a request for counsel brings about the same result until a lawyer is procured. Finally, there are a miscellany of minor directives, for example, the burden of proof of waiver is on the State, admissions and exculpatory statements are treated just like confessions, withdrawal of a waiver is always permitted, and so forth.

"While the fine points of this scheme are far less clear than the Court admits, the tenor is quite apparent. The new rules are not designed to guard against police brutality or other unmistakably banned forms of coercion. Those who use third-degree tactics and deny them in court are equally able and destined to lie as skillfully about warnings and waivers. Rather, the thrust of the new rules is to negate all pressures, to reinforce the nervous or ignorant suspect, and ultimately to discourage any confession at all. The aim in short is toward "voluntariness" in a utopian sense, or to view it from a different angle, voluntariness with a vengeance.

"To incorporate this notion into the Constitution requires a strained reading of history and precedent and a disregard of the very pragmatic concerns that alone may on occasion justify such strains. I believe that reasoned examination will show that the Due Process Clauses provide an adequate tool for coping with confessions and that, even if the Fifth Amendment privilege against self-incrimination be invoked, its precedents taken as a whole do not sustain the present rules. "Viewed as a choice based on pure policy, these new rules prove to be a highly debatable, if not one-sided, appraisal of the competing interests, imposed over widespread objection, at the very time when judicial restraint is most called for by the circumstances.

"On March 3, 1963, an 18-year-old girl was kidnapped and forcibly raped near Phoenix, Arizona. Ten days later, on the morning of March 13, petitioner Miranda was arrested and taken to the police station. At this time Miranda was 23 years old, indigent, and educated to the extent of completing half the ninth grade. He had 'an emotional illness' of the schizophrenic type, according to the doctor who eventually examined him; the doctor's report also stated that Miranda was 'alert and oriented as to time, place, and person,' intelligent within normal limits, competent to stand trial, and sane within the legal definition. At the police station, the victim picked Miranda out of a lineup, and two officers then took him into a separate room to interrogate him, starting about 11:30 a. m. Though at first denying his guilt, within a short time Miranda gave a detailed oral confession and then wrote out in his own hand and signed a brief statement admitting and describing the crime. All this was accomplished in two hours or less without any force, threats or promises and - I will assume this though the record is uncertain . . . without any effective warnings at all.

"In conclusion: *Nothing in the letter or the spirit of the Constitution or in the precedents squares with the heavy-handed and one-sided action that is so precipitously taken by the Court in the name of fulfilling its constitutional responsibilities.* The foray which the Court makes today brings to mind the wise and farsighted words of Mr. Justice Jackson in *Douglas v. Jeannette*: *'This Court is forever adding new stories to the temples of constitutional law, and the temples have a way of collapsing when one story too many is added.'*

81.

MR. JUSTICE WHITE, with whom MR. JUSTICE HARLAN and MR. JUSTICE STEWART join, dissenting:

"The proposition that the privilege against self-incrimination forbids in-custody interrogation without the warnings specified in the majority opinion and without a clear waiver of counsel has no significant support in the history of the privilege or in the language of the Fifth Amendment. As for the English authorities and the common-law history, the privilege, firmly established in the second half of the seventeenth century, was never applied except to prohibit compelled judicial interrogations. The rule excluding coerced confessions matured about 100 years later, "[b]ut there is nothing in the reports to suggest that the theory has its roots in the privilege against self-incrimination. And so far as the cases reveal, the privilege, as such, seems to have been given effect only in judicial proceedings, including the preliminary examinations by authorized magistrates.

"Our own constitutional provision provides that no person 'shall be compelled in any criminal case to be a witness against himself.' These words, when '[c]onsidered in the light to be shed by grammar and the dictionary . . . appear to signify simply that nobody shall be compelled to give oral testimony against himself in a criminal proceeding under way in which he is defendant.' And there is very little in the surrounding circumstances of the adoption of the Fifth Amendment or in the provisions of the then existing state constitutions or in state practice which would give the constitutional provision any broader meaning....

"In this court also it has been settled that the mere fact that the confession is made to a police officer, while the accused was under arrest in or out of prison, or was drawn out by his questions, does not necessarily render the confession involuntary, but, as one of the circumstances, such imprisonment or interrogation may be taken into account in determining whether or not the statements of the prisoner were voluntary.

"Counsel for the accused insist that there cannot be a voluntary statement, a free open confession, while a defendant is confined and in irons under an accusation of having committed a capital offence. We have not been referred to any authority in support of that position. It is true that the fact of a prisoner being in custody at the time he makes a confession is a circumstance not to be overlooked, because it bears upon the inquiry whether the confession was voluntarily made or was extorted by threats or violence or made under the influence of fear. But confinement or imprisonment is not in itself sufficient to justify the exclusion of a confession, if it appears to have been voluntary, and was not obtained by putting the prisoner in fear or by promises.

"The fact that [a defendant] is in custody and manacled does not necessarily render his statement involuntary, nor is that necessarily the effect of popular excitement shortly preceding. . . . And it is laid down that it is not essential to the admissibility of a confession that it should appear that the person was warned that what he said would be used against him, but on the contrary, if the confession was voluntary, it is sufficient though it appear that he was not so warned.

"Only a tiny minority of our judges who have dealt with the question, including today's majority, have considered in-custody interrogation, without more, to be a violation of the Fifth Amendment. And this Court, as every member knows, has left standing literally thousands of criminal convictions that rested at least in part on confessions taken in the course of interrogation by the police after arrest.

"That the Court's holding today is neither compelled nor even strongly suggested by the language of the Fifth Amendment, is at odds with American and English legal history, and involves a departure from a long line of precedent does not prove either that the Court has exceeded its powers or that the Court is wrong or unwise in its present reinterpretation of the Fifth Amendment.

"It does, however, underscore the obvious - that the Court has not discovered or found the law in making today's decision, nor has it derived it from some irrefutable sources; what it has done is to make new law and new public policy in much the same way that it has in the course of interpreting other great clauses of the Constitution. This is what the Court historically has done. Indeed, it is what it must do and will continue to do until and unless there is some fundamental change in the constitutional distribution of governmental powers.

"We may inquire what are the textual and factual bases of this new fundamental rule. To reach the result announced on the grounds it does, the Court must stay within the confines of the Fifth Amendment, which forbids self-incrimination only if compelled. Hence the core of the Court's opinion is that because of the 'compulsion inherent in custodial surroundings, no statement obtained from [a] defendant [in custody] can truly be the product of his free choice,' absent the use of adequate protective devices as described by the Court. *However, the Court does not point to any sudden inrush of new knowledge requiring the rejection of 70 years' experience. Nor does it assert that its novel conclusion reflects a changing consensus among state courts, or that a succession of cases had steadily eroded the old rule and proved it unworkable.*

"Rather than asserting new knowledge, the Court concedes that it cannot truly know what occurs during custodial questioning, because of the innate secrecy of such proceedings. It extrapolates a picture of what it conceives to be the norm from police investigatorial manuals, published in 1959 and 1962 or earlier, without any attempt to allow for adjustments in police practices that may have occurred in the wake of more recent decisions of state appellate tribunals or this Court. But even if the relentless application of the described procedures could lead to involuntary confessions, it most assuredly does not follow that each and every case will disclose this kind of interrogation or this kind of consequence.

"Insofar as appears from the Court's opinion, it has not examined a single transcript of any police interrogation, let alone the interrogation that took place in any one of these cases which it decides today. Judged by any of the standards for empirical investigation utilized in the social sciences the factual basis for the Court's premise is patently inadequate.

"Although in the Court's view in-custody interrogation is inherently coercive, the Court says that the spontaneous product of the coercion of arrest and detention is still to be deemed voluntary. An accused, arrested on probable cause, may blurt out a confession which will be admissible despite the fact that he is alone and in custody, without any showing that he had any notion of his right to remain silent or of the consequences of his admission. Yet, under the Court's rule, if the police ask him a single question such as 'Do you have anything to say?' or 'Did you kill your wife?' his response, if there is one, has somehow been compelled, even if the accused has been clearly warned of his right to remain silent.

"Common sense informs us to the contrary. While one may say that the response was 'involuntary' in the sense the question provoked or was the occasion for the response and thus the defendant was induced to speak out when he might have remained silent if not arrested and not questioned, it is patently unsound to say the response is compelled.

"Today's result would not follow even if it were agreed that to some extent custodial interrogation is inherently coercive. The test has been whether the totality of circumstances deprived the defendant of a 'free choice to admit, to deny, or to refuse to answer,' and whether physical or psychological coercion was of such a degree that 'the defendant's will was overborne at the time he confessed,' The duration and nature of incommunicado custody, the presence or absence of advice concerning the defendant's constitutional rights, and the granting or refusal of requests to communicate with lawyers, relatives or friends have all been rightly regarded as important data bearing on the basic inquiry.

"But it has never been suggested, until today, that such questioning was so coercive and accused persons so lacking in hardihood that the very first response to the very first question following the commencement of custody must be conclusively presumed to be the product of an overborne will.

"All of this makes very little sense in terms of the compulsion which the Fifth Amendment proscribes. That amendment deals with compelling the accused himself. It is his free will that is involved. Confessions and incriminating admissions, as such, are not forbidden evidence; only those which are compelled are banned.

"I doubt that the Court observes these distinctions today. By considering any answers to any interrogation to be compelled regardless of the content and course of examination and by escalating the requirements to prove waiver, the Court not only prevents the use of compelled confessions but for all practical purposes forbids interrogation except in the presence of counsel. "That is, instead of confining itself to protection of the right against compelled self-incrimination the Court has created a limited Fifth Amendment right to counsel - or, as the Court expresses it, a 'need for counsel to protect the Fifth Amendment privilege . . . .' *The focus then is not on the will of the accused but on the will of counsel and how much influence he can have on the accused. Obviously there is no warrant in the Fifth Amendment for thus installing counsel as the arbiter of the privilege.*

"*In sum, for all the Court's expounding on the menacing atmosphere of police interrogation procedures, it has failed to supply any foundation for the conclusions it draws or the measures it adopts.*

"Criticism of the Court's opinion, however, cannot stop with a demonstration that the factual and textual bases for the rule it propounds are, at best, less than compelling. Equally relevant is an assessment of the rule's consequences measured against community values. The Court's duty to assess the consequences of its action is not satisfied by the utterance of the truth that a value of our system of criminal justice is 'to respect the inviolability of the human personality' and to require government to produce the evidence against the accused by its own independent labors.

"More than the human dignity of the accused is involved; the human personality of others in the society must also be preserved. Thus the values reflected by the privilege are not the sole desideratum; society's interest in the general security is of equal weight.

"The obvious underpinning of the Court's decision is a deep-seated distrust of all confessions. As the Court declares that the accused may not be interrogated without counsel present, absent a waiver of the right to counsel, and as the Court all but admonishes the lawyer to advise the accused to remain silent, the result adds up to a judicial judgment that evidence from the accused should not be used against him in any way, whether compelled or not.

"This is the not so subtle overtone of the opinion - that it is inherently wrong for the police to gather evidence from the accused himself. And this is precisely the nub of this dissent. I see nothing wrong or immoral, and certainly nothing unconstitutional, in the police's asking a suspect whom they have reasonable cause to arrest whether or not he killed his wife or in confronting him with the evidence on which the arrest was based, at least where he has been plainly advised that he may remain completely silent.

"Until today, 'the admissions or confessions of the prisoner, when voluntarily and freely made, have always ranked high in the scale of incriminating evidence.' Particularly when corroborated, as where the police have confirmed the accused's disclosure of the hiding place of implements or fruits of the crime, such confessions have the highest reliability and significantly contribute to the certitude with which we may believe the accused is guilty. Moreover, it is by no means certain that the process of confessing is injurious to the accused. To the contrary it may provide psychological relief and enhance the prospects for rehabilitation.

"This is not to say that the value of respect for the inviolability of the accused's individual personality should be accorded no weight or that all confessions should be indiscriminately admitted. This Court has long read the Constitution to proscribe compelled confessions, a salutary rule from which there should be no retreat. But I see no sound basis, factual or otherwise, and the Court gives none, for concluding that the present rule against the receipt of coerced confessions is inadequate for the task of sorting out inadmissible evidence and must be replaced by the per se rule which is now imposed. Even if the new concept can be said to have advantages of some sort over the present law, they are far outweighed by its likely undesirable impact on other very relevant and important interests.

"The most basic function of any government is to provide for the security of the individual and of his property...These ends of society are served by the criminal laws which for the most part are aimed at the prevention of crime. Without the reasonably effective performance of the task of preventing private violence and retaliation, it is idle to talk about human dignity and civilized values.

"And what about the accused who has confessed or would confess in response to simple, noncoercive questioning and whose guilt could not otherwise be proved? Is it so clear that release is the best thing for him in every case? Has it so unquestionably been resolved that in each and every case it would be better for him not to confess and to return to his environment with no attempt whatsoever to help him? I think not. It may well be that in many cases it will be no less than a callous disregard for his own welfare as well as for the interests of his next victim.

"There is another aspect to the effect of the Court's rule on the person whom the police have arrested on probable cause. The fact is that he may not be guilty at all and may be able to extricate himself quickly and simply if he were told the circumstances of his arrest and were asked to explain. This effort, and his release, must now await the hiring of a lawyer or his appointment by the court, consultation with counsel and then a session with the police or the prosecutor. Similarly, where probable cause exists to arrest several suspects, as where the body of the victim is discovered in a house having several residents, it will often be true that a suspect may be cleared only through the results of interrogation of other suspects. Here too the release of the innocent may be delayed by the Court's rule."

This judicial overreaching and wholesale rewriting of the 5th Amendment in *Miranda* is but another instance of the illegitimate doctrine of applying the Bill of Rights, in this case the 5th Amendment, to the states. This is clearly contrary to the intention of the drafters of both the 5th and 14th amendments.

The following is a list, not necessarily complete, of the extent to which the Court has determined which portions of the Bill of Rights have been "incorporated" by the 14th Amendment Due Process Clause so as to be applicable to the states.

The 1st Amendment- its regulation as to speech, religion, and association applies to the states pursuant to *West Virginia State Board of Education v. Barnette* (1943*), Everson v. Board of Education* (1947) *and Edwards v. California* (1963).

In the *Everson* case of 1947, the Court held for the first time, by ignoring previous precedents, that a wall of separation between church and state must be kept high and impregnable.

In 1962, in *Engle v. Vitale*, the court outlawed prayer in public schools.

In 1963, in *Abington v.Schemepp*, the Court outlawed bible reading in the public school system.

In 1965, the Court outlawed a student's right to bow his head and pray audibly for his food.

In 1967, the Court outlawed a nursery rhyme which did not mention the word God. The court held that even though the word God was not contained in this nursery rhyme, if someone were to hear it, it might cause them to think of God and it is therefore unconstitutional.

In 1980, in *Stone v. Graham*, the Court held that the posting of the Ten Commandments in our public schools was illegal. The Court held that "If the posted copies of the Ten Commandments are to have any effect at all it will be to induce the school children to read them, and if they read them they may meditate upon them and perhaps venerate and obey them. This is not a permissible objective."

In 1992, in *Lee v. Weisman*, the Court held it unconstitutional to have an invocation or prayer at a school graduation.

Regardless of whether one agrees or disagrees with these decisions, the issue is whether "nine lawyers in robes" often only five of the nine, are entitled to render these monumental decisions for over 300 million people of this country.

I submit they had, and have, no such authority as the Constitution did not and does not grant them such power and such feigned power exists only because of the Court's rewriting the Constitution in favor of granting the Court this power to apply the Bill of Rights to the states.

The 2nd Amendment - *McDonald v. City of Chicago* (2010), concluded that the Fourteenth Amendment incorporates the Second Amendment right, recognized in *District of Columbia v. Heller* (2008), to keep and bear arms for the purpose of self-defense. *Bruen* case (2022) recognized the right of individuals to carry a loaded gun in public for self-defense.

The 4th Amendment- Arrest and Search has the same application to the states as federal pursuant to *Mapp v.Ohio* ((1961) *and Ker v. California* (1963).

The 5th Amendment- regarding indictment, *Hurtado v. California* (1884) and *Alexander v. Louisiana* (1972); Double Jeopardy, *Benton v. Maryland* (1969) and *Ashe v. Swenson* (1970); Privilege Against Self-incrimination, *Malloy v. Hogan* (1964) and *California v. Byers* (1971).

The 6th Amendment- Speedy trial, *Klopfer v. North Carolina* (1967); Public Trial, *In re Oliver* (1948); Jury Trial, *Duncan v. Louisiana* (1968); Notice of Charge, *In re Gault* (1967); Confrontation of Witnesses, *Pointer v. Texas* (1965) and *Parker v. Gladden* (1966); Compulsory Process for Obtaining Witnesses, *Washington v. Texas* (1967); Right to Counsel, *Gideon v. Wainwright* (1963).

The 8th Amendment- Cruel and Unusual Punishment, *Furman v. Georgia,* (1972) holding the death penalty unconstitutional in cases where the penalty may be selectively and capriciously applied.

Hence, the Court has literally "taken over" the Bill of Rights and applied them to the states, notwithstanding the fact that the drafters of the 14th Amendment Due Process Clause had no such intention.

No discussion of the 14th Amendment, Due Process clause would be complete without referring to its historical underpinnings. To that end, the following is presented:

In pertinent part, the clause states, ... *"that no state shall deprive any person of life, liberty, or property without due process of law"*...

The Constitution requires a two-thirds vote to submit an amendment for *ratification.* While the *submission* was by two-thirds of those present, this two-thirds was obtained only by excluding, under reconstruction acts, representatives of ten confederate states, notwithstanding the fact that the Constitution also provides that each state shall have at least one representative in the House....

Consequently, it follows that the 14th Amendment was never legally *submitted.* However, assuming the *submission* to be legal, it is equally clear that the 14th Amendment was never legally *ratified.* Adoption under the Constitution required *ratification* by at lease three-fourths, or 28, of the 37 states then in existence.

Kentucky, Delaware and Maryland rejected the amendment outright. The amendment was not ratified by California until 1959. New Jersey and Ohio initially ratified it but both later withdrew their ratifications. All ten of the Southern states immediately rejected it. The amendment failed for lack of sufficient votes.

Congress then enacted, over President Johnson's veto, the Reconstruction Act of 1867, which declared that no legal government existed in the ten southern states, and placed them all under military occupation....

Congress then demanded that each excluded state ratify the amendment in order to enjoy the status of a state, including representation in Congress. Only under this duress was the 14th Amendment finally "ratified".

The above is a paraphrase of the historical note provided by *Merrill, How To Lose A Federal Republic Without Even Half Trying,* 29 Oklahoma Law Review 577, 581 (1976). And of course this note applies to the entire 14th Amendment of which the Due Process clause is only a part.

What Alexander Hamilton presaged in Federalist 84 regarding misconstruing the Bill of Rights, has, in a sense, indeed come to pass...Hamilton, in pertinent part, said:

". . . I go further, and affirm, that bills of rights, in the sense and in the extent in which they are contended for, are not only unnecessary in the proposed constitution, but would even be dangerous. They would contain various exceptions to powers which are not granted, and on this various account, would afford a colourable pretext to claim more than were granted. For why declare that things shall not be done which there is no power to do? Why for instance, should it be said, that the liberty of the press shall not be restrained, when no power is given by which restrictions may be imposed? I will not contend that such a provision would confer a regulating power, but it is evident that it would furnish, to men disposed to usurp, a plausible pretence for claiming that power. They might urge with a semblance of reason, that the constitution ought not to be charged with the absurdity of providing against the abuse of an authority, which was not given, and that the provision of restraining the liberty of the press afforded a clear implication, that a power to prescribe proper regulations concerning it, was intended to be vested in the national government. This may serve as a specimen of the numerous handles which would be given to the doctrine of constructive powers, by the indulgence of an injudicious zeal for bills of rights. . . ."

Of course Hamilton could not have known the extent to which the Bill of Rights were to be applied to the states, by ". . . men disposed to usurp. . . by the indulgence of an injudicious zeal for bills of rights. . . ." Ironically, had Hamilton's view prevailed, and there had been enacted no Bill of Rights, the Supreme Court would have possessed one less ". . . pretence for claiming that power. . ."

"The Constitution does not provide a cure for every social ill, nor does it vest judges with a mandate to try to remedy every social problem.."   Plyler v. Doe (1982)

CHAPTER 6

EQUAL PROTECTION OR SUBJECTIVE ADJUDICATION

The 14th Amendment provides: "No state shall...deny to any person within its jurisdiction the equal protection of the laws." This was ratified in 1868.

Perhaps I was a bit hasty in describing, in Chapter 5, the 14th Amendment Due Process Clause as the most insidious device utilized by the Supreme Court to emasculate the states and the People of these United States.

There is another scheme, which might enjoy such accolade, employed by the Supreme Court to further deprive the states and the People of the right to govern themselves. This involves the 14th Amendment, Equal Protection clause. This chapter is concerned with this clause which was ratified in 1868 as part of the post-civil-war package of three amendments, the 13th, 14th and 15th.

The 13th, in 1865, abolished slavery in the United States and its territories. The 15th, in 1870, granted the right to vote to the former slaves. The 14th was concerned with granting other rights to the former slaves to include citizenship, due process and equal protection.

What follows will show how early-on, the Court adhered very closely to the intention of the drafters of the 14th A E/P clause, but as time went on and the composition of the court changed, the Court realized that since they were the ultimate authority as to what the Constitution "actually" meant, they could invent theories and doctrines and tests *ad nauseam*, to suit their collective agenda, and their rulings would go unchallenged.

They were right, and the Court has been adrift for considerable time. It's now time for us to right their course.

It must be recognized that almost all statutes and regulations discriminate among people, i.e., virtually none treats all people equally.

Although without constitutional authority, the Court has taken it upon itself to develop several tests to determine whether a law before it passes constitutional muster.

The test utilized early-on was the "rational basis' test. This test presumed the validity of the law and unless those challenging the law could show its lack of rationality, it was deemed constitutional.

Then the Court invented the so-called "strict scrutiny" test, which presumed *un*constitutionality unless the government could show a "compelling" reason for the law. This test was created to deal with situations involving a "suspect class" or "fundamental right."

Then, the court created a third test, termed the "intermediate level of scrutiny". This test was utilized to fill the gap between the earlier two tests, and was used by the Court when, in their judgment, it became necessary to find a law unconstitutional, and the then-existing tests would prove inadequate.

Examples of each of these tests follow:

An early case, *Mugler v. Kansas* (1887), made clear that certain areas were strictly within the unique power of the states, i.e., health, safety and morals. These powers were described as the states' "police powers."

Mugler was a case involving the sale and manufacture of intoxicating beverages and whether the State of Kansas could outlaw same. The Supreme Court said it could, based on the state's "police powers."

It wasn't long until the Court began to erode the police powers of the states. *In Lochner v. New York* (1905), the Court stated that any legislation regarding health, safety, morals and general welfare were reserved for the states "and with such conditions the 14th Amendment was not designed to interfere."

However, it determined that the state of New York exceeded the police powers as Lochner was concerned with the state's power to limit the number of hours per week a man could agree, or be requested, to work. The Court stated that the legislation had no connection to health, safety or morals and ruled that the law was unconstitutional.

In 1908, in *Muller v. Oregon*, the Court upheld an Oregon statute which limited the hours a woman could work in a factory or laundry to 10 hours a day. The Court stated that Oregon was justified in treating women differently than men. There was no mention of Equal Protection. This is consistent with the original intent of the drafters of the Equal Protection clause.

Please recall that the purpose of the 14th Amendment E/qual Protection clause was to ensure that the former slaves were treated equally with non-slaves, and nothing more.

In 1948 in *Goesaert v. Cleary*, the issue presented was whether the State of Michigan could forbid a female to be licensed as a bartender unless she were the wife or daughter of the male owner of a licensed liquor establishment. The statute was upheld and the majority opinion was written by Justice Frankfurter.

Justice Frankfurter:

"The claim...is that Michigan cannot forbid females generally from being barmaids and at the same time make an exception in favor of the wives and daughters of the owners of liquor establishments. Beguiling as the subject is, it need not detain us long. To ask whether or not the Equal Protection of the Laws Clause of the Fourteenth Amendment barred Michigan from making the classification the State has made between wives and daughters of owners of liquor places and wives and daughters of non-owners, is one of those rare instances where to state the question is in effect to answer it.

"We are, to be sure, dealing with a historic calling. We meet the alewife, sprightly and ribald, in Shakespeare, but centuries before him she played a role in the social life of England.

"The Fourteenth Amendment did not tear history up by the roots, and the regulation of the liquor traffic is one of the oldest and most untrammeled of legislative powers. Michigan could, beyond question, forbid all women from working behind a bar. This is so despite the vast changes in the social and legal position of women. The fact that women may now have achieved the virtues that men have long claimed as their prerogatives and now indulge in vices that men have long practiced, does not preclude the States from drawing a sharp line between the sexes, certainly, in such matters as the regulation of the liquor traffic... The Constitution does not require legislatures to reflect sociological insight, or shifting social standards, any more than it requires them to keep abreast of the latest scientific standards.

"While Michigan may deny to all women opportunities for bartending, Michigan cannot play favorites among women without rhyme or reasons. The Constitution in enjoining the equal protection of the laws upon States precludes irrational discrimination as between persons or groups of persons in the incidence of a law. But the Constitution does not require situations 'which are different in fact or opinion to be treated in law as though they were the same.'

"Since bartending by women may, in the allowable legislative judgment, give rise to moral and social problems against which it may devise preventive measures, the legislature need not go to the full length of prohibition if it believes that as to a defined group of females other factors are operating which either eliminate or reduce the moral and social problems otherwise calling for prohibition. Michigan evidently believes that the oversight assured through ownership of a bar by a barmaid's husband or father minimizes hazards that may confront a barmaid without such protecting oversight.

"This Court is certainly not in a position to gainsay such belief by the Michigan legislature. If it is entertainable, as we think it is, Michigan has not violated its duty to afford equal protection of its laws. We cannot cross-examine either actually or argumentatively the mind of Michigan legislators nor question their motives. Since the line they have drawn is not without a basis in reason, we cannot give ear to the suggestion that the real impulse behind this legislation was an unchivalrous desire of male bartenders to try to monopolize the calling. Suffice it to say that ... a statute is not invalid under the Constitution because it might have gone farther than it did, or because it may not succeed in bringing about the result that it tends to produce. Nor is it unconstitutional for Michigan to withdraw from women the occupation of bartending because it allows women to serve as waitresses where liquor is dispensed. The District Court has sufficiently indicated the reasons that may have influenced the legislature in allowing women to be waitresses in a liquor establishment over which a man's ownership provides control. Nothing need be added to what was said below as to the other grounds on which the Michigan law was assailed. Judgment affirmed.

Mr. Justice RUTLEDGE, with whom Mr. Justice DOUGLAS and Mr. Justice MURPHY join, dissenting:

"While the equal protection clause does not require a legislature to achieve 'abstract symmetry' or to classify with 'mathematical nicety,'' that clause does require lawmakers to refrain from invidious distinctions of the sort drawn by the statute challenged in this case.

"The statute arbitrarily discriminates between male and female owners of liquor establishments. A male owner, although he himself is always absent from his bar, may employ his wife and daughter as barmaids. A female owner may neither work as a barmaid herself nor employ her daughter in that position, even if a man is always present in the establishment to keep order. This inevitable result of the classification belies the assumption that the statute was motivated by a legislative solicitude for the moral and physical well-being of women who, but for the law, would be employed as barmaids. Since there could be no other conceivable justification for such discrimination against women owners of liquor establishments, the statute should be held invalid as a denial of equal protection."

So, as of 1948 the Court was still adhering to the true intention of the 14th A E/P clause and was not extending its reach beyond laws involving the treatment of former slaves.

As is characteristic, however, the dissent, without elaboration, stated that since the statute treated women differently than men it was a denial of *equal protection*. This was a trial-balloon to see what reaction it would garner. After some period of adjustment, it would eventually come around full-circle and become the law of the land.

U.S. SUPREME COURT
HARPER V. VIRGINIA STATE BOARD OF ELECTIONS
383 U.S. 663 (1966)

This case made the much-anticipated, marked departure from the original meaning and intent of the 14th A E/P clause, i.e., to ensure that the former slave was now treated as a free person.

In this case, the Court held that a poll tax was a violation of said clause because ... " the right to vote is too precious, too fundamental to be so burdened or conditioned [as to apply to it a poll tax]..."

In order to support their decision, the Court simply rewrote the 14th A E/P clause and applied it to a poll tax by referring to previous cases which were themselves clear departures from the actual text and obvious meaning of the amendment.

This was nothing more than judicial activism on the part of the Court showing disrespect and disdain for the drafters of the amendment and for the Constitution itself. Fortunately there was in their midst several justices who honored their oath and adhered to their proper role as justices, i.e.,to exercise judicial restraint and to recognize that the role of any judicial officer was to remain passive in the sense that they do not write the law, they simply apply the law as written.

The Constitution, which created their position, assigns the power to write laws to the legislative branch of the Federal Government via Article I.

The role of applying the law to the facts, is assigned to the judicial branch, Article III. And the role of enforcing the law is assigned to the executive branch, Article II.

In dissent, Justice Black wrote:

"In *Breedlove v. Suttles*, 1937, a few weeks after I took my seat as a member of this Court, we unanimously upheld the right of the State of Georgia to make payment of its state poll tax a prerequisite to voting in state elections....I joined the Court's judgment in *Butler v. Thompson*, upholding... the Virginia state poll tax law challenged here against the same equal protection challenges.

"Since the Breedlove and Butler cases were decided, the Federal Constitution has not been amended in the only way it could constitutionally have been, that is, as provided in Article V of the Constitution. I would adhere to the holding of those cases.

"The Court, however, overrules *Breedlove* in part, but its opinion reveals that it does so not by using its limited power to interpret the original meaning of the Equal Protection Clause, but by giving that clause a new meaning which it believes represents a better governmental policy.

"From this action I dissent.

"It should be pointed out at once that the Court's decision is to no extent based on a finding that the Virginia law as written or as applied is being used as a device or mechanism to deny Negro citizens of Virginia the right to vote on account of their color....

"If the record could support a finding that the law as written or applied has such an effect, the law would of course be unconstitutional as a violation of the Fourteenth and Fifteenth Amendments.

"What the Court ... holds is that the Equal Protection Clause necessarily bars all States from making payment of a state tax, any tax, a prerequisite to voting. I think the interpretation that this Court gave the Equal Protection Clause in *Breedlove* was correct. The mere fact that a law results in treating some groups differently from others does not, of course, automatically amount to a violation of the Equal Protection Clause.

"To bar a State from drawing any distinctions in the application of its laws would practically paralyze the regulatory power of legislative bodies.

"Consequently, the constitutional command for a state to afford 'equal protection of the laws' sets a goal not attainable by the invention and application of a precise formula. Voting laws are no exception to this principle. All voting laws treat some persons differently from others in some respects. Some bar a person from voting who is under 21 years of age; others bar those under 18. Some bar convicted felons or the insane, and some have attached a freehold or other property qualification for voting.

"The *Breedlove* case upheld a poll tax which was imposed on men but was not equally imposed on women and minors, and the Court today does not overrule that part of Breedlove which approved those discriminatory provisions. And...this Court held that state laws which disqualified the illiterate from voting did not violate the Equal Protection Clause. From these cases and all the others decided by this Court interpreting the Equal Protection Clause it is clear that some discriminatory voting qualifications can be imposed without violating the Equal Protection Clause.

"A study of our cases shows that this Court has refused to use the general language of the Equal Protection Clause as though it provided a handy instrument to strike down state laws which the Court feels are based on bad governmental policy. The equal protection cases carefully analyzed boil down to the principle that distinctions drawn and even discriminations imposed by state laws do not violate the Equal Protection Clause so long as these distinctions and discriminations are not 'irrational,' 'irrelevant,' 'unreasonable,' "arbitrary,' or 'invidious.'

"*These vague and indefinite terms do not, of course, provide a precise formula or an automatic mechanism for deciding cases arising under the Equal Protection Clause.* The restrictive connotations of these terms ... are a plain recognition of the fact that under a proper interpretation of the Equal Protection Clause States are to have the broadest kind of leeway in areas where they have a general constitutional competence to act.

"In view of the purpose of the terms to restrain the courts from a wholesale invalidation of state laws under the Equal Protection Clause it would be difficult to say that the poll tax requirement is 'irrational' or 'arbitrary' or works 'invidious discriminations.'

"State poll tax legislation can 'reasonably,' 'rationally' and without an 'invidious' or evil purpose to injure anyone be found to rest on a number of state policies including (1) the State's desire to collect its revenue, and (2) its belief that voters who pay a poll tax will be interested in furthering the State's welfare when they vote.

"Certainly it is rational to believe that people may be more likely to pay taxes if payment is a prerequisite to voting. And if history can be a factor in determining the 'rationality' of discrimination in a state law...then whatever may be our personal opinion, history is on the side of 'rationality' of the State's poll tax policy. Property qualifications existed in the Colonies and were continued by many States after the Constitution was adopted.

"Although I join the Court in disliking the policy of the poll tax, this is not in my judgment a justifiable reason for holding this poll tax law unconstitutional. Such a holding on my part would, in my judgment, be an exercise of power which the Constitution does not confer upon me.

"Another reason for my dissent from the Court's judgment and opinion is that it seems to be using the old 'natural-law-due-process formula' to justify striking down state laws as violations of the Equal Protection Clause. I have heretofore had many occasions to express my strong belief that there is no constitutional support whatever for this Court to use the Due Process Clause as though it provided a blank check to alter the meaning of the Constitution as written so as to add to it substantive constitutional changes which a majority of the Court at any given time believes are needed to meet present-day problems.

"Nor is there in my opinion any more constitutional support for this Court to use the Equal Protection Clause, as it has today, to write into the Constitution its notions of what it thinks is good governmental policy.

"If basic changes as to the respective powers of the state and national governments are needed, I prefer to let those changes be made by amendment as Article V of the Constitution provides.

"For a majority of this Court to undertake that task, whether purporting to do so under the Due Process or the Equal Protection Clause amounts, in my judgment, to an exercise of power the Constitution makers with foresight and wisdom refused to give the Judicial Branch of the Government.

"I have in no way departed from the view I expressed in Adamson v. California (1947), that the 'natural-law-due-process formula' under which courts make the Constitution mean what they think it should at a given time "has been used in the past, and can be used in the future, to license this Court, in considering regulatory legislation, to roam at large in the broad expanses of policy and morals and to trespass, all too freely, on the legislative domain of the States as well as the Federal Government.

"The Court denies that it is using the 'natural-law-due-process formula.' It says that its invalidation of the Virginia law 'is founded not on what we think governmental policy should be, but on what the Equal Protection Clause requires.' I find no statement in the Court's opinion, however, which advances even a plausible argument as to why the alleged discriminations which might possibly be effected by Virginia's poll tax law are 'irrational,' 'unreasonable,' 'arbitrary,' or 'invidious' or have no relevance to a legitimate policy which the State wishes to adopt.

"The Court gives no reason at all to discredit the long-standing beliefs that making the payment of a tax a prerequisite to voting is an effective way of collecting revenue and that people who pay their taxes are likely to have a far greater interest in their government. The Court's failure to give any reasons to show that these purposes of the poll tax are 'irrational,' 'unreasonable,' 'arbitrary,' or 'invidious' is a pretty clear indication to me that none exist.

"I can only conclude that the primary, controlling, predominant, if not the exclusive reason for declaring the Virginia law unconstitutional is the Court's deep-seated hostility and antagonism, which I share, to making payment of a tax a prerequisite to voting. The Court's justification for consulting its own notions rather than following the original meaning of the Constitution, as I would, apparently is based on the belief of the majority of the Court that for this Court to be bound by the original meaning of the Constitution is an intolerable and debilitating evil; that our Constitution should not be 'shackled to the political theory of a particular era,' and that to save the country from the original Constitution the Court must have constant power to renew it and keep it abreast of this Court's more enlightened theories of what is best for our society.

"It seems to me that this is an attack not only on the great value of our Constitution itself but also on the concept of a written constitution which is to survive through the years as originally written unless changed through the amendment process which the Framers wisely provided.

"Moreover, when a 'political theory' embodied in our Constitution becomes outdated, it seems to me that a majority of the nine members of this Court are not only without constitutional power but are far less qualified to choose a new constitutional political theory than the people of this country proceeding in the manner provided by Article V.

"The people have not found it impossible to amend their Constitution to meet new conditions. *The Equal Protection Clause itself is the product of the people's desire to use their constitutional power to amend the Constitution to meet new problems.*

"Moreover, the people, in section 5 of the Fourteenth Amendment, designated the governmental tribunal they wanted to provide additional rules to enforce the guarantees of that Amendment. The branch of Government they chose was not the Judicial Branch but the Legislative.

Section 5 states: *The Congress* shall have power to enforce, by appropriate legislation, the provisions of this article.

"I have no doubt at all that Congress has the power [through] section 5 to pass legislation to abolish the poll tax in order to protect the citizens of this country if it believes that the poll tax is being used as a device to deny voters equal protection of the laws.

"But this legislative power which was granted to Congress by section 5 of the Fourteenth Amendment is limited to Congress.

"All of the amendments derive much of their force from this latter provision. It is not said the judicial power of the general government shall extend to enforcing the prohibitions and to protecting the rights and immunities guaranteed. *It is not said that branch of the government shall be authorized to declare void any action of a State in violation of the prohibitions. It is the power of Congress which has been enlarged.*

"Congress is authorized to enforce the prohibitions by appropriate legislation. Some legislation is contemplated to make the amendments fully effective. Whatever legislation is appropriate, that is, adapted to carry out the objects the amendments have in view, whatever tends to enforce submission to the prohibitions they contain, and to secure to all persons the enjoyment of perfect equality of civil rights and the equal protection of the laws against State denial or invasion, if not prohibited, is brought within the domain of congressional power.Thus section 5 of the Fourteenth Amendment in accordance with our constitutional structure of government authorizes the Congress to pass definitive legislation to protect Fourteenth Amendment rights which it has done many times. For Congress to do this fits in precisely with the division of powers originally entrusted to the three branches of government - Executive, Legislative, and Judicial.

"But for us to undertake in the guise of constitutional interpretation to decide the constitutional policy question of this case amounts, in my judgment, to a plain exercise of power which the Constitution has denied us but has specifically granted to Congress. I cannot join in holding that the Virginia state poll tax law violates the Equal Protection Clause.

MR. JUSTICE HARLAN, whom MR. JUSTICE STEWART joins, dissenting.

"The final demise of state poll taxes, already totally proscribed by the Twenty-Fourth Amendment with respect to federal elections and abolished by the States themselves in all but four States with respect to state elections, is perhaps in itself not of great moment. But the fact that the *coup de grace* has been administered by this Court instead of being left to the affected States or to the federal political process should be a matter of continuing concern to all interested in maintaining the proper role of this tribunal under our scheme of government...

"My disagreement with the present decision is that in holding the Virginia poll tax violative of the Equal Protection Clause the Court has departed from long-established standards governing the application of that clause.

"The Equal Protection Clause prevents States from arbitrarily treating people differently under their laws. Whether any such differing treatment is to be deemed arbitrary depends on whether or not it reflects an appropriate differentiating classification among those affected, the clause has never been thought to require equal treatment of all persons despite differing circumstances.

"The test evolved by this Court for determining whether an asserted justifying classification exists is whether such a classification can be deemed to be founded on some rational and otherwise constitutionally permissible state policy...and until recently it has been followed in all kinds of 'equal protection' cases.

"But today in holding unconstitutional state poll taxes and property qualifications for voting,...the Court reverts to the highly subjective judicial [decision]...and goes no further than to say that the electoral franchise is 'precious' and 'fundamental,' and to conclude that '[t]o introduce wealth or payment of a fee as a measure of a voter's qualifications is to introduce a capricious or irrelevant factor.'

"These are of course captivating phrases, but they are wholly inadequate to satisfy the standard governing adjudication of the equal protection issue: Is there a rational basis for Virginia's poll tax as a voting qualification? I think the answer to that question is undoubtedly "yes." Property qualifications and poll taxes have been a traditional part of our political structure. In the Colonies the franchise was generally a restricted one. Over the years these and other restrictions were gradually lifted, primarily because popular theories of political representation had changed. Often restrictions were lifted only after wide public debate. The issue of woman suffrage, for example, raised questions of family relationships, of participation in public affairs, of the very nature of the type of society in which Americans wished to live; eventually a consensus was reached, which culminated in the Nineteenth Amendment no more than 45 years ago.

"Similarly with property qualifications, it is only by fiat that it can be said, especially in the context of American history, that there can be no rational debate as to their advisability. Most of the early Colonies had them; many of the States have had them during much of their histories; and, whether one agrees or not, arguments have been and still can be made in favor of them.

"For example, it is certainly a rational argument that payment of some minimal poll tax promotes civic responsibility, weeding out those who do not care enough about public affairs to pay $1.50 or thereabouts a year for the exercise of the franchise. It is also arguable, indeed it was probably accepted as sound political theory by a large percentage of Americans through most of our history, that people with some property have a deeper stake in community affairs, and are consequently more responsible, more educated, more knowledgeable, more worthy of confidence, than those without means, and that the community and Nation would be better managed if the franchise were restricted to such citizens.

"Nondiscriminatory and fairly applied literacy tests, upheld by this Court...find justification on very similar grounds.

"These viewpoints, to be sure, ring hollow on most contemporary ears. Their lack of acceptance today is evidenced by the fact that nearly all of the States, left to their own devices, have eliminated property or poll-tax qualifications; by the cognate fact that Congress and three-quarters of the States quickly ratified the

Twenty-Fourth Amendment; and by the fact that rules such as the 'pauper exclusion' in Virginia law have never been enforced.

"*Property and poll-tax qualifications, very simply, are not in accord with current egalitarian notions of how a modern democracy should be organized. It is of course entirely fitting that legislatures should modify the law to reflect such changes in popular attitudes.*

"*However, it is all wrong, in my view, for the Court to adopt the political doctrines popularly accepted at a particular moment of our history and to declare all others to be irrational and invidious, barring them from the range of choice by reasonably minded people acting through the political process.*

"It was not too long ago that Mr. Justice Holmes felt impelled to remind the Court that the Due Process Clause of the Fourteenth Amendment does not enact the laissez-faire theory of society. The times have changed, and perhaps it is appropriate to observe that neither does the Equal Protection Clause of that Amendment rigidly impose upon America an ideology of unrestrained egalitarianism. I would affirm the decision of the District Court. "

Comes now *Shapiro v. Thompson:* As will be seen, this is another example of the brazen attitude of those on the SC who believe they "know better" than the People and simply ignore the legislature and rewrite the Constitution as they see fit. This, I might add is not the opinion of the author, to be dismissed out of hand by the establishment, but irrefutable proof has as its source the decisions of the justices themselves.

Please read on and be informed. . .

U.S.SUPREME COURT
SHAPIRO V. THOMPSON
394 U.S. 618 (1969)

"These appeals are from decisions of three-judge District Courts holding unconstitutional Connecticut, Pennsylvania, or District of Columbia statutory provisions which deny welfare assistance to persons who are residents and meet all other eligibility requirements except that they have not resided within the jurisdiction for at least a year immediately preceding their applications for assistance.

"Appellees' main contention ... is that the prohibition of benefits to residents of less than one year creates a classification which constitutes an invidious discrimination denying them equal protection of the laws.

"Appellants argue that the waiting period is needed to preserve the fiscal integrity of their public assistance programs, as persons who require welfare assistance during their first year of residence are likely to become continuing burdens on welfare programs. Appellants also seek to justify the classification as a permissible attempt to discourage indigents from entering a State solely to

101.

obtain larger benefits, and to distinguish between new and old residents on the basis of the tax contributions they have made to the community. Certain appellants rely in addition on the following administrative and related governmental objectives: facilitating the planning of welfare budgets, providing an objective test of residency, minimizing the opportunity for recipients fraudulently to receive payments from more than one jurisdiction, and encouraging early entry of new residents into the labor force. Connecticut and Pennsylvania also argue that Congress approved the imposition of the one-year requirement in 402 (b) of the Social Security Act.

"There is no dispute that the effect of the waiting-period requirement in each case is to create two classes of needy resident families indistinguishable from each other except that one is composed of residents who have resided a year or more, and the second of residents who have resided less than a year, in the jurisdiction. On the basis of this sole difference the first class is granted and the second class is denied welfare aid upon which may depend the ability of the families to obtain the very means to subsist - food, shelter, and other necessities of life. In each case, the District Court found that appellees met the test for residence in their jurisdictions, as well as all other eligibility requirements except the requirement of residence for a full year prior to their applications. On reargument, appellees' central contention is that the statutory prohibition of benefits to residents of less than a year creates a classification which constitutes an invidious discrimination denying them equal protection of the laws. We agree. The interests which appellants assert are promoted by the classification either may not constitutionally be promoted by government or are not compelling governmental interests.

"Primarily, appellants justify the waiting-period requirement as a protective device to preserve the fiscal integrity of state public assistance programs. It is asserted that people who require welfare assistance during their first year of residence in a State are likely to become continuing burdens on state welfare programs. Therefore, the argument runs, if such people can be deterred from entering the jurisdiction by denying them welfare benefits during the first year, state programs to assist long-time residents will not be impaired by a substantial influx of indigent newcomers. "There is weighty evidence that exclusion from the jurisdiction of the poor who need or may need relief was the specific objective of these provisions...

"We do not doubt that the one-year waiting-period device is well suited to discourage the influx of poor families in need of assistance. An indigent who desires to migrate, resettle, find a new job, and start a new life will doubtless hesitate if he knows that he must risk making the move without the possibility of falling back on state welfare assistance during his first year of residence, when his need may be most acute. But the purpose of inhibiting migration by needy persons into the State is constitutionally impermissible.

102.

"This Court long ago recognized that the nature of our Federal Union and our constitutional concepts of personal liberty unite to require that all citizens be free to travel throughout the length and breadth of our land uninhibited by statutes, rules, or regulations which unreasonably burden or restrict this movement....

"For all the great purposes for which the Federal government was formed, we are one people, with one common country. We are all citizens of the United States; and, as members of the same community, must have the right to pass and repass through every part of it without interruption, as freely as in our own States."

"We have no occasion to ascribe the source of this right to travel interstate to a particular constitutional provision. It suffices that, as MR. JUSTICE STEWART said for the Court in *United States v. Guest* (1966):

"The constitutional right to travel from one State to another . . . occupies a position fundamental to the concept of our Federal Union. It is a right that has been firmly established and repeatedly recognized.

". . . *[T]he right finds no explicit mention in the Constitution.* The reason, it has been suggested, is that a right so elementary was conceived from the beginning to be a necessary concomitant of the stronger Union the Constitution created. In any event, freedom to travel throughout the United States has long been recognized as a basic right under the Constitution."

"Thus, the purpose of deterring the in-migration of indigents cannot serve as justification for the classification created by the one-year waiting period, since that purpose is constitutionally impermissible. If a law has "no other purpose . . . than to chill the assertion of constitutional rights by penalizing those who choose to exercise them, then it [is] patently unconstitutional.

"Alternatively, appellants argue that even if it is impermissible for a State to attempt to deter the entry of all indigents, the challenged classification may be justified as a permissible state attempt to discourage those indigents who would enter the State solely to obtain larger benefits. We observe first that none of the statutes before us is tailored to serve that objective...

"More fundamentally, a State may no more try to fence out those indigents who seek higher welfare benefits than it may try to fence out indigents generally. Implicit in any such distinction is the notion that indigents who enter a State with the hope of securing higher welfare benefits are somehow less deserving than indigents who do not take this consideration into account. But we do not perceive why a mother who is seeking to make a new life for herself and her children should be regarded as less deserving because she considers, among others factors, the level of a State's public assistance. Surely such a mother is no less deserving than a mother who moves into a particular State in order to take advantage of its better educational facilities.

"Appellants argue further that the challenged classification may be sustained as an attempt to distinguish between new and old residents on the basis of the contribution they have made to the community through the payment of taxes. We have difficulty seeing how longterm residents who qualify for welfare are making a greater present contribution to the State in taxes than indigent residents who have recently arrived. If the argument is based on contributions made in the past by the long-term residents, there is some question, as a factual matter, whether this argument is applicable in Pennsylvania where the record suggests that some 40% of those denied public assistance because of the waiting period had lengthy prior residence in the State. But we need not rest on the particular facts of these cases. Appellants' reasoning would logically permit the State to bar new residents from schools, parks, and libraries or deprive them of police and fire protection. Indeed it would permit the State to apportion all benefits and services according to the past tax contributions of its citizens. The Equal Protection Clause prohibits such an apportionment of state services.

"We recognize that a State has a valid interest in preserving the fiscal integrity of its programs. It may legitimately attempt to limit its expenditures, whether for public assistance, public education, or any other program. But a State may not accomplish such a purpose by invidious distinctions between classes of its citizens. It could not, for example, reduce expenditures for education by barring indigent children from its schools. Similarly, in the cases before us, appellants must do more than show that denying welfare benefits to new residents saves money. The saving of welfare costs cannot justify an otherwise invidious classification.   ? ?In sum, neither deterrence of indigents from migrating to the State nor limitation of welfare benefits to those regarded as contributing to the State is a constitutionally permissible state objective.

"Appellants next advance as justification certain administrative and related governmental objectives allegedly served by the waiting-period requirement. They argue that the requirement (1) facilitates the planning of the welfare budget; (2) provides an objective test of residency; (3) minimizes the opportunity for recipients fraudulently to receive payments from more than one jurisdiction; and (4) encourages early entry of new residents into the labor force.

"At the outset, we reject appellants' argument that a mere showing of a rational relationship between the waiting period and these four admittedly permissible state objectives will suffice to justify the classification. The waiting-period provision denies welfare benefits to otherwise eligible applicants solely because they have recently moved into the jurisdiction. But in moving from State to State or to the District of Columbia appellees were exercising a constitutional right, and any classification which serves to penalize the exercise of that right, unless shown to be necessary to promote a compelling governmental interest, is unconstitutional. The argument that the waiting-period requirement facilitates budget predictability is wholly unfounded. The records in all three cases are utterly devoid of evidence that either State or the District of Columbia in fact uses the one-year requirement as a means to predict the number of people who will require assistance in the budget year...

"The argument that the waiting period serves as an administratively efficient rule of thumb for determining residency similarly will not withstand scrutiny. The residence requirement and the one-year waiting-period requirement are distinct and independent prerequisites for assistance under these three statutes, and the facts relevant to the determination of each are directly examined by the welfare authorities. Before granting an application, the welfare authorities investigate the applicant's employment, housing, and family situation and in the course of the inquiry necessarily learn the facts upon which to determine whether the applicant is a resident.

"Similarly, there is no need for a State to use the one-year waiting period as a safeguard against fraudulent receipt of benefits; for less drastic means are available, and are employed, to minimize that hazard. Of course, a State has a valid interest in preventing fraud by any applicant, whether a newcomer or a long-time resident. It is not denied, however, that the investigations now conducted entail inquiries into facts relevant to that subject. In addition, cooperation among state welfare departments is common. The District of Columbia, for example, provides interim assistance to its former residents who have moved to a State which has a waiting period. As a matter of course, District officials send a letter to the welfare authorities in the recipient's new community "to request the information needed to continue assistance." A like procedure would be an effective safeguard against the hazard of double payments. Since double payments can be prevented by a letter or a telephone call, it is unreasonable to accomplish this objective by the blunderbuss method of denying assistance to all indigent newcomers for an entire year. "Pennsylvania suggests that the one-year waiting period is justified as a means of encouraging new residents to join the labor force promptly. But this logic would also require a similar waiting period for long-term residents of the State. A state purpose to encourage employment provides no rational basis for imposing a one-year waiting-period restriction on new residents only.

"We conclude therefore that appellants in these cases do not use and have no need to use the one-year requirement for the governmental purposes suggested. Thus, even under traditional equal protection tests a classification of welfare applicants according to whether they have lived in the State for one year would seem irrational and unconstitutional. But, of course, the traditional criteria do not apply in these cases. Since the classification here touches on the fundamental right of interstate movement, its constitutionality must be judged by the stricter standard of whether it promotes a compelling state interest. Under this standard, the waiting-period requirement clearly violates the Equal Protection Clause.

"Connecticut and Pennsylvania argue, however, that the constitutional challenge to the waiting-period requirements must fail because Congress expressly approved the imposition of the requirement by the States as part of the jointly funded AFDC program...

"But even if we were to assume, *arguendo,* that Congress did approve the imposition of a one-year waiting period, it is the responsive state legislation which infringes constitutional rights. By itself 402 (b) has absolutely no restrictive effect. It is therefore not that statute but only the state requirements which pose the constitutional question.

"Finally, even if it could be argued that the constitutionality of 402 (b) is somehow at issue here, it follows from what we have said that the provision, insofar as it permits the one-year waiting-period requirement, would be unconstitutional. Congress may not authorize the States to violate the Equal Protection Clause. Perhaps Congress could induce wider state participation in school construction if it authorized the use of joint funds for the building of segregated schools. "But could it seriously be contended that Congress would be constitutionally justified in such authorization by the need to secure state cooperation? Congress is without power to enlist state cooperation in a joint federal-state program by legislation which authorizes the States to violate the Equal Protection Clause.

"The waiting-period requirement in the District of Columbia Code involved is also unconstitutional even though it was adopted by Congress as an exercise of federal power. In terms of federal power, the discrimination created by the one-year requirement violates the Due Process Clause of the Fifth Amendment. '[W]hile the Fifth Amendment contains no equal protection clause, it does forbid discrimination that is `so unjustifiable as to be violative of due process.' For the reasons we have stated in invalidating the Pennsylvania and Connecticut provisions, the District of Columbia provision is also invalid - the Due Process Clause of the Fifth Amendment prohibits Congress from denying public assistance to poor persons otherwise eligible solely on the ground that they have not been residents of the District of Columbia for one year at the time their applications are filed.

"Accordingly, the judgments are affirmed.

MR. JUSTICE HARLAN, dissenting.

"In upholding the equal protection argument, the Court has applied an equal protection doctrine of relatively recent vintage: the rule that statutory classifications which either are based upon certain 'suspect' criteria or affect 'fundamental rights' will be held to deny equal protection unless justified by a "compelling" governmental interest. The 'compelling interest' doctrine, which today is articulated more explicitly than ever before, constitutes an increasingly significant exception to the long-established rule that a statute does not deny equal protection if it is rationally related to a legitimate governmental objective.

"The 'compelling interest' doctrine has two branches. The branch which requires that classifications based upon 'suspect' criteria be supported by a compelling interest apparently had its genesis in cases involving racial classifications.

"Today the list apparently has been further enlarged to include classifications based upon recent interstate movement, and perhaps those based upon the exercise of any constitutional right... I think that this branch of the 'compelling interest' doctrine is sound when applied to racial classifications, for historically the Equal Protection Clause was largely a product of the desire to eradicate legal distinctions founded upon race. However, I believe that the more recent extensions have been unwise.

"The second branch of the 'compelling interest' principle is even more troublesome. For it has been held that a statutory classification is subject to the 'compelling interest' test if the result of the classification may be to affect a 'fundamental right,'regardless of the basis of the classification.

"I think this branch of the 'compelling interest' doctrine particularly unfortunate and unnecessary. It is unfortunate because it creates an exception which threatens to swallow the standard equal protection rule. Virtually every state statute affects important rights...

"[T]o extend the 'compelling interest' rule to all cases in which such rights are affected would go far toward making this Court a 'super-legislature.'

"This branch of the doctrine is also unnecessary. When the right affected is one assured by the Federal Constitution, any infringement can be dealt with under the [appropriate] clause.

"But when a statute affects only matters not mentioned in the Federal Constitution and is not arbitrary or irrational, I must reiterate that I know of nothing which entitles this Court to pick out particular human activities, characterize them as 'fundamental,' and give them added protection under an unusually stringent equal protection test...

Hence, we see again that the court simply ignores the true intention of the drafters of the 14th Amendment Equal Protection clause, which one will recall, *was solely to ensure that the former slave was treated equally with the non-slave.*

There is no mention in this case that those denied welfare benefits were of any particular racial make up. The only restriction to being granted welfare, assuming other requirements were met, was that the applicant have been a resident for one year. Hence, as pointed out by the dissent, there was no violation of the 14th Amendment Equal Protection clause.

It is also noteworthy that the Court admits that there is no explicit constitutional right to travel from state to state. However, it argues by fiat or by conclusion that nevertheless there is such a constitutional right and such a right

107.

is fundamental and because it is 'fundamental.' to interfere with such a right as the states have in this case, must be unconstitutional.

In making such an unsupported argument, the Court ignores a truism too fundamental, to borrow a phrase, to need stating. That truism is that prior to the existence of the Constitution and the creation of the Federal government by said document, the states held all the rights, i.e., the states could pass any law they wished except for those which were denied them through their own respective constitutions.

Now, once the Federal Government came into being the states had an additional limitation on their rights, i.e., those imposed by the U.S. Constitution. Hence, if the states were not forbidden to do a particular thing, they retained the power to so do. Since there was, and is, no prohibition in the U.S. Constitution, regarding one's right to travel from state to state, such a right predates the Constitution and has existed and continues to exist without any grant of such right from the U.S.Constitution or the Supreme Court.

In other words, it is not necessary to find such a right in the U.S. Constitution in order for the people of this country to possess such a right. Such a right existed before the document and the federal government, were created.

The Court's arrogant attempt to find such a right and by their grace grant it to the People is exactly backwards....the People need no one, including the Supreme Court, to grant us a right which we have always possessed and maintained since 1776. The arrogance of the Court to so do is stunning.

We don't need no stinkin' badges. . . .

The following case is presented primarily to show the absolute, undisguised arrogance of the Supreme Court as exemplified in excerpts of Justice Marshall's dissent. Excerpts, from the majority opinion, immediately follow:

U.S. SUPREME COURT
SAN ANTONIO SCHOOL DISTRICT v. RODRIGUEZ
411 U.S. 1 (1973)

"The financing of public elementary and secondary schools in Texas is a product of state and local participation. Almost half of the revenues are derived from a largely state-funded program designed to provide a basic minimum educational offering in every school. Each district supplements state aid through an ad valorem tax on property within its jurisdiction. Appellees brought this class action on behalf of schoolchildren said to be members of poor families who reside in school districts having a low property tax base, making the claim that the Texas system's reliance on local property taxation favors the more affluent and violates equal protection requirements because of substantial interdistrict disparities in per-pupil expenditures resulting primarily from differences in the value of assessable property among the districts. The District Court, finding that wealth is a "suspect" classification and that education is a "fundamental" right, concluded that the system could be upheld only upon a showing, which appellants failed to make, that there was a compelling state interest for the system. The court also concluded that appellants failed even to ... demonstrate a reasonable or rational basis for the State's system ..."

The lower court held that the law was unconstitutional under the Equal Protection clause of the 14th amendment. The U.S. Supreme Court reversed.

"This, then, establishes the framework for our analysis. *We must decide, first, whether the Texas system of financing public education operates to the disadvantage of some suspect class or impinges upon a fundamental right explicitly or implicitly protected by the Constitution, thereby requiring strict judicial scrutiny.*

"If so, the judgment of the District Court should be affirmed. If not, the Texas scheme must still be examined to determine whether it rationally furthers some legitimate, articulated state purpose and therefore does not constitute an invidious discrimination in violation of the Equal Protection Clause of the Fourteenth Amendment...

"We are unable to agree that this case, which in significant aspects is sui generis, may be so neatly fitted into the conventional mosaic of constitutional analysis under the Equal Protection Clause. Indeed, for the several reasons that follow, we find neither the suspect-classification nor the fundamental-interest analysis persuasive...

"The lesson of [previous] cases in addressing the question now before the Court is plain. It is not the province of this Court to create substantive constitutional rights in the name of guaranteeing equal protection of the laws. Thus, the key to discovering whether education is 'fundamental' is not to be found in comparisons of the relative societal significance of education as opposed to subsistence or housing. Nor is it to be found by weighing whether education is as important as the right to travel. *Rather, the answer lies in assessing whether there is a right to education explicitly or implicitly guaranteed by the Constitution....*

"*We do not denigrate the importance of decent, safe, and sanitary housing. But the Constitution does not provide judicial remedies for every social and economic ill.* We are unable to perceive in that document any constitutional guarantee of access to dwellings of a particular quality or any recognition of the right of a tenant to occupy the real property of his landlord beyond the term of his lease, without the payment of rent . . . . Absent constitutional mandate.

"*Education, of course, is not among the rights afforded explicit protection under our Federal Constitution. Nor do we find any basis for saying it is implicitly so protected.* As we have said, the undisputed importance of education will not alone cause this Court to depart from the usual standard for reviewing a

109.

State's social and economic legislation. It is appellees' contention, however, that education is distinguishable from other services and benefits provided by the State because it bears a peculiarly close relationship to other rights and liberties accorded protection under the Constitution. Specifically, they insist that education is itself a fundamental personal right because it is essential to the effective exercise of First Amendment freedoms and to intelligent utilization of the right to vote. In asserting a nexus between speech and education, appellees urge that the right to speak is meaningless unless the speaker is capable of articulating his thoughts intelligently and persuasively. The 'marketplace of ideas' is an empty forum for those lacking basic communicative tools. Likewise, they argue that the corollary right to receive information becomes little more than a hollow privilege when the recipient has not been taught to read, assimilate, and utilize available knowledge.

"We have carefully considered each of the arguments supportive of the District Court's finding that education is a fundamental right or liberty and have found those arguments unpersuasive. In one further respect we find this a particularly inappropriate case in which to subject state action to strict judicial scrutiny. The present case, in another basic sense, is significantly different from any of the cases in which the Court has applied strict scrutiny to state or federal legislation touching upon constitutionally protected rights.

"It should be clear, for the reasons stated above and in accord with the prior decisions of this Court, that this is not a case in which the challenged state action must be subjected to the searching judicial scrutiny reserved for laws that create suspect classifications or impinge upon constitutionally protected rights.

"We need not rest our decision, however, solely on the inappropriateness of the strict-scrutiny test. A century of Supreme Court adjudication under the Equal Protection Clause affirmatively supports the application of the traditional standard of review, which requires only that the State's system be shown to bear some rational relationship to legitimate state purposes. This case represents far more than a challenge to the manner in which Texas provides for the education of its children. We have here nothing less than a direct attack on the way in which Texas has chosen to raise and disburse state and local tax revenues. *We are asked to condemn the State's judgment in conferring on political subdivisions the power to tax local property to supply revenues for local interests. In so doing, appellees would have the Court intrude in an area in which it has traditionally deferred to state legislatures. This Court has often admonished against such interferences with the State's fiscal policies under the Equal Protection Clause:*

"*Thus, we stand on familiar ground when we continue to acknowledge that the Justices of this Court lack both the expertise and the familiarity with local problems so necessary to the making of wise decisions with respect to the raising and disposition of public revenues.*

110.

"Yet, we are urged to direct the States either to alter drastically the present system or to throw out the property tax altogether in favor of some other form of taxation. No scheme of taxation, whether the tax is imposed on property, income, or purchases of goods and services, has yet been devised which is free of all discriminatory impact. *In such a complex arena in which no perfect alternatives exist, the Court does well not to impose too rigorous a standard of scrutiny lest all local fiscal schemes become subjects of criticism under the Equal Protection Clause.*

"The foregoing considerations buttress our conclusion that Texas' system of public school finance is an inappropriate candidate for strict judicial scrutiny. These same considerations are relevant to the determination whether that system, with its conceded imperfections, nevertheless bears some rational relationship to a legitimate state purpose. It is to this question that we next turn our attention.

"In sum, to the extent that the Texas system of school financing results in unequal expenditures between children who happen to reside in different districts, we cannot say that such disparities are the product of a system that is so irrational as to be invidiously discriminatory. Texas has acknowledged its shortcomings and has persistently endeavored - not without some success - to ameliorate the differences in levels of expenditures without sacrificing the benefits of local participation. The Texas plan is not the result of hurried, ill-conceived legislation. It certainly is not the product of purposeful discrimination against any group or class. On the contrary, it is rooted in decades of experience in Texas and elsewhere, and in major part is the product of responsible studies by qualified people. In giving substance to the presumption of validity to which the Texas system is entitled,... it is important to remember that at every stage of its development it has constituted a "rough accommodation" of interests in an effort to arrive at practical and workable solutions. One also must remember that the system here challenged is not peculiar to Texas or to any other State. In its essential characteristics, the Texas plan for financing public education reflects what many educators for a half century have thought was an enlightened approach to a problem for which there is no perfect solution. *We are unwilling to assume for ourselves a level of wisdom superior to that of legislators, scholars, and educational authorities in 50 States, especially where the alternatives proposed are only recently conceived and nowhere yet tested.* The constitutional standard under the Equal Protection Clause is whether the challenged state action rationally furthers a legitimate state purpose or interest. .. We hold that the Texas plan abundantly satisfies this standard.

"These practical considerations, of course, play no role in the adjudication of the constitutional issues presented here. But they serve to highlight the wisdom of the traditional limitations on this Court's function. The consideration and initiation of fundamental reforms with respect to state taxation and education are matters reserved for the legislative processes of the various States, *and we do no violence to the values of federalism and separation of powers by staying our hand.*

"We hardly need add that this Court's action today is not to be viewed as placing its judicial imprimatur on the status quo. The need is apparent for reform in tax systems which may well have relied too long and too heavily on the local property tax. And certainly innovative thinking as to public education, its methods, and its funding is necessary to assure both a higher level of quality and greater uniformity of opportunity. These matters merit the continued attention of the scholars who already have contributed much by their challenges. *But the ultimate solutions must come from the lawmakers and from the democratic pressures of those who elect them.*

"Reversed.

MR. JUSTICE STEWART, concurring.

"The method of financing public schools in Texas, as in almost every other State, has resulted in a system of public education that can fairly be described as chaotic and unjust. 1 It does not follow, however, and I cannot find, that this system violates the Constitution of the United States. I join the opinion and judgment of the Court because I am convinced that any other course would mark an extraordinary departure from principled adjudication under the Equal Protection Clause of the Fourteenth Amendment. *The uncharted directions of such a departure are suggested, I think, by the imaginative dissenting opinion my Brother MARSHALL has filed today.*

"Unlike other provisions of the Constitution, the Equal Protection Clause confers no substantive rights and creates no substantive liberties The function of the Equal Protection Clause, rather, is simply to measure the validity of classifications created by state laws...

"There is hardly a law on the books that does affect some people differently from others...

State legislatures are presumed to have acted within their constitutional power despite the fact that, in practice, their laws result in some inequality. A statutory discrimination will not be set aside if any state of facts reasonably may be conceived to justify it....

"This doctrine is no more than a specific application of one of the first principles of constitutional adjudication - the basic presumption of the constitutional validity of a duly enacted state or federal law...

"Under the Equal Protection Clause, this presumption of constitutional validity disappears when a State has enacted legislation whose purpose or effect is to create classes based upon criteria that, in a constitutional sense, are inherently 'suspect.' Because of the historic purpose of the Fourteenth Amendment, the prime example of such a 'suspect' classification is one that is based upon race. But there are other classifications that, at least in some settings, are also 'suspect' - for example, those based upon national origin, alienage, indigency, or illegitimacy...

"Moreover, quite apart from the Equal Protection Clause, a state law that impinges upon a substantive right or liberty created or conferred by the Constitution is, of course, presumptively invalid, whether or not the law's purpose or effect is to create any classifications. For example, a law that provided that newspapers could be published only by people who had resided in the State for five years could be superficially viewed as invidiously discriminating against an identifiable class in violation of the Equal Protection Clause. But, more basically, such a law would be invalid simply because it abridged the freedom of the press. Numerous cases in this Court illustrate this principle...

"Finally, the Texas system impinges upon no substantive constitutional rights or liberties.

MR. JUSTICE BRENNAN, dissenting.

"Although I agree with my Brother WHITE that the Texas statutory scheme is devoid of any rational basis, and for that reason is violative of the Equal Protection Clause, *I also record my disagreement with the Court's rather distressing assertion that a right may be deemed 'fundamental' for the purposes of equal protection analysis only if it is 'explicitly or implicitly guaranteed by the Constitution.'* As my Brother MARSHALL convincingly demonstrates, our prior cases stand for the proposition that 'fundamentality' is, in large measure, a function of the right's importance in terms of the effectuation of those rights which are in fact constitutionally guaranteed. Thus, '[a]s the nexus between the specific constitutional guarantee and the non-constitutional interest draws closer, the nonconstitutional interest becomes more fundamental and the degree of judicial scrutiny applied when the interest is infringed on a discriminatory basis must be adjusted accordingly.'

"Here, there can be no doubt that education is inextricably linked to the right to participate in the electoral process and to the rights of free speech and association guaranteed by the First Amendment. This being so, any classification affecting education must be subjected to strict judicial scrutiny, and since even the State concedes that the statutory scheme now before us cannot pass constitutional muster under this stricter standard of review, I can only conclude that the Texas school-financing scheme is constitutionally invalid.

MR. JUSTICE WHITE, with whom MR. JUSTICE DOUGLAS and MR. JUSTICE BRENNAN join, dissenting...

"The Equal Protection Clause permits discriminations between classes but requires that the classification bear some rational relationship to a permissible object sought to be attained by the statute. It is not enough that the Texas system before us seeks to achieve the valid, rational purpose of maximizing local initiative; the means chosen by the State must also be rationally related to the end sought to be achieved. As the Court stated just last term in Weber v. Aetna Casualty & Surety Co.:

"The tests to determine the validity of state statutes under the Equal Protection Clause have been variously expressed, but this Court requires, at a minimum, that a statutory classification bear some rational relationship to a legitimate state purpose...

"Neither Texas nor the majority heeds this rule. If the State aims at maximizing local initiative and local choice, by permitting school districts to resort to the real property tax if they choose to do so, it utterly fails in achieving its purpose in districts with property tax bases so low that there is little if any opportunity for interested parents, rich or poor, to augment school district revenues. "Requiring the State to establish only that unequal treatment is in furtherance of a permissible goal, without also requiring the State to show that the means chosen to effectuate that goal are rationally related to its achievement, makes equal protection analysis no more than an empty gesture. In my view, the parents and children in Edgewood, and in like districts, suffer from an invidious discrimination violative of the Equal Protection Clause...

"There is no difficulty in identifying the class that is subject to the alleged discrimination and that is entitled to the benefits of the Equal Protection Clause. I need go no farther than the parents and children in the Edgewood district, who are plaintiffs here and who assert that they are entitled to the same choice as Alamo Heights to augment local expenditures for schools but are denied that choice by state law. This group constitutes a class sufficiently definite to invoke the protection of the Constitution. They are as entitled to the protection of the Equal Protection Clause as were the voters in allegedly under represented counties in the reapportionment cases. Texas candidate filing fee on equal protection grounds was upheld, we noted that the victims of alleged discrimination wrought by the filing fee 'cannot be described by reference to discrete and precisely defined segments of the community as is typical of inequities challenged under the Equal Protection Clause, but concluded that 'we would ignore reality were we not to recognize that this system falls with unequal weight on voters, as well as candidates, according to their economic status.'

"Similarly, in the present case we would blink reality to ignore the fact that school districts, and students in the end, are differentially affected by the Texas school-financing scheme with respect to their capability to supplement the Minimum Foundation School Program. At the very least, the law discriminates against those children and their parents who live in districts where the per-pupil tax base is sufficiently low to make impossible the provision of comparable school revenues by resort to the real property tax which is the only device the State extends for this purpose.

MR. JUSTICE MARSHALL, with whom MR. JUSTICE DOUGLAS concurs, dissenting.

"The Court today decides, in effect, that a State may constitutionally vary the quality of education which it offers its children in accordance with the amount of taxable wealth located in the school districts within which they reside. The majority's decision represents an abrupt departure from the mainstream of recent state and federal court decisions concerning the unconstitutionality of state educational financing schemes dependent upon taxable local wealth. More unfortunately, though, the majority's holding can only be seen as a retreat from our historic commitment to equality of educational opportunity and as unsupportable acquiescence in a system which deprives children in their earliest years of the chance to reach their full potential as citizens. The Court does this despite the absence of any substantial justification for a scheme which arbitrarily channels educational resources in accordance with the fortuity of the amount of taxable wealth within each district.

"In my judgment, the right of every American to an equal start in life, so far as the provision of a state service as important as education is concerned, is far too vital to permit state discrimination on grounds as tenuous as those presented by this record. Nor can I accept the notion that it is sufficient to remit these appellees to the vagaries of the political process which, contrary to the majority's suggestion, has proved singularly unsuited to the task of providing a remedy for this discrimination. I, for one, am unsatisfied with the hope of an ultimate 'political' solution sometime in the indefinite future while, in the meantime, countless children unjustifiably receive inferior educations that 'may affect their hearts and minds in a way unlikely ever to be undone.' *Brown v . Board of Education* (1954). I must therefore respectfully dissent...

"This Court has repeatedly held that state discrimination which either adversely affects a 'fundamental interest,' or is based on a distinction of a suspect character, must be carefully scrutinized to ensure that the scheme is necessary to promote a substantial, legitimate state interest. The majority today concludes, however, that the Texas scheme is not subject to such a strict standard of review under the Equal Protection Clause. Instead, in its view, the Texas scheme must be tested by nothing more than that lenient standard of rationality which we have traditionally applied to discriminatory state action in the context of economic and commercial matters. By so doing, the Court avoids the telling task of searching for a substantial state interest which the Texas financing scheme, with its variations in taxable district property wealth, is necessary to further. I cannot accept such an emasculation of the Equal Protection Clause in the context of this case.

"To begin, I must once more voice my disagreement with the Court's rigidified approach to equal protection analysis. The Court apparently seeks to establish today that equal protection cases fall into one of two neat categories which dictate the appropriate standard of review - strict scrutiny or mere rationality. But this Court's decisions in the field of equal protection defy such easy categorization. A principled reading of what this Court has done reveals that it has applied a spectrum of standards in reviewing discrimination allegedly violative of the Equal Protection Clause. This spectrum clearly comprehends variations in the degree of care with which the Court will scrutinize particular classifications, depending, I believe, on the constitutional and societal importance of the interest adversely affected and the recognized invidiousness of the basis upon which the particular classification is drawn. I find in fact that many of the Court's recent decisions embody the very sort of reasoned approach to equal protection analysis for which I previously argued - that is, an approach in which 'concentration [is] placed upon the character of the classification in question, the relative importance to individuals in the class discriminated against of the governmental benefits that they do not receive, and the asserted state interests in support of the classification.'

"I therefore cannot accept the majority's labored efforts to demonstrate that fundamental interests, which call for strict scrutiny of the challenged classification, encompass only established rights which we are somehow bound to recognize from the text of the Constitution itself. To be sure, some interests which the Court has deemed to be fundamental for purposes of equal protection analysis are themselves constitutionally protected rights. Thus, discrimination against the guaranteed right of freedom of speech has called for strict judicial scrutiny.Further, every citizen's right to travel interstate, although nowhere expressly mentioned in the Constitution, has long been recognized as implicit in the premises underlying that document: the right 'was conceived from the beginning to be a necessary concomitant of the stronger Union the Constitution created.'

"Consequently, the Court has required that a state classification affecting the constitutionally protected right to travel must be 'shown to be necessary to promote a compelling governmental interest.' But it will not do to suggest that the 'answer' to whether an interest is fundamental for purposes of equal protection analysis is always determined by whether that interest 'is a right . . . explicitly or implicitly guaranteed by the Constitution,'

"I would like to know where the Constitution guarantees the right to procreate, or the right to vote in state elections, or the right to an appeal from a criminal conviction. These are instances in which, due to the importance of the interests at stake, the Court has displayed a strong concern with the existence of discriminatory state treatment. But the Court has never said or indicated that

116.

these are interests which independently enjoy full-blown constitutional protection.

"Thus, the Court refused to recognize a substantive constitutional guarantee of the right to procreate. Nevertheless, ...held that 'strict scrutiny' of state discrimination affecting procreation 'is essential,' for '[m]arriage and procreation are fundamental to the very existence and survival of the race.' Recently, in *Roe v. Wade* (1973), the importance of procreation has, indeed, been explained on the basis of its intimate relationship with the constitutional right of privacy which we have recognized....

"Similarly, the right to vote in state elections has been recognized as a 'fundamental political right,' because the Court concluded very early that it is 'preservative of all rights.' For this reason, 'this Court has made clear that a citizen has a constitutionally protected right to participate in elections on an equal basis with other citizens in the jurisdiction.' *The final source of such protection from inequality in the provision of the state franchise is, of course, the Equal Protection Clause.* Yet it is clear that whatever degree of importance has been attached to the state electoral process when unequally distributed, the right to vote in state elections has itself never been accorded the stature of an independent constitutional guarantee.

"The majority is, of course, correct when it suggests that the process of determining which interests are fundamental is a difficult one. But I do not think the problem is insurmountable. And "I certainly do not accept the view that the process need necessarily degenerate into an unprincipled, subjective 'picking-and-choosing' between various interests or that it must involve this Court in creating 'substantive constitutional rights in the name of guaranteeing equal protection of the laws,' *Although not all fundamental interests are constitutionally guaranteed, the determination of which interests are fundamental should be firmly rooted in the text of the Constitution.* The task in every case should be to determine the extent to which constitutionally guaranteed rights are dependent on interests not mentioned in the Constitution. As the nexus between the specific constitutional guarantee and the nonconstitutional interest draws closer, the nonconstitutional interest becomes more fundamental and the degree of judicial scrutiny applied when the interest is infringed on a discriminatory basis must be adjusted accordingly. Thus, it cannot be denied that interests such as procreation, the exercise of the state franchise, and access to criminal appellate processes are not fully guaranteed to the citizen by our Constitution. But these interests have nonetheless been afforded special judicial consideration in the face of discrimination because they are, to some extent, interrelated with constitutional guarantees. "Procreation is now

117.

understood to be important because of its interaction with the established constitutional right of privacy. The exercise of the state franchise is closely tied to basic civil and political rights inherent in the First Amendment. And access to criminal appellate processes enhances the integrity of the range of rights implicit in the Fourteenth Amendment guarantee of due process of law. Only if we closely protect the related interests from state discrimination do we ultimately ensure the integrity of the constitutional guarantee itself. This is the real lesson that must be taken from our previous decisions involving interests deemed to be fundamental.

"The effect of the interaction of individual interests with established constitutional guarantees upon the degree of care exercised by this Court in reviewing state discrimination affecting such interests is amply illustrated by our decision last term in *Eisenstadt v. Baird* (1972). In *Baird*, the Court struck down as violative of the Equal Protection Clause a state statute which denied unmarried persons access to contraceptive devices on the same basis as married persons. The Court purported to test the statute under its traditional standard whether there is some rational basis for the discrimination effected. In the context of commercial regulation, the Court has indicated that the Equal Protection Clause 'is offended only if the classification rests on grounds wholly irrelevant to the achievement of the State's objective.' this lenient standard is further weighted in the State's favor by the fact that '[a] statutory discrimination will not be set aside if any state of facts reasonably may be conceived [by the Court] to justify it.'

"But in *Baird* the Court clearly did not adhere to these highly tolerant standards of traditional rational review. For although there were conceivable state interests intended to be advanced by the statute - e. g., deterrence of premarital sexual activity and regulation of the dissemination of potentially dangerous articles - the Court was not prepared to accept these interests on their face, but instead proceeded to test their substantiality by independent analysis. Such close scrutiny of the State's interests was hardly characteristic of the deference shown state classifications in the context of economic interests. Yet I think the Court's action was entirely appropriate, for access to and use of contraceptives bears a close relationship to the individual's constitutional right of privacy.

"A similar process of analysis with respect to the invidiousness of the basis on which a particular classification is drawn has also influenced the Court as to the appropriate degree of scrutiny to be accorded any particular case. The highly suspect character of classifications based on race, nationality, or alienage is well established. The reasons why such classifications call for close judicial scrutiny

118.

are manifold. Certain racial and ethnic groups have frequently been recognized as 'discrete and insular minorities' who are relatively powerless to protect their interests in the political process. Moreover, race, nationality, or alienage is 'in most circumstances irrelevant' to any constitutionally acceptable legislative purpose, Instead, lines drawn on such bases are frequently the reflection of historic prejudices rather than legislative rationality. It may be that all of these considerations, which make for particular judicial solicitude in the face of discrimination on the basis of race, nationality, or alienage, do not coalesce - or at least not to the same degree - in other forms of discrimination. Nevertheless, these considerations have undoubtedly influenced the care with which the Court has scrutinized other forms of discrimination.

"Status of birth, like the color of one's skin, is something which the individual cannot control, and should generally be irrelevant in legislative considerations. Yet illegitimacy has long been stigmatized by our society. *Hence, discrimination on the basis of birth - particularly when it affects innocent children - warrants special judicial consideration.*

"*Since the Court now suggests that only interests guaranteed by the Constitution are fundamental for purposes of equal protection analysis, and since it rejects the contention that public education is fundamental, it follows that the Court concludes that public education is not constitutionally guaranteed.* It is true that this Court has never deemed the provision of free public education to be required by the Constitution. Indeed, it has on occasion suggested that state-supported education is a privilege bestowed by a State on its citizens. Nevertheless, the fundamental importance of education is amply indicated by the prior decisions of this Court, by the unique status accorded public education by our society, and by the close relationship between education and some of our most basic constitutional values...

"Today, education is perhaps the most important function of state and local governments. Compulsory school attendance laws and the great expenditures for education both demonstrate our recognition of the importance of education to our democratic society. It is required in the performance of our most basic public responsibilities, even service in the armed forces. It is the very foundation of good citizenship. Today it is a principal instrument in awakening the child to cultural values, in preparing him for later professional training, and in helping him to adjust normally to his environment. . . .

"Only last Term, the Court recognized that '[p]roviding public schools ranks at the very apex of the function of a State.' This is clearly borne out by the fact that in 48 of our 50 States the provision of public education is mandated by the state constitution. No other state function is so uniformly recognized as an essential element of our society's well-being. In large measure, the explanation for the special importance attached to education must rest, as the Court recognized in on the facts that 'some degree of education is necessary to prepare citizens to participate effectively and intelligently in our open political system . . .,' and that 'education prepares individuals to be self-reliant and self-sufficient participants in society.' Both facets of this observation are suggestive of the substantial relationship which education bears to guarantees of our Constitution.

"Education directly affects the ability of a child to exercise his First Amendment rights, both as a source and as a receiver of information and ideas, whatever interests he may pursue in life...The opportunity for formal education may not necessarily be the essential determinant of an individual's ability to enjoy throughout his life the rights of free speech and association guaranteed to him by the First Amendment. But such an opportunity may enhance the individual's enjoyment of those rights, not only during but also following school attendance. Thus, in the final analysis, 'the pivotal position of education to success in American society and its essential role in opening up to the individual the central experiences of our culture lend it an importance that is undeniable...

"The only justification offered by appellants to sustain the discrimination in educational opportunity caused by the Texas financing scheme is local educational control. Presented with this justification, the District Court concluded that '[n]ot only are defendants unable to demonstrate compelling state interests for their classifications based upon wealth, they fail even to establish a reasonable basis for these classifications.'... I must agree with this conclusion.

U.S. SUPREME COURT
PLYLER v. DOE
457 U.S. 202 (1982)

Held:

A Texas statute which withholds from local school districts any state funds for the education of children who were not "legally admitted" into the United States, and which authorizes local school districts to deny enrollment to such children, violates the Equal Protection Clause of the Fourteenth Amendment.

JUSTICE BRENNAN delivered the opinion of the Court.

"The question presented by these cases is whether, consistent with the Equal Protection Clause of the Fourteenth Amendment, Texas may deny to undocumented school-age children the free public education that it provides to children who are citizens of the United States or legally admitted aliens.

"Since the late 19th century, the United States has restricted immigration into this country. Unsanctioned entry into the United States is a crime, and those who have entered unlawfully are subject to deportation. But despite the existence of these legal restrictions, a substantial number of persons have succeeded in unlawfully entering the United States, and now live within various States, including the State of Texas.

"In May 1975, the Texas Legislature revised its education laws to withhold from local school districts any state funds for the education of children who were not 'legally admitted' into the United States. The 1975 revision also authorized local school districts to deny enrollment in their public schools to children not 'legally admitted' to the country. These cases involve constitutional challenges to those provisions.

"The Fourteenth Amendment provides that '[n]o State shall . . . deprive any person of life, liberty, or property, without due process of law; nor deny to any person within its jurisdiction the equal protection of the laws.' (Emphasis added.) Appellants argue at the outset that undocumented aliens, because of their immigration status, are not 'persons within the jurisdiction' of the State of Texas, and that they therefore have no right to the equal protection of Texas law. We reject this argument. Whatever his status under the immigration laws, an alien is surely a 'person' in any ordinary sense of that term. Aliens, even aliens whose presence in this country is unlawful, have long been recognized as 'persons' guaranteed due process of law by the Fifth and Fourteenth Amendments... Indeed, we have clearly held that the Fifth Amendment protects aliens whose presence in this country is unlawful from invidious discrimination by the Federal Government.

"Appellants seek to distinguish our prior cases, emphasizing that the Equal Protection Clause directs a State to afford its protection to persons within its jurisdiction while the Due Process Clauses of the Fifth and Fourteenth Amendments contain no such assertedly limiting phrase. In appellants' view, persons who have entered the United States illegally are not "within the jurisdiction" of a State even if they are present within a State's boundaries and subject to its laws. "Neither our cases nor the logic of the Fourteenth Amendment supports that constricting construction of the phrase 'within its jurisdiction.' We have never suggested that the class of persons who might avail themselves of the equal protection guarantee is less than coextensive with that entitled to due process. To the contrary, we have recognized that both provisions were fashioned to protect an identical class of persons, and to reach every exercise of state authority.

121.

"The Fourteenth Amendment to the Constitution is not confined to the protection of citizens. It says: 'Nor shall any state deprive any person of life, liberty, or property without due process of law; nor deny to any person within its jurisdiction the equal protection of the laws.' These provisions are universal in their application, to all persons within the territorial jurisdiction, without regard to any differences of race, of color, or of nationality; and the protection of the laws is a pledge of the protection of equal laws.'

"In concluding that 'all persons within the territory of the United States,' including aliens unlawfully present, may invoke the Fifth and Sixth Amendments to challenge actions of the Federal Government, we reasoned from the understanding that the Fourteenth Amendment was designed to afford its protection to all within the boundaries of a State. Our cases applying the Equal Protection Clause reflect the same territorial theme.

"Manifestly, the obligation of the State to give the protection of equal laws can be performed only where its laws operate, that is, within its own jurisdiction. It is there that the equality of legal right must be maintained. That obligation is imposed by the Constitution upon the States severally as governmental entities, - each responsible for its own laws establishing the rights and duties of persons within its borders.

"There is simply no support for appellants' suggestion that 'due process' is somehow of greater stature than 'equal protection' and therefore available to a larger class of persons. To the contrary, each aspect of the Fourteenth Amendment reflects an elementary limitation on state power. To permit a State to employ the phrase 'within its jurisdiction' in order to identify subclasses of persons whom it would define as beyond its jurisdiction, thereby relieving itself of the obligation to assure that its laws are designed and applied equally to those persons, would undermine the principal purpose for which the Equal Protection Clause was incorporated in the Fourteenth Amendment. The Equal Protection Clause was intended to work nothing less than the abolition of all caste-based and invidious class-based legislation. That objective is fundamentally at odds with the power the State asserts here to classify persons subject to its laws as nonetheless excepted from its protection.

"Although the congressional debate concerning 1 of the Fourteenth Amendment was limited, that debate clearly confirms the understanding that the phrase 'within its jurisdiction' was intended in a broad sense to offer the guarantee of equal protection to all within a State's boundaries, and to all upon whom the State would impose the obligations of its laws. Indeed, it appears from those debates that Congress, by using the phrase "person within its jurisdiction," sought expressly to ensure that the equal protection of the laws was provided to the alien population....

"Is it not essential to the unity of the people that the citizens of each State shall be entitled to all the privileges and immunities of citizens in the several States? Is it not essential to the unity of the Government and the unity of the people that all persons, whether citizens or strangers, within this land, shall have equal protection in every State in this Union in the rights of life and liberty and property ?

"Senator Howard, also a member of the Joint Committee of Fifteen, and the floor manager of the Amendment in the Senate, was no less explicit about the broad objectives of the Amendment, and the intention to make its provisions applicable to all who 'may happen to be' within the jurisdiction of a State:

"The last two clauses of the first section of the amendment disable a State from depriving not merely a citizen of the United States, but any person, whoever he may be, of life, liberty, or property without due process of law, or from denying to him the equal protection of the laws of the State. This abolishes all class legislation in the States and does away with the injustice of subjecting one caste of persons to a code not applicable to another. . . . It will, if adopted by the States, forever disable every one of them from passing laws trenching upon those fundamental rights and privileges which pertain to citizens of the United States, and to all persons who may happen to be within their jurisdiction.

"Use of the phrase 'within its jurisdiction' thus does not detract from, but rather confirms, the understanding that the protection of the Fourteenth Amendment extends to anyone, citizen or stranger, who is subject to the laws of a State, and reaches into every corner of a State's territory. That a person's initial entry into a State, or into the United States, was unlawful, and that he may for that reason be expelled, cannot negate the simple fact of his presence within the State's territorial perimeter. Given such presence, he is subject to the full range of obligations imposed by the State's civil and criminal laws. And until he leaves the jurisdiction - either voluntarily, or involuntarily in accordance with the Constitution and laws of the United States - he is entitled to the equal protection of the laws that a State may choose to establish.

"Our conclusion that the illegal aliens who are plaintiffs in these cases may claim the benefit of the Fourteenth Amendment's guarantee of equal protection only begins the inquiry. The more difficult question is whether the Equal Protection Clause has been violated by the refusal of the State of Texas to reimburse local school boards for the education of children who cannot demonstrate that their presence within the United States is lawful, or by the

123.

imposition by those school boards of the burden of tuition on those children. It is to this question that we now turn.

"The Equal Protection Clause directs that 'all persons similarly circumstanced shall be treated alike.' The initial discretion to determine what is 'different' and what is 'the same' resides in the legislatures of the States. A legislature must have substantial latitude to establish classifications that roughly approximate the nature of the problem perceived, that accommodate competing concerns both public and private, and that account for limitations on the practical ability of the State to remedy every ill. In applying the Equal Protection Clause to most forms of state action, we thus seek only the assurance that the classification at issue bears some fair relationship to a legitimate public purpose...

"These well-settled principles allow us to determine the proper level of deference to be afforded. Undocumented aliens cannot be treated as a suspect class because their presence in this country in violation of federal law is not a "constitutional irrelevancy." Nor is education a fundamental right; a State need not justify by compelling necessity every variation in the manner in which education is provided to its population, *San Antonio Independent School Dist. v. Rodriguez.*

"But more is involved in these cases...The stigma of illiteracy will mark them for the rest of their lives. By denying these children a basic education, we deny them the ability to live within the structure of our civic institutions, and foreclose any realistic possibility that they will contribute in even the smallest way to the progress of our Nation. In determining the rationality of the law, we may appropriately take into account its costs to the Nation and to the innocent children who are its victims. In light of these countervailing costs, the discrimination contained in the law can hardly be considered rational unless it furthers some substantial goal of the State.

"It is the State's principal argument, and apparently the view of the dissenting Justices, that the undocumented status of these children vel non establishes a sufficient rational basis for denying them benefits that a State might choose to afford other residents. The State notes that while other aliens are admitted 'on an equality of legal privileges with all citizens under non-discriminatory laws,' the asserted right of these children to an education can claim no implicit congressional imprimatur. Indeed, in the State's view, Congress' apparent disapproval of the presence of these children within the United States, and the evasion of the federal regulatory program that is the mark of undocumented status, provides authority for its decision to impose upon them special disabilities. Faced with an equal protection challenge respecting the treatment of aliens, we agree that the courts must be attentive to congressional policy; the

124.

exercise of congressional power might well affect the State's prerogatives to afford differential treatment to a particular class of aliens. But we are unable to find in the congressional immigration scheme any statement of policy that might weigh significantly in arriving at an equal protection balance concerning the State's authority to deprive these children of an education.

"The Constitution grants Congress the power to 'establish an uniform Rule of Naturalization.' Art. I., 8, cl. 4. Drawing upon this power, upon its plenary authority with respect to foreign relations and international commerce, and upon the inherent power of a sovereign to close its borders, Congress has developed a complex scheme governing admission to our Nation and status within our borders. *The obvious need for delicate policy judgments has counseled the Judicial Branch to avoid intrusion into this field.* But this traditional caution does not persuade us that unusual deference must be shown the classification embodied herein. The States enjoy no power with respect to the classification of aliens. This power is 'committed to the political branches of the Federal Government.' Although it is 'a routine and normally legitimate part' of the business of the Federal Government to classify on the basis of alien status, and to 'take into account the character of the relationship between the alien and this country,' only rarely are such matters relevant to legislation by a State.

"As we recognized in *De Canas v. Bica* (1976), the States do have some authority to act with respect to illegal aliens, at least where such action mirrors federal objectives and furthers a legitimate state goal. In *De Canas*, the State's program reflected Congress' intention to bar from employment all aliens except those possessing a grant of permission to work in this country. In contrast, there is no indication that the disability imposed by the law corresponds to any identifiable congressional policy. The State does not claim that the conservation of state educational resources was ever a congressional concern in restricting immigration. More importantly, the classification reflected in the law does not operate harmoniously within the federal program.

"To be sure, like all persons who have entered the United States unlawfully, these children are subject to deportation. But there is no assurance that a child subject to deportation will ever be deported. An illegal entrant might be granted federal permission to continue to reside in this country, or even to become a citizen. In light of the discretionary federal power to grant relief from deportation, a State cannot realistically determine that any particular undocumented child will in fact be deported until after deportation proceedings have been completed. It would of course be most difficult for the State to justify a denial of education to a child enjoying an inchoate federal permission to remain.

"We are reluctant to impute to Congress the intention to withhold from these children, for so long as they are present in this country through no fault of their own, access to a basic education. In other contexts, undocumented status, coupled with some articulable federal policy, might enhance state authority with respect to the treatment of undocumented aliens. But in the area of special constitutional sensitivity presented by these cases, and in the absence of any contrary indication fairly discernible in the present legislative record, we perceive no national policy that supports the State in denying these children an elementary education. The State may borrow the federal classification. But to justify its use as a criterion for its own discriminatory policy, the State must demonstrate that the classification is reasonably adapted to 'the purposes for which the state desires to use it.' We therefore turn to the state objectives that are said to support the law herein discussed.

"Finally, appellants suggest that undocumented children are appropriately singled out because their unlawful presence within the United States renders them less likely than other children to remain within the boundaries of the State, and to put their education to productive social or political use within the State. Even assuming that such an interest is legitimate, it is an interest that is most difficult to quantify. The State has no assurance that any child, citizen or not, will employ the education provided by the State within the confines of the State's borders. In any event, the record is clear that many of the undocumented children disabled by this classification will remain in this country indefinitely, and that some will become lawful residents or citizens of the United States. It is difficult to understand precisely what the State hopes to achieve by promoting the creation and perpetuation of a subclass of illiterates within our boundaries, surely adding to the problems and costs of unemployment, welfare, and crime. It is thus clear that whatever savings might be achieved by denying these children an education, they are wholly insubstantial in light of the costs involved to these children, the State, and the Nation.

"If the State is to deny a discrete group of innocent children the free public education that it offers to other children residing within its borders, that denial must be justified by a showing that it furthers some substantial state interest. No such showing was made here. Accordingly, the judgment of the Court of Appeals in each of these cases is

Affirmed.

JUSTICE MARSHALL, concurring.

"While I join the Court opinion, I do so without in any way retreating from my opinion in *San Antonio Independent School District v. Rodriguez* (1973). I continue to believe that an individual's interest in education is fundamental, and that this view is amply supported "by the unique status accorded public education by our society, and by the close relationship between education and some of our most basic constitutional values.'Furthermore, I believe that the facts of these cases demonstrate the wisdom of rejecting a rigidified approach to equal protection analysis, and of employing an approach that allows for varying levels of scrutiny depending upon 'the constitutional and societal importance of the interest adversely affected and the recognized invidiousness of the basis upon which the particular classification is drawn.' It continues to be my view that a class-based denial of public education is utterly incompatible with the Equal Protection Clause of the Fourteenth Amendment.

JUSTICE BLACKMUN, concurring.

"I join the opinion and judgment of the Court.

"Like JUSTICE POWELL, I believe that the children involved in this litigation 'should not be left on the streets uneducated.' I write separately, however, because in my view the nature of the interest at stake is crucial to the proper resolution of these cases.

"The 'fundamental rights' aspect of the Court's equal protection analysis - the now-familiar concept that governmental classifications bearing on certain interests must be closely scrutinized - has been the subject of some controversy. Justice Harlan, for example, warned that "[v]irtually every state statute affects important rights. . . . [T]o extend the `compelling interest' rule to all cases in which such rights are affected would go far toward making this Court a `super-legislature.' Others have noted that strict scrutiny under the Equal Protection Clause is unnecessary when classifications infringing enumerated constitutional rights are involved, for 'a state law that impinges upon a substantive right or liberty created or conferred by the Constitution is, of course, presumptively invalid, whether or not the law's purpose or effect is to create any classifications.' Still others have suggested that fundamental rights are not properly a part of equal protection analysis at all, because they are unrelated to any defined principle of equality.

"These considerations, combined with doubts about the judiciary's ability to make fine distinctions in assessing the effects of complex social policies, led the Court in *Rodriguez* to articulate a firm rule: *fundamental rights are those that 'explicitly or implicitly [are] guaranteed by the Constitution.'* It therefore squarely rejected the notion that 'an ad hoc determination as to the social or economic importance' of a given interest is relevant to the level of scrutiny accorded classifications involving that interest, and made clear that '[i]t is not the province of this Court to create substantive constitutional rights in the name of guaranteeing equal protection of the laws.'

127.

"I joined JUSTICE POWELL'S opinion for the Court in *Rodriguez*, and I continue to believe that it provides the appropriate model for resolving most equal protection disputes. Classifications infringing substantive constitutional rights necessarily will be invalid, if not by force of the Equal Protection Clause, then through operation of other provisions of the Constitution. Conversely, classifications bearing on nonconstitutional interests - even those involving "the most basic economic needs of impoverished human beings,' - generally are not subject to special treatment under the Equal Protection Clause, because they are not distinguishable in any relevant way from other regulations in 'the area of economics and social welfare.'

"With all this said, however, I believe the Court's experience has demonstrated that the Rodriguez formulation does not settle every issue of 'fundamental rights' arising under the Equal Protection Clause. Only a pedant would insist that there are no meaningful distinctions among the multitude of social and political interests regulated by the States, and *Rodriguez* does not stand for quite so absolute a proposition. To the contrary, *Rodriguez* implicitly acknowledged that certain interests, though not constitutionally guaranteed, must be accorded a special place in equal protection analysis. Thus, the Court's decisions long have accorded strict scrutiny to classifications bearing on the right to vote in state elections, and *Rodriguez* confirmed the constitutional underpinnings of the right to equal treatment in the voting process. Yet, the right to vote, *per se*, is not a constitutionally protected right. Instead, regulation of the electoral process receives unusual scrutiny because the right to exercise the franchise in a free and unimpaired manner is preservative of other basic civil and political rights.

"In other words, the right to vote is accorded extraordinary treatment because it is, in equal protection terms, an extraordinary right: a citizen cannot hope to achieve any meaningful degree of individual political equality if granted an inferior right of participation in the political process. "Those denied the vote are relegated, by state fiat, in a most basic way to second-class status.

It is arguable, of course, that the Court never should have applied fundamental rights doctrine in the fashion outlined above. Justice Harlan, for one, maintained that strict equal protection scrutiny was appropriate only when racial or analogous classifications were at issue...But it is too late to debate that point, and I believe that accepting the principle of the voting cases - the idea that state classifications bearing on certain interests pose the risk of allocating rights in a fashion inherently contrary to any notion of 'equality'- dictates the outcome here. As both JUSTICE POWELL and THE CHIEF JUSTICE observe, the Texas scheme inevitably will create 'a subclass of illiterate persons.' Where I differ with THE CHIEF JUSTICE is in my conclusion that this makes the statutory scheme unconstitutional as well as unwise.

"In my view, when the State provides an education to some and denies it to others, it immediately and inevitably creates class distinctions of a type fundamentally inconsistent with those purposes, mentioned above, of the Equal Protection Clause. Children denied an education are placed at a permanent and insurmountable competitive disadvantage, for an uneducated child is denied even the opportunity to achieve. And when those children are members of an identifiable group, that group - through the State's action - will have been converted into a discrete underclass. Other benefits provided by the State, such as housing and public assistance, are of course important; to an individual in immediate need, they may be more desirable than the right to be educated. But classifications involving the complete denial of education are in a sense unique, for they strike at the heart of equal protection values by involving the State in the creation of permanent class distinctions. In a sense, then, denial of an education is the analogue of denial of the right to vote: the former relegates the individual to second-class social status; the latter places him at a permanent political disadvantage.

"This conclusion is fully consistent with *Rodriguez*. The Court there reserved judgment on the constitutionality of a state system that 'occasioned an absolute denial of educational opportunities to any of its children,' noting that "no charge fairly could be made that the system [at issue in *Rodriguez*] fails to provide each child with an opportunity to acquire . . . basic minimal skills.' And it cautioned that in a case 'involv[ing] the most persistent and difficult questions of educational policy, . . . [the] Court's lack of specialized knowledge and experience counsels against premature interference with the informed judgments made at the state and local levels.' Thus *Rodriguez* held, and the Court now reaffirms, that 'a State need not justify by compelling necessity every variation in the manner in which education is provided to its population.'

"Similarly, *it is undeniable that education is not a 'fundamental right' in the sense that it is constitutionally guaranteed*. Here, however, the State has undertaken to provide an education to most of the children residing within its borders. And, in contrast to the situation in Rodriguez, it does not take an advanced degree to predict the effects of a complete denial of education upon those children targeted by the State's classification. In such circumstances, the voting decisions suggest that the State must offer something more than a rational basis for its classification.

"Concededly, it would seem ironic to discuss the social necessity of an education in a case that concerned only undocumented aliens 'whose very presence in the state and this country is illegal.' But because of the nature of the federal immigration laws and the pre-eminent role of the Federal Government in regulating immigration, the class of children here is not a monolithic one. Thus, the District Court in the *Alien Children Education case* found as a factual matter that a significant number of illegal aliens will remain in this country permanently, that some of the children involved in this litigation are 'documentable,'and that '[m]any of the undocumented children are not deportable. None of the named plaintiffs is under an order of deportation.' As the Court's alienage cases demonstrate, these children may not be denied rights that are granted to citizens, excepting only those rights bearing on political interests. And, as JUSTICE POWELL notes, the structure of the immigration statutes makes it impossible for the State to determine which aliens are entitled to residence, and which eventually will be deported. Indeed, any attempt to do so would involve the State in the administration of the immigration laws. Whatever the State's power to classify deportable aliens, then - and whatever the Federal Government's ability to draw more precise and more acceptable alienage classifications - the statute at issue here sweeps within it a substantial number of children who will in fact, and who may well be entitled to, remain in the United States. Given the extraordinary nature of the interest involved, this makes the classification here fatally imprecise. And, as the Court demonstrates, the Texas legislation is not otherwise supported by any substantial interests.

"Because I believe that the Court's carefully worded analysis recognizes the importance of the equal protection and pre-emption interests I consider crucial, I join its opinion as well as its judgment.

JUSTICE POWELL, concurring.

"I join the opinion of the Court, and write separately to emphasize the unique character of the cases before us.

"The classification in question severely disadvantages children who are the victims of a combination of circumstances. Access from Mexico into this country, across our 2,000-mile border, is readily available and virtually uncontrollable. Illegal aliens are attracted by our employment opportunities, and perhaps by other benefits as well. This is a problem of serious national proportions, as the Attorney General recently has recognized. *Perhaps because of the intractability of the problem, Congress - vested by the Constitution with the responsibility of protecting our borders and legislating with respect to aliens - has not provided effective leadership in dealing with this problem.* It therefore is certain that illegal aliens will continue to enter the United States and, as the record makes clear, an unknown percentage of them will remain here. I agree with the Court that their children should not be left on the streets uneducated.

"Although the analogy is not perfect, our holding today does find support in decisions of this Court with respect to the status of illegitimates, where we said: '[V]isiting . . . condemnation on the head of an infant' for the misdeeds of the parents is illogical, unjust, and 'contrary to the basic concept of our system that legal burdens should bear some relationship to individual responsibility or wrongdoing.'

"In these cases, the State of Texas effectively denies to the school-age children of illegal aliens the opportunity to attend the free public schools that the State makes available to all residents. They are excluded only because of a status resulting from the violation by parents or guardians of our immigration laws and the fact that they remain in our country unlawfully. The appellee children are innocent in this respect. They can 'affect neither their parents' conduct nor their own status.'

"Our review in a case such as these is properly heightened. The classification at issue deprives a group of children of the opportunity for education afforded all other children simply because they have been assigned a legal status due to a violation of law by their parents. These children thus have been singled out for a lifelong penalty and stigma. A legislative classification that threatens the creation of an underclass of future citizens and residents cannot be reconciled with one of the fundamental purposes of the Fourteenth Amendment. In these unique circumstances, the Court properly may require that the State's interests be substantial and that the means bear a 'fair and substantial relation' to these interests.

"In my view, the State's denial of education to these children bears no substantial relation to any substantial state interest. Both of the District Courts found that an uncertain but significant percentage of illegal alien children will remain in Texas as residents and many eventually will become citizens. The discussion by the Court, of the State's purported interests demonstrates that they are poorly served by the educational exclusion. Indeed, the interests relied upon by the State would seem to be insubstantial in view of the consequences to the State itself of wholly uneducated persons living indefinitely within its borders. By contrast, access to the public schools is made available to the children of lawful residents without regard to the temporary nature of their residency in the particular Texas school district The Court of Appeals and the District Courts that addressed these cases concluded that the classification could not satisfy even the bare requirements of rationality. One need not go so far to conclude that the exclusion of appellees' class of children from state-provided education is a type of punitive discrimination based on status that is impermissible under the Equal Protection Clause.

131.

"In reaching this conclusion, I am not unmindful of what must be the exasperation of responsible citizens and government authorities in Texas and other States similarly situated. Their responsibility, if any, for the influx of aliens is slight compared to that imposed by the Constitution on the Federal Government So long as the ease of entry remains inviting, and the power to deport is exercised infrequently by the Federal Government, the additional expense of admitting these children to public schools might fairly be shared by the Federal and State Governments. But it hardly can be argued rationally that anyone benefits from the creation within our borders of a subclass of illiterate persons many of whom will remain in the State, adding to the problems and costs of both State and National Governments attendant upon unemployment, welfare, and crime."

After having read the majority opinion immediately preceding, replete with its version of rewriting the 14th Amendment, E/P clause, applying it to situations not intended by the drafters of said clause, please read, reread and savor the following dissent.

CHIEF JUSTICE BURGER, with whom JUSTICE WHITE, JUSTICE REHNQUIST, and JUSTICE O'CONNOR join, dissenting.

"Were it our business to set the Nation's social policy, I would agree without hesitation that it is senseless for an enlightened society to deprive any children - including illegal aliens - of an elementary education. I fully agree that it would be folly - and wrong - to tolerate creation of a segment of society made up of illiterate persons, many having a limited or no command of our language. However, the Constitution does not constitute us as "Platonic Guardians" nor does it vest in this Court the authority to strike down laws because they do not meet our standards of desirable social policy, 'wisdom,' or 'common sense.' *We trespass on the assigned function of the political branches under our structure of limited and separated powers when we assume a policymaking role as the Court does today.*

"The Court makes no attempt to disguise that it is acting to make up for Congress' lack of 'effective leadership' in dealing with the serious national problems caused by the influx of uncountable millions of illegal aliens across our borders. The failure of enforcement of the immigration laws over more than a decade and the inherent difficulty and expense of sealing our vast borders have combined to create a grave socioeconomic dilemma. It is a dilemma that has not yet even been fully assessed, let alone addressed. *However, it is not the function of the Judiciary to provide 'effective leadership' simply because the political branches of government fail to do so.*

132.

"The Court's holding today manifests the justly criticized judicial tendency to attempt speedy and wholesale formulation of 'remedies' for the failures - or simply the laggard pace - of the political processes of our system of government. *The Court employs, and in my view abuses, the Fourteenth Amendment in an effort to become an omnipotent and omniscient problem solver.*

"*That the motives for doing so are noble and compassionate does not alter the fact that the Court distorts our constitutional function to make amends for the defaults of others.*

"In a sense, the Court's opinion rests on such a unique confluence of theories and rationales that it will likely stand for little beyond the results in these particular cases. Yet the extent to which the Court departs from principled constitutional adjudication is nonetheless disturbing.

"I have no quarrel with the conclusion that the Equal Protection Clause of the Fourteenth Amendment applies to aliens who, after their illegal entry into this country, are indeed physically 'within the jurisdiction' of a state. However, as the Court concedes, this 'only begins the inquiry.' The Equal Protection Clause does not mandate identical treatment of different categories of persons.

"*The dispositive issue in these cases, simply put, is whether, for purposes of allocating its finite resources, a state has a legitimate reason to differentiate between persons who are lawfully within the state and those who are unlawfully there.* The distinction the State of Texas has drawn - based not only upon its own legitimate interests but on *classifications established by the Federal Government in its immigration laws and policies - is not unconstitutional.*

"The Court acknowledges that, except in those cases when state classifications disadvantage a 'suspect class' or impinge upon a 'fundamental right,' the Equal Protection Clause permits a state 'substantial latitude' in distinguishing between different groups of persons. *Moreover, the Court expressly - and correctly - rejects any suggestion that illegal aliens are a suspect class, or that education is a fundamental right. Yet by patching together bits and pieces of what might be termed quasi-suspect-class and quasi-fundamental-rights analysis, the Court spins out a theory custom-tailored to the facts of these cases.*

The majority again synthesized a new test or doctrine suited for the particular facts of this case, often referred to as subjective adjudication. Again it ignored the actual text of the Constitution . . . and ignored the clearly established law up to that point.

Burger's dissent continues:

"In the end, we are told little more than that the level of scrutiny employed to strike down the Texas law applies only when illegal alien children are deprived of a public education. *If ever a court was guilty of an unabashedly result-oriented approach, this case is a prime example.*

"The Court first suggests that these illegal alien children, although not a suspect class, are entitled to special solicitude under the Equal Protection Clause because they lack 'control' over or 'responsibility' for their unlawful entry into this country. Similarly, the Court appears to take the position that the law is presumptively 'irrational' because it has the effect of imposing 'penalties' on 'innocent' children. However, the Equal Protection Clause does not preclude legislators from classifying among persons on the basis of factors and characteristics over which individuals may be said to lack 'control.' Indeed, in some circumstances persons generally, and children in particular, may have little control over or responsibility for such things as their ill health, need for public assistance, or place of residence. Yet a state legislature is not barred from considering, for example, relevant differences between the mentally healthy and the mentally ill, or between the residents of different counties simply because these may be factors unrelated to individual choice or to any 'wrongdoing.' *The Equal Protection Clause protects against arbitrary and irrational classifications, and against invidious discrimination stemming from prejudice and hostility; it is not an all-encompassing 'equalizer' designed to eradicate every distinction for which persons are not 'responsible.'*

"The Court does not presume to suggest that appellees' purported lack of culpability for their illegal status prevents them from being deported or otherwise 'penalized' under federal law. Yet would deportation be any less a 'penalty' than denial of privileges provided to legal residents? *Illegality of presence in the United States does not - and need not - depend on some amorphous concept of 'guilt' or 'innocence' concerning an alien's entry. Similarly, a state's use of federal immigration status as a basis for legislative classification is not necessarily rendered suspect for its failure to take such factors into account.*

"*The Court's analogy to cases involving discrimination against illegitimate children is grossly misleading.* The State has not thrust any disabilities upon appellees due to their 'status of birth.' Rather, appellees' status is predicated upon the circumstances of their concededly illegal presence in this country, and is a direct result of Congress' obviously valid exercise of its 'broad constitutional powers' in the field of immigration and naturalization. U.S. Const.,Art. I, 8, cl. 4. *This Court has recognized that in allocating governmental benefits to a given class of aliens, one 'may take into account the character of the relationship between the alien and this country.' When that 'relationship' is a federally prohibited one, there can, of course, be no presumption that a state has a*

134.

constitutional duty to include illegal aliens among the recipients of its governmental benefits.

"The second strand of the Court's analysis rests on the premise that, although public education is not a constitutionally guaranteed right, 'neither is it merely some governmental `benefit' indistinguishable from other forms of social welfare legislation.' Whatever meaning or relevance this opaque observation might have in some other context it simply has no bearing on the issues at hand. Indeed, it is never made clear what the Court's opinion means on this score.

"The importance of education is beyond dispute. Yet we have held repeatedly that the importance of a governmental service does not elevate it to the status of a 'fundamental right' for purposes of equal protection analysis. In *San Antonio Independent School Dist.*, Justice Powell, speaking for the Court, expressly rejected the proposition that state laws dealing with public education are subject to special scrutiny under the Equal Protection Clause. Moreover, the Court points to no meaningful way to distinguish between education and other governmental benefits in this context. Is the Court suggesting that education is more 'fundamental' than food, shelter, or medical care ?

"The Equal Protection Clause guarantees similar treatment of similarly situated persons, but it does not mandate a constitutional hierarchy of governmental services. *Justice Powell, speaking for the Court in San Antonio Independent School Dist.,put it well in stating that to the extent this Court raises or lowers the degree of 'judicial scrutiny' in equal protection cases according to a transient Court majority's view of the societal importance of the interest affected, we 'assum[e] a legislative role and one for which the Court lacks both authority and competence.' Yet that is precisely what the Court does today.*

"The central question in these cases, as in every equal protection case not involving truly fundamental rights 'explicitly or implicitly guaranteed by the Constitution,' is whether there is some legitimate basis for a legislative distinction between different classes of persons. The fact that the distinction is drawn in legislation affecting access to public education - as opposed to legislation allocating other important governmental benefits, such as public assistance, health care, or housing - cannot make a difference in the level of scrutiny applied.

"Once it is conceded - as the Court does - that illegal aliens are not a suspect class, and that education is not a fundamental right, our inquiry should focus on and be limited to whether the legislative classification at issue bears a rational relationship to a legitimate state purpose.

"The State contends primarily that the law serves to prevent undue depletion of its limited revenues available for education, and to preserve the fiscal integrity of

135.

the State's school-financing system against an ever-increasing flood of illegal aliens - aliens over whose entry or continued presence it has no control. Of course such fiscal concerns alone could not justify discrimination against a suspect class or an arbitrary and irrational denial of benefits to a particular group of persons. Yet I assume no Member of this Court would argue that prudent conservation of finite state revenues is *per se* an illegitimate goal. Indeed, the numerous classifications this Court has sustained in social welfare legislation were invariably related to the limited amount of revenues available to spend on any given program or set of programs. The significant question here is whether the requirement of tuition from illegal aliens who attend the public schools - as well as from residents of other states, for example - is a rational and reasonable means of furthering the State's legitimate fiscal ends.

"Without laboring what will undoubtedly seem obvious to many, it simply is not 'irrational' for a state to conclude that it does not have the same responsibility to provide benefits for persons whose very presence in the state and this country is illegal as it does to provide for persons lawfully present. By definition, illegal aliens have no right whatever to be here, and the state may reasonably, and constitutionally, elect not to provide them with governmental services at the expense of those who are lawfully in the state, we held that a State may protect its 'fiscal interests and lawfully resident labor force from the deleterious effects on its economy resulting from the employment of illegal aliens.' And only recently this Court made clear that a State has a legitimate interest in protecting and preserving the quality of its schools and 'the right of its own bona fide residents to attend such institutions on a preferential tuition basis.' The Court has failed to offer even a plausible explanation why illegality of residence in this country is not a factor that may legitimately bear upon the bona fides of state residence and entitlement to the benefits of lawful residence.

"It is significant that the Federal Government has seen fit to exclude illegal aliens from numerous social welfare programs, such as the food stamp program, the old-age assistance, aid to families with dependent children, aid to the blind, aid to the permanently and totally disabled, and supplemental security income programs, the Medicare hospital insurance benefits program, and the Medicaid hospital insurance benefits for the aged and disabled program.

"Although these exclusions do not conclusively demonstrate the constitutionality of the State's use of the same classification for comparable purposes, at the very least they tend to support the rationality of excluding illegal alien residents of a state from such programs so as to preserve the state's finite revenues for the benefit of lawful residents.

136.

"The Court maintains - as if this were the issue - that 'barring undocumented children from local schools would not necessarily improve the quality of education provided in those schools. "However, the legitimacy of barring illegal aliens from programs such as Medicare or Medicaid does not depend on a showing that the barrier would 'improve the quality' of medical care given to persons lawfully entitled to participate in such programs. Modern education, like medical care, is enormously expensive, and there can be no doubt that very large added costs will fall on the State or its local school districts as a result of the inclusion of illegal aliens in the tuition-free public schools.

"The State may, in its discretion, use any savings resulting from its tuition requirement to 'improve the quality of education' in the public school system, or to enhance the funds available for other social programs, or to reduce the tax burden placed on its residents; each of these ends is 'legitimate.' The State need not show, as the Court implies, that the incremental cost of educating illegal aliens will send it into bankruptcy, or have a `grave impact on the quality of education, that is not dispositive under a "rational basis' scrutiny. In the absence of a constitutional imperative to provide for the education of illegal aliens, the State may 'rationally' choose to take advantage of whatever savings will accrue from limiting access to the tuition-free public schools to its own lawful residents, excluding even citizens of neighboring States.

"Denying a free education to illegal alien children is not a choice I would make were I a legislator. Apart from compassionate considerations, the long-range costs of excluding any children from the public schools may well outweigh the costs of educating them. But that is not the issue; the fact that there are sound policy arguments against the Texas Legislature's choice does not render that choice an unconstitutional one.

"The Constitution does not provide a cure for every social ill, nor does it vest judges with a mandate to try to remedy every social problem. Moreover, when this Court rushes in to remedy what it perceives to be the failings of the political processes, it deprives those processes of an opportunity to function.

"When the political institutions are not forced to exercise constitutionally allocated powers and responsibilities, those powers, like muscles not used, tend to atrophy. Today's cases, I regret to say, present yet another example of unwarranted judicial action which in the long run tends to contribute to the weakening of our political processes. Congress, 'vested by the Constitution with the responsibility of protecting our borders and legislating with respect to aliens,' bears primary responsibility for addressing the problems occasioned by the millions of illegal aliens flooding across our southern border. Similarly, it is for Congress, and not this Court, to assess the 'social costs borne by our Nation when select groups are denied the means to absorb the values and skills upon which our social order rests.'

"While the 'specter of a permanent caste' of illegal Mexican residents of the United States is indeed a disturbing one, it is but one segment of a larger problem, which is for the political branches to solve. I find it difficult to believe that Congress would long tolerate such a self-destructive result - that it would fail to deport these illegal alien families or to provide for the education of their children. *Yet instead of allowing the political processes to run their course - albeit with some delay - the Court seeks to do Congress' job for it, compensating for congressional inaction. It is not unreasonable to think that this encourages the political branches to pass their problems to the Judiciary.*

"The solution to this seemingly intractable problem is to defer to the political processes, unpalatable as that may be to some. James Bradley Thayer's observed:

"The exercise of [the power of judicial review], even when unavoidable, is always attended with a serious evil, namely, that the correction of legislative mistakes comes from the outside, and the people thus lose the political experience, and the moral education and stimulus that comes from fighting the question out in the ordinary way, and correcting their own errors. The tendency of a common and easy resort to this great function, now lamentably too common, is to dwarf the political capacity of the people, and to deaden its sense of moral responsibility."

Hence, the decisions of the Supreme Court, in interpreting the 14th Amendment, Equal Protection Clause of 1868, began as one of strict adherence to the text, as in the *Slaughterhouse Cases* of 1872, contemporaneous with said amendment, through various and "improved" tests to the *Plyler* case of 1982, wherein the Court literally invented a *newer*, hybrid test to fit the facts of the case and to insure the result that the Texas statute would be declared unconstitutional thus continuing its micromanaging of the states.

"The phrase, 'subject to its jurisdiction' was intended to exclude from its operation children of ministers, consuls, and citizens or subjects of foreign States born within the United States."   Slaughter-House case (1872)

CHAPTER 7

CITIZENSHIP AND ANCHOR BABIES

The 14th Amendment, Section 1, states in pertinent part, "All persons born or naturalized in the United States, *and subject to the jurisdiction thereof*, are citizens of the United States and of the States wherein they reside."

During the original debate over this citizenship clause of the 14th amendment, Senator Jacob M.Howard of Michigan, the author of the Citizenship Clause, described the clause as excluding American Indians who maintain their tribal ties, and "persons born in the United States who are [of] foreigners, aliens, [and] who belong to the families of ambassadors or foreign ministers."

In any event, the Supreme Court, in the *Slaughterhouse* case of 1872, early-on defined the clause, ..."and subject to the jurisdiction thereof..."

This opinion was handed down on the heels of the 14th Amendment's ratification in 1868.

The Slaughterhouse cases:

U.S. SUPREME COURT

IN RE SLAUGHTER-HOUSE CASES

83 U.S. 36 (1872)

"To...establish a clear and comprehensive definition of citizenship which should declare what should constitute citizenship of the United States, and also citizenship of a State, the first clause of the first section was framed. 'All persons born or naturalized in the United States, *and subject to the jurisdiction thereof*, are citizens of the United States and of the State wherein they reside.'

"The first observation we have to make on this clause is, that it puts at rest both the questions which we stated to have been the subject of differences of opinion. It declares that persons may be citizens of the United States without regard to their citizenship of a particular State, and it overturns the *Dred Scott* decision by making all persons born within the United States and subject to its jurisdiction citizens of the United States. That its main purpose was to establish the citizenship of the negro can admit of no doubt.

"The phrase, 'subject to its jurisdiction' was intended to exclude from its operation children of ministers, consuls, and citizens or subjects of foreign States born within the United States."

139.

In *Elk v. Wilkins* (1884) the meaning of the clause was again tested regarding whether anyone born in the United States would be a citizen regardless of the parents' nationality.

In *Elk*, the Supreme Court held that children of Native Americans were *not* citizens, despite the fact that they were born in the United States.

The *Elk v. Wilkins* case*:*

U.S. SUPREME COURT

ELK v. WILKINS

112 U.S. 94 (1884)

This is an action brought by an Indian who claims he was born within the United States and that by virtue of the fourteenth amendment to the Constitution of the United States, he is a citizen of the United States, and entitled to the right and privilege of citizens of the United States and that he is entitled to vote.

The court held:

"The question then is, whether an Indian, born a member of one of the Indian tribes within the United States, is, merely by reason of his birth within the United States, and of his afterwards voluntarily separating himself from his tribe and taking up his residence among white citizens, a citizen of the United States, within the meaning of the first section of the fourteenth amendment of the constitution.

"Under the constitution of the United States, as originally established, 'Indians not taxed' were excluded from the persons according to whose numbers representatives and direct taxes were apportioned among the several states; and congress had and exercised the power to regulate commerce with the Indian tribes, and the members thereof, whether within or without the boundaries of one of the states of the Union.

"The Indian tribes, being within the territorial limits of the United States, were not, strictly speaking, foreign states; but they were alien nations, distinct political communities, with whom the United States might and habitually did deal, as they thought fit, either through treaties made by the president and senate, or through acts of congress in the ordinary forms of legislation. *The members of those tribes owed immediate allegiance to their several tribes, and were not part of the people of the United States.* They were in a dependent condition, a state of pupilage, resembling that of a ward to his guardian. Indians and their property, exempt from taxation by treaty or statute of the United States, could not be taxed by any state. General acts of congress did not apply to Indians, unless so expressed as to clearly manifest an intention to include them.

140.

"... 'They (the Indian tribes) may without doubt, like the subjects of any foreign government, be naturalized by the authority of congress, and become citizens of a state, and of the United States; and if an individual should leave his nation or tribe, and take up his abode among the white population, he would be entitled to all the rights and privileges which would belong to an emigrant from any other foreign people.'

"*But an emigrant from any foreign state cannot become a citizen of the United States without a formal renunciation of his old allegiance, and an acceptance by the United States of that renunciation through such form of naturalization as may be required law.*

"This section contemplates two sources of citizenship, and two sources only: birth and naturalization. The persons declared to be citizens are 'all persons born or naturalized in the United States, and subject to the jurisdiction thereof.' *The evident meaning of these last words is, not merely subject in some respect or degree to the jurisdiction of the United States, but completely subject to their political jurisdiction, and owing them direct and immediate allegiance.*

"And the words relate to the time of birth in the one case, as they do to the time of naturalization in the other. Persons not thus subject to the jurisdiction of the United States at the time of birth cannot become so afterwards, except by being naturalized, either individually, as by proceedings under the naturalization acts; or collectively, as by the force of a treaty by which foreign territory is acquired.

"Indians born within the territorial limits of the United States, members of, and owing immediate allegiance to, one of the Indiana tribes, (an alien though dependent power,) although in a geographical sense born in the United States, are no more 'born in the United States and subject to the jurisdiction thereof,' within the meaning of the first section of the fourteenth amendment, than the children of subjects of any foreign government born within the domain of that government, or the children born within the United States, of ambassadors or other public ministers of foreign nations.

"This view is confirmed by the second section of the fourteenth amendment, which provides that 'representatives shall be apportioned among the several states according to their respective numbers, counting the whole number of persons in each state, excluding Indians not taxed.' Slavery having been abolished, and the persons formerly held as slaves made citizens, this clause fixing the apportionment of representatives has abrogated so much of the corresponding clause of the original constitution as counted only three-fifths of such persons.

141.

" *But Indians not taxed are still excluded from the count, for the reason that they are not citizens.* Their absolute exclusion from the basis of representation, in which all other persons are now included, is wholly inconsistent with their being considered citizens. So the further provision of the second section for a proportionate reduction of the basis of the representation of any state in which the right to vote for presidential electors, representatives in congress, or executive or judicial officers or members of the legislature of a state, is denied, except for participation in rebellion or other crime, to 'any of the male inhabitants of such state, being twenty-one years of age and citizens of the United States,' cannot apply to a denial of the elective franchise to Indians not taxed, who form no part of the people entitled to representation.

"It is also worthy of remark that the language used, about the same time, by the very congress which framed the fourteenth amendment, in the first section of the civil rights act of April 9, 1866, declaring who shall be citizens of the United States, is 'all persons born in the United States, *and not subject to any foreign power, excluding Indians not taxed.*' Such Indians, then, not being citizens by birth, can only become citizens in the second way mentioned in the fourteenth amendment, by being 'naturalized in the United States,' by or under some treaty or statute.

"The treaty of 1867 with the Kansas Indians strikingly illustrates the principle that *no one can become a citizen of a nation without its consent, and directly contradicts the supposition that a member of an Indian tribe can at will be alternately a citizen of the United States and a member of the tribe.*

"Since the ratification of the fourteenth amendment, congress has passed several acts for naturalizing Indians of certain tribes, which would have been superfluous if they were, or might become without any action of the government, citizens of the United States.

"But the question whether any Indian tribes, or any members thereof, should be admitted to the privileges and responsibilities of citizenship, is a question to be decided by the nation whose wards they are and whose citizens they seek to become, *and not by each Indian for himself.* "... *an Indian cannot make himself a citizen of the United States without the consent and co-operation of the government.* The fact that he has abandoned his nomadic life or tribal relations, and adopted the habits and manners of civilized people, may be a good reason why he should be made a citizen of the United States, but does not of itself make him one. *To be a citizen of the United States is a political privilege which no one, not born to, can assume without its consent in some form.*

"The plaintiff, not being a citizen of the United States under the fourteenth amendment of the constitution, has been deprived of no right secured by the fifteenth amendment, and cannot maintain this action.

Judgment affirmed."

So, as of 1884, the Supreme Court applied the 14th Amendment citizenship clause as written, i.e., *"The phrase, 'subject to its jurisdiction' was intended to exclude from its operation children of ministers, consuls, and citizens or subjects of foreign States born within the United States."*

However, in 1898, the Supreme Court, in the case of *United States v. Wong Kim Ark,* regarding children of non-citizen legal residents of Chinese ancestry born in United States ruled that the children *were* U.S. citizens.

In doing so, the Court ignored the previous cases defining citizenship; reinstated the feudal system existing in England at the time of the American revolution, which was rejected by the founding fathers; ignored a treaty between the United States and China to the effect that neither country permitted the other's children to become citizens of their country, either by birth or naturalization process. This is most clearly evidenced by the dissent as follows:

Here now, excerpts from the most-outrageous, *United States v. Wong Kim Ark*:

U.S. SUPREME COURT
U.S. v. WONG KIM ARK
169 U.S. 649 (1898)

"This was a writ of habeas corpus, issued October 2, 1895, by the district court of the United States for the Northern district of California, to the collector of customs at the port of San Francisco, in behalf of Wong Kim Ark, who alleged that he was a citizen of the United States, of more than 21 years of age, and was born at San Francisco in 1873, of parents of Chinese descent, and subjects of the emperor of China, but domiciled residents at San Francisco; and that, on his return to the United States on the steamship Coptic, in August, 1895, from a temporary visit to China, he applied to said collector of customs for permission to land, and was by the collector refused such permission, and was restrained of his liberty by the collector, and by the general manager of the steamship company acting under his direction, in violation of the constitution and laws of the United States, not by virtue of any judicial order or proceeding, but solely upon the pretense that he was not a citizen of the United States.

"The facts of this case, as agreed by the parties, are as follows: Wong Kim Ark was born in 1873, in the city of San Francisco, in the state of California and United States of America, and was and is a laborer. His father and mother were

143.

persons of Chinese descent, *and subjects of the emperor of China.* They were at the time of his birth domiciled residents of the United States, having previously established and are still enjoying a permanent domicile and residence therein at San Francisco. They continued to reside and remain in the United States until 1890, when they departed for China; and, during all the time of their residence in the United States, they were engaged in business, and were never employed in any diplomatic or official capacity under the emperor of China.

"Wong Kim Ark, ever since his birth, has had but one residence, to wit, in California, within the United States and has there resided, claiming to be a citizen of the United States, and has never lost or changed that residence, or gained or acquired another residence; and neither he, nor his parents acting for him, ever renounced his allegiance to the United States, or did or committed any act or thing to exclude him therefrom. In 1890 (when he must have been about 17 years of age) he departed for China, on a temporary visit, and with the intention of returning to the United States, and did return thereto by sea in the same year, and was permitted by the collector of customs to enter the United States, upon the sole ground that he was a native-born citizen of the United States.

"After such return, he remained in the United States, claiming to be a citizen thereof, until 1894, when he (being about 21 years of age, but whether a little above or a little under that age does not appear) again departed for China on a temporary visit, and with the intention of returning to the United States; and he did return thereto, by sea, in August, 1895, and applied to the collector of customs for permission to land, and was denied such permission, upon the sole ground that he was not a citizen of the United States.

"It is conceded that, if he is a citizen of the United States, the acts of congress known as the 'Chinese Exclusion Acts,' prohibiting persons of the Chinese race, and especially Chinese laborers, from coming into the United States, do not and cannot apply to him.

"The question presented by the record is whether a child born in the United States, of parents of Chinese descent, who at the time of his birth *are subjects of the emperor of China*, but have a permanent domicile and residence in the United States, and are there carrying on business, and are not employed in any diplomatic or official capacity under the emperor of China, becomes at the time of his birth a citizen of the United States, by virtue of the first clause of the fourteenth amendment of the constitution: 'All persons born or naturalized in the United States, and *subject to the jurisdiction thereof*, are citizens of the United States and of the state wherein they reside.

144.

"The evident intention, and the necessary effect, of the submission of this case to the decision of the court upon the facts agreed by the parties, were to present for determination the single question, stated at the beginning of this opinion, namely, whether a child born in the United States, of parents of Chinese descent, who, at the time of his birth, *are subjects of the emperor of China*, but have a permanent domicile and residence in the United States, and are there carrying on business, and are not employed in any diplomatic or official capacity under the emperor of China, becomes at the time of his birth a citizen of the United States. For the reasons above stated, this court is of opinion that the question must be answered in the affirmative.

"Order affirmed."

Now, a most cogent Dissent:

Mr. Chief Justice FULLER, with whom concurred Mr. Justice HARLAN, dissenting.

"I cannot concur in the opinion and judgment of the court in this case.

"The proposition is that a child born in this country of parents who were not citizens of the United States, and under the laws of their own country and of the United States could not become such,- as was the fact from the beginning of the government in respect of the class of aliens to which the parents in this instance belonged,-is, from the moment of his birth, a citizen of the United States, by virtue of the first clause of the fourteenth amendment, any act of congress to the contrary notwithstanding.

"The argument is that although the constitution prior to that amendment nowhere attempted to define the words 'citizens of the United States' and 'natural-born citizen,' as used therein, yet that it must be interpreted in the light of the English common-law rule which made the place of birth the criterion of nationality; that that rule 'was in force in all the [sic] English colonies upon this continent down to the time of the Declaration of Independence, and in the United States afterwards, and continued to prevail under the constitution as originally established'; and 'that, before the enactment of the civil rights act of 1866 and the adoption of the constitutional amendment, all white persons, at least, born within the sovereignty of the United States, whether children of citizens or of foreigners, excepting only children of ambassadors or public ministers of a foreign government, were native-born citizens of the United States.'

"Thus, the fourteenth amendment is held to be merely declaratory, except that it brings all persons, irrespective of color, within the scope of the alleged rule, and puts that rule beyond the control of the legislative power.

145.

"If the conclusion of the majority opinion is correct, then the children of citizens of the United States, who have been born abroad since July 28, 1868, when the amendment was declared ratified, were and are aliens, unless they have or shall, on attaining majority, become citizens by naturalization in the United States; and no statutory provision to the contrary is of any force or effect. And children who are aliens by descent, but born on our soil, are exempted from the exercise of the power to exclude or to expel aliens, or any class of aliens, so often maintained by this court,-an exemption apparently disregarded by the acts in respect of the exclusion of persons of Chinese descent.

"The English common-law rule, which it is insisted was in force after the Declaration of Independence, was that 'every person born within the dominions of the crown, no matter whether of English or of o reign parents, and, in the latter case, whether the parents were settled or merely temporarily sojourning in the country, was an English subject; save only the children of foreign ambassadors (who were excepted because their fathers carried their own nationality with them), or a child born to a foreigner during the hostile occupation of any part of the territories of England.'

"The tie which bound the child to the crown was indissoluble.The nationality of his parents had no bearing on his nationality. Though born during a temporary stay of a few days, the child was irretrievably a British subject.

"The rule was the outcome of the connection in feudalism between the individual and the soil on which he lived, and the allegiance due was that of liege men to their liege lord. It was not local and temporary, as was the obedience to the laws owed by aliens within the dominions of the crown, but permanent and indissoluble, and not to be canceled by any change of time or place or circumstances.

"And it is this rule, pure and simple, which it is asserted determined citizenship of the United States during the entire period prior to the passage of the act of April 9, 1866, and the ratification of the fourteenth amendment, and governed the meaning of the words, 'citizen of the United States' and 'natural-born citizen,' used in the constitution as originally framed and adopted. I submit that no such rule obtained during the period referred to, and that those words bore no such construction; that the act of April 9, 1866, expressed the contrary rule; that the fourteenth amendment prescribed the same rule as the act; and that, if that amendment bears the construction now put upon it, it imposed the English common-law rule on this country for the first time, and made it 'absolute and unbending,' just as Great Britain was being relieved from its inconveniences.

"Obviously, where the constitution deals with common-law rights and uses common-law phraseology, its language should be read in the light of the

146.

common law; but when the question arises as to what constitutes citizenship of the nation, involving, as it does, international relations, and political as contradistinguished from civil status, international principles must be considered; and, unless the municipal law of England appears to have been affirmatively accepted, it cannot be allowed to control in the matter of construction.

"Nationality is essentially a political idea, and belongs to the sphere of public law. Hence Mr. Justice Story said that the incapacities of femes covert, at common law, 'do not reach their political rights, nor prevent their acquiring or losing a national character. Those political rights do not stand upon the mere doctrines of municipal law, applicable to ordinary transactions, but stand upon the more general principles of the law of nations.'...

"Before the Revolution, the views of the publicists had been thus put by Vattel: *'The natives, or natural-born citizens, are those born in the country, of parents who are citizens.* As the society cannot exist and perpetuate itself otherwise than by the children of the citizens, those children naturally follow the condition of their fathers, and succeed to all their rights. The society is supposed to desire this, in consequence of what it owes to its own preservation; and it is presumed, as matter of course, that each citizen, on entering into society, reserves to his children the right of becoming members of it. The country of the fathers is h erefore [sic] that of the children; and these become true citizens merely by their tacit consent. We shall soon see whether, on their coming to the years of discretion, they may renounce their right, and what they owe to the society in which they were born.

" *I say that, in order to be of the country, it is necessary that a person be born of a father who is a citizen; for, if he is born there of a foreigner, it will be only the place of his birth, and not his country.'* 'The true bond which connects the child with the body politic is not the matter of an inanimate piece of land, but the moral relations of his parentage. ... The place of birth produces no change in the rule that children follow the condition of their fathers, for it is not naturally the place of birth that gives rights, but extraction.'

"And to the same effect are the modern writers, as, for instance, Bar, who says: 'To what nation a person belongs is by the laws of all nations closely dependent on descent. It is almost a universal rule that the citizenship of the parents determines it,-that of the father where children are lawful, and, where they are bastards, that of their mother, without regard to the place of their birth; and that must necessarily be recognized as the correct canon, since nationality is in its essence dependent on descent.'

147.

"The framers of the constitution were familiar with the distinctions between the Roman law and the feudal law, between obligations based on territoriality and those based on the personal and invisible character of origin; *and there is nothing to show that in the matter of nationality they intended to adhere to principles derived from regal government, which they had just assisted in overthrowing.*

"Manifestly, when the sovereignty of the crown was thrown off, and an independent government established, every rule of the common law, and every statute of England obtaining in the colonies, in derogation of the principles on which the new government was founded, was abrogated.

"The states, for all national purposes embraced in the constitution, became one, united under the same sovereign authority, and governed by the same laws; but they retained their jurisdiction over all persons and things within their territorial limits, except where surrendered to the general government or restrained by the constitution, and protection to life, liberty, and property rested primarily with them. So far as the *jus commune*, or 'folk right,' relating to the rights of persons, was concerned, the colonies regarded it as their birthright, and adopted such parts of it as they found applicable to their condition.

"They became sovereign and independent states, and, when the republic was created, each of the 13 states had its own local usages, customs, and common law, *while in respect of the national government there necessarily was no general, independent, and separate common law of the United States, nor has there ever been....*As to the *jura coronae*, including therein the obligation of allegiance, the extent to which these ever were applicable in this country depended on circumstances; and it would seem quite clear that the rule making locality of birth the criterion of citizenship, because creating a permanent tie of allegiance, no more survived the American Revolution than the same rule survived the French Revolution.

"Doubtless, before the latter event, in the progress of monarchical power, the rule which involved the principle of liege homage may have become the rule of Europe; but that idea never had any basis in the United States.

"As Chief Justice Taney observed, though in a different connection: 'It is true that most of the states have adopted the principles of English jurisprudence, so far as it concerns private and individual rights. And, when such rights are in question, we habitually refer to the English decisions, not only with respect, but in many cases as authoritative. But, in the distribution of political power between the great departments of government, there is such a wide difference between the power conferred on the president of the United States and the authority and

148.

sovereignty which belong to the English crown, that it would be altogether unsafe to reason from any supposed resemblance between them, either as regards conquest in war or any other subject where the rights and powers of the executive arm of the government are brought into question. *Our own constitution and form of government must be our only guide.'*

"And Mr. Lawrence, in his edition of Wheaton, makes this comment: 'There is, it is believed, as great a difference between the territorial allegiance claimed by an hereditary sovereign on feudal principles and the personal right of citizenship participated in by all the members of a political community, according to American institutions, as there is between the authority and sovereignty of the queen of England and the power of the American president; and the inapplicability of English precedents is as clear in the one case as in the other. The same view, with particular application to naturalization, was early taken by the American commentator on Blackstone. "Blackstone distinguished allegiance into two sorts,-the one, natural and perpetual; the other, local and temporary. 'Natural allegiance,' so called, was allegiance resulting from birth in subjection to the crown, and indelibility was an essential, vital, and necessary characteristic.

"The royal commission to inquire into the laws of naturalization and allegiance was created May 21, 1868; and, in their report, the commissioners, among other things, say: 'The allegiance of a natural-born British subject is regarded by the common law as indelible. We are of opinion that this doctrine of the common law is neither reasonable nor convenient. It is at variance with those principles on which the rights and duties of a subject should be deemed to rest; it conflicts with that freedom of action which is now recognized as most conducive to the general good, as well as to individual happiness and prosperity; *and it is especially inconsistent with the practice of a state which allows to its subjects absolute freedom of emigration..'*

"However, the commission, by a majority, declined to recommend the abandonment of the rule altogether, though 'clearly of opinion that it ought not to be, as it now is, absolute and unbending,' but recommended certain modifications which were carried out in subsequent legislation.

"But from the Declaration of Independence to this day, the United States have rejected the doctrine of indissoluble allegiance, and maintained the general right of expatriation, to be exercised in subordination to the public interests, and subject to regulation.

"As early as the act of January 29, 1795, applicants for naturalization were required to take, not simply an oath to support the constitution of the United States, but of absolute renunciation and abjuration of all allegiance and fidelity

149.

to every foreign prince or state, and particularly to the prince or state of which they were before the citizens or subjects.

"St. 3 Jac. I. c. 4, provided that promising obedience to any other prince, state, or potentate subjected the person so doing to be adjudged a traitor, and to suffer the penalty of high treason; and in respect of the act of 1795 Lord Grenville wrote to our minister, Rufus King: 'No British subject can, by such a form of renunciation as that which is prescribed in the American law of naturalization, devest himself of his allegiance to his sovereign. Such a declaration of renunciation made by any of the king's subjects would, instead of operating as a protection to them, be considered an act highly criminal on their part.'

"Nevertheless, congress has persisted from 1795 in rejecting the English rule, and in requiring the alien, who would become a citizen of the United States, in taking on himself the ties binding him to our government, to affirmatively sever the ties that bound him to any other.

"The subject was examined at length in 1856, in an opinion given the secretary of state by Atty. Gen. Cushing, where the views of the writers on international law and those expressed in cases in the federal and state courts are largely set forth, and the attorney general says: 'The doctrine of absolute and perpetual allegiance, the root of the denial of the right of any emigration, is inadmissible in the United States. It was a matter involved in, and settled for us by, the Revolution, which founded the American Union.

"'Moreover, the right of expatriation, under fixed circumstances of time and of manner, being expressly asserted in the legislatures of several of our states, and affirmed by decisions of their courts, must be considered as thus made a part of the fundamental law of the United States.' "Expatriation included not simply the leaving of one's native country, but the becoming naturalizen [sic] in the country adopted as a future residence. The emigration which the United States encouraged was that of those who could become incorporate with its people, make its flag their own, and aid in the accomplishment of a common destiny; and it was obstruction to such emigration that made one of the charges against the crown in the Declaration... The right of expatriation was recognized as a practical and fundamental doctrine of America. There was no uniform rule so far as the states were severally concerned, and none such assumed in respect of the United States.

"In 1859, Atty. Gen. Black thus advised the president (9 Ops. Attys. Gen. 356): 'The natural right of every free person, who owes no debts and is not guilty of any crime, to leave the country of his birth in good faith and for an honest purpose, the privilege of throwing off his natural allegiance, and substituting

150.

another allegiance in its place,-the general right, in one word, of expatriation,-is incontestable. I know that the common law of England denies it; that the judicial decisions of that country are opposed to it; and that some of our own courts, misled by British authority, have expressed, though not very decisively, the same opinion. But all this is very far from settling the question. *The municipal code of England is not one of the sources from which we derive our knowledge of international law. We take it from natural reason and justice, from writers of known wisdom, and from the practice of civilized nations. All these are opposed to the doctrine of perpetual allegiance.'*

"In the opinion of the attorney general, the United States, in recognizing the right of expatriation, declined, from the beginning, to accept the view that rested the obligation of the citizen on feudal principles, and proceeded on the law of nations, which was in direct conflict therewith.

"And the correctness of this conclusion was specifically affirmed not many years after, when the right, as the natural and inherent right of all people and fundamental in this country, was declared by congress in the act of July 27, 1868, carried forward into sections 1999 and 2000 of the Revised Statutes, in 1874.It is beyond dispute that the most vital constituent of the English common-law rule has always been rejected in respect of citizenship of the United States.

"Whether it was also the rule at common law that the children of British subjects born abroad were themselves British subjects-nationalit being attributed to parentage instead of locality-has been variously determined. If this were so, of course the statute of Edw. III. was declaratory, as was the subsequent legislation. But if not, then such children were aliens, and the statute of 7 Anne and subsequent statutes must be regarded as in some sort acts of naturalization. On the other hand, it seems to me that the rule, 'Partus sequitur patrem,' has always applied to children of our citizens born abroad, and that the acts of congress on this subject are clearly declaratory, passed out of abundant caution, to obviate misunderstandings which might arise from the prevalence of the contrary rule elsewhere.

"Section 1993 of the Revised Statutes provides that children so born 'are declared to be citizens of the United States; but the rights of citizenship shall not descend to children whose fathers never resided in the United States.' Thus a limitation is prescribed on the passage of citizenship by descent beyond the second generation if then surrendered by permanent nonresidence, and this limitation was contained in all the acts from 1790 down. Section 2172 provides that such children shall 'be considered as citizens thereof.'

"The language of the statute of 7 Anne is quite different in providing that 'the children of all natural-born subjects born out of the ligeance of her majesty, her heirs and successors, shall be deemed, adjudged, and taken to be natural-born subjects of this kingdom, to all intents, constructions, and purposes whatsoever.'

"In my judgment, the children of our citizens born abroad were always natural-born citizens from the standpoint of this government. If not, and if the correct view is that they were aliens, but collectively naturalized under the acts of congress which recognized them as natural born, then those born since the fourteenth imendment are not citizens at all unless they have become such by individual compliance with the general laws for the naturalization of aliens, because they are not naturalized 'in the United States.'

"By the fifth clause of the first section of article 2 of the constitution it is provided that 'no person except a natural-born citizen, or a citizen of the United States, at the time of the adoption of the constitution, shall be eligible to the office of president; neither shall any person be eligible to that office who shall not have attained to the age of thirty-five years, and been fourteen years a resident within the United States.'

"In the convention it was, says Mr. Bancroft, 'objected that no number of years could properly prepare a foreigner for that place; but as men of other lands had spilled their blood in the cause of the United States, and had assisted at every stage of the formation of their institutions, on the 7th of September it was unanimously settled that foreign-born residents of fourteen years who should be citizens at the time of the formation of the constitution are eligible to the office of president.'

"Considering the circumstances surrounding the framing of the constitution, I submit that it is unreasonable to conclude that 'naturalborn citizen' applied to everybody born within the geographical tract known as the United States, irrespective of circumstances; and that the children of foreigners, happening to be born to them while passing through the country, whether of royal parentage or not, or whether of the Mongolian, Malay, or other race, were eligible to the presidency, while children of our citizens, born abroad, were not.

"By the second clause of the second section of article 1 it is provided that 'no person shall be a representative who shall not have attained to the age of twenty-five years, and been seven years a citizen of the United States, and who shall not, when elected, be an inhabitant of that state of which he shall be chosen'; and by the third clause of section 3, that 'no person shall be a senator who shall not have attained to the age of thirty years, and been nine yer a citizen of the United States, and who shall not, when elected, be an inhabitant of that state for which he shall be chosen.' At that time the theory largely obtained, as stated by Mr. Justice Story, in his Commentaries on the Constitution (section 1693), 'that every citizen of a state is ipso facto a citizen of the United States.'

152.

"Mr. Justice Curtis, in *Dred Scott v. Sandford*, expressed the opinion that under the constitution of the United States 'every free person born on the soil of a state, who is a citizen of that state by force of its constitution or laws, is also a citizen of the United States.' And he said: 'Among the powers unquestionably possessed by the several states was that of determining what persons should and what persons should not be citizens. It was practicable to confer on the government of the Union this entire power. It embraced what may, well enough for the purpose now in view, be divided into three parts: First, the power to remove the disabilities of alienage, either by special acts in reference to each individual case, or by establishing a rule of naturalization to be administered and applied by the courts; second, determining what persons should enjoy the privileges of citizenship, in respect to the internal affairs of the several states; third, what native-born persons should be citizens of the United States.

"The first-named power, that of establishing a uniform rule of naturalization, was granted; and here the grant, according to its terms, stopped. Construing a constitution containing only limited and defined powers of government, the argument derived from this definite and re stricted power to establish a rule of naturalization must be admitted to be exceedingly strong. I do not say it is necessarily decisive. It might be controlled by other parts of the constitution. But when this particular subject of citizenship was under consideration, and, in the clause specially intended to define the extent of power concerning it, we find a particular part of this entire power separated from the residue, and conferred on the general government, there arises a strong presumption that this is all which is granted, and that the residue is left to the states and to the people. And this presumption is, in my opinion, converted into a certainty, by an examination of all such other clauses of the constitution as touch this subject.

"But in that case Mr. Chief Justice Taney said: 'The words 'people of the United States' and 'citizens' are synonymous terms, and mean the same thing. They both describe the political body who, according to our republican institutions, form the sovereignty, and who hold the power and conduct the government through their representatives. They are what we familiarly call the 'sovereign people,' and every citizen is one of this people and a constituent member of this sovereignty.... In discussing this question, we must not confound the rights of citizenship which a state may confer within its own limits, and the rights of citizenship as a member of the Union. It does not by any means follow, because he has all the rights and privileges of a citizen of a state, that he must be a citizen of the United States. He may have all of the rights and privileges of a citizen of a state, and yet not be entitled to the rights and privileges of a citizen in any other state; for, previous to the adoption of the constitution of the United

153.

States, every state had the undoubted right to confer on whomsoever it pleased the character of citizen and to endow him with all its rights.

"But this character, of course, was confined to the boundaries of the state, and gave him no rights or privileges in other states beyond those secured to him by the laws of nations and the comity of states. Nor have the several states surrendered the power of conferring these rights and privileges by adopting the constitution of the United States. Each state may still confer them upon an alien, or any one it thinks proper, or upon any class or description of persons; yet he would not be a citizen in the sense in which that word is used in the constitution of the United States, nor entitled to sue as such in one of its courts, nor to the privileges and immunities of a citizen in the other states. The rights which he would acquire would be restricted to the state which gave them. The constitution has conferred on congress the right to establish a uniform rule of naturalization, and this right is evidently exclusive, and has always been held by this court to be so.

"Consequently, no state, since the adoption of the constitution, can by naturalizing an alien invest him with the rights and privileges secured to a citizen of a state under the federal government, although, so far as the state alone was concerned, he would undoubtedly be entitled to the rights of a citizen, and clothed with all the rights and immunities which the constitution and laws of the state attached to that character.

"Plainly, the distinction between citizenship of the United States and citizenship of a state, thus pointed out, involved then, as now, the complete rights of the citizen internationally as contradistinguished from those of persons not citizens of the United States.

"The English common-law rule recognized no exception in the instance of birth during the mere temporary or accidental sojourn of the parents. As allegiance sprang from the place of birth regardless of parentage, and supervened at the moment of birth, the inquiry whether the parents were permanently or only temporarily within the realm was wholly immaterial. And it is settled in England that the question of domicile is entirely distinct from that of allegiance. The one relates to the civil, and the other to the political, status.

"But a different view as to the effect of permanent abode on nationality has been expressed in this country.

"In his work on Conflict of Laws (section 48), Mr. Justice Story, treating the subject as one of public law, said: 'Persons who are born in a country are generally deemed to be citizens of that country. A reasonable qualification of the rule would seem to be that it should not apply to the children of parents who were in itinere in the country, or who were abiding there for temporary purposes, as for health or curiosity or occasional business. It would be difficult, however, to assert that, in the present state of public law, such a qualification is universally established.'

"Undoubtedly, all persons born in a country are presumptively citizens thereof, but the presumption is not irrebuttable.

"In his Lectures on Constitutional Law, Mr. Justice Miller remarked: 'If a stranger or traveler passing through or temporarily residing in this country, who has not himself been naturalized, and who claims to owe no allegiance to our government, has a child born here, which goes out of the country with its father, such child is not a citizen of the United States, because it was not subject to its jurisdiction.'

"The civil rights act became a law April 9, 1866 and provided 'that all persons born in the United States, and not subject to any foreign power, excluding Indians not taxed, are hereby declared to be citizens of the United States.' And this was re-enacted June 22, 1874.

"The words 'not subject to any foreign power' do not in themselves refer to mere territorial jurisdiction, for the persons referred to are persons born in the United States. All such persons are undoubtedly subject to the territorial jurisdiction of the United States, and yet the act concedes that, nevertheless, they may be subject to the political jurisdiction of a foreign government. In other words, by the terms of the act, all persons born in the United States, and not owing allegiance to any foreign power, are citizens.

"The allegiance of children so born is not the local allegiance arising from their parents merely being domiciled in the country; and it is single, and not double, allegiance. Indeed, double allegiance, in the sense of double nationality, has no place in our law, and the existence of a man without a country is not recognized.

"But it is argued that the words 'and not subject to any foreign power' should be construed as excepting from the operation of the statute only the children of public ministers and of aliens born during hostile occupation.

"Was there any necessity of excepting them? And, if there were others described by the words, why should the language be construed to exclude them?

"Whether the immunity of foreign ministers from local allegiance rests on the fiction of extraterritoriality or on the waiver of territorial jurisdiction, by receiving them as representatives of other sovereignties, the result is the same.

"They do not owe allegiance otherwise than to their own governments, and their children cannot be regarded as born within any other.

"And this is true as to the children of aliens within territory in hostile occupation, who necessarily are not under the protection of, nor bound to render

155.

obedience to, the sovereign whose domains are invaded; but it is not pretended that the children of citizens of a government so situated would not become its citizens at their birth, as the permanent allegiance of their parents would not be severed by the mere fact of the enemy's possession.

"If the act of 1866 had not contained the words 'and not subject to any foreign power,' the children neither of public ministers nor of aliens in territory in hostile occupation would have been included within its terms on any proper construction, for their birth would not have subjected them to ties of allegiance, whether local and temporary, or general and permanent.

"There was no necessity as to them for the insertion of the words, although they were embraced by them.

"But there were others in respect of whom the exception was needed, namely, the children of aliens, whose parents owed local and temporary allegiance merely, remaining subject to a foreign power by virtue of the tie of permanenta llegiance, which they had not severed by formal abjuration or equivalent conduct, and some of whom were not permitted to do so if they would. "And it was to prevent the acquisition of citizenship by the children of such aliens merely by birth within the geographical limits of the United States that the words were inserted.

"Two months after the statute was enacted, on June 16, 1866, the fourteenth amendment was proposed, and declared ratified July 28, 1868. The first clause of the first section reads: 'All persons born or naturalized in the United States and subject to the jurisdiction thereof, are citizens of the United States and of the state wherein they reside.' *The act was passed and the amendment proposed by the same congress, and it is not open to reasonable doubt that the words 'subject to the jurisdiction thereof,' in the amendment, were used as synonymous with the words 'and not subject to any foreign power,' of the act.*

"The jurists and statesmen referred to in the majority opinion, notably Senators Trumbull and Reverdy Johnson, concurred in that view, Senator Trumbull saying: *'What do we mean by 'subject to the jurisdiction of the United States'? Not owing allegiance to anybodyelse; that is what it means'.* And Senator Johnson: 'Now, all that this amendment provides is that all persons born within the United States, and not subject to some foreign power (for that, no doubt, is the meaning of the committee who have brought the matter before us), shall be considered as citizens of the United States.'

"This was distinctly so ruled in *Elk v. Wilkins*, and no reason is perceived why the words were used if they apply only to that obedience which all persons not possessing immunity therefrom must pay the laws of the country in which they happen to be.

156.

"Dr. Wharton says that the words 'subject to the jurisdiction' must be construed in the sense which international law attributes to them, but that the children of our citizens born abroad, and of foreigners born in the United States, have the right, on arriving at full age, to elect one allegiance, and repudiate the other....

"The point, however, before us, is whether permanent allegiance is imposed at birth without regard to circumstances,-permanent until thrown off and another allegiance acquired by formal acts; not local and determined by a mere change of domicile.

"The fourteenth amendment came before the court in the *Slaughter-House Cases* (1872) -the cases having been brought up by writ of error in May, 1870, and it was held that the first clause was intended to define citizenship of the United States and citizenship of a state, which definitions recognized the distinction between the one and the other; that the privileges and immunities of citizens of the states embrace generally those fundamental civil rights for the security of which organized society was instituted, and which remain, with certain exceptions mentioned in the federal constitution, under the care of the state governments; while the privileges and immunities of citizens of the United States are those which arise out of the nature and essential character of the national government, the provisions of its constitution, or its laws and treaties made in pursuance thereof; and that it is the latter which are placed under the protection of congress by the second clause.

"And Mr. Justice Miller, delivering the opinion of the court, in analyzing the first clause, observed that 'the phrase 'subject to the jurisdiction thereof' was intended to exclude from its operation children of ministers, consuls, and citizens or subjects of foreign states, born within the United States.'

"That eminent judge did not have in mind the distinction between persons charged with diplomatic functions and those who were not, but was well aware that consuls are usually the citizens or subjects of the foreign states from which they come, and that, indeed, the appointment of natives of the places where the consular service is required, though permissible, has been pronounced objectionable in principle.

"His view was that the children of 'citizens or subjects of foreign states' owing permanent allegiance elsewhere, and only local obedience here, are not otherwise subject to the jurisdiction of the United States than are their parents....

"I do not insist that, although what was said was deemed essential to the argument and a necessary part of it, the point was definitively disposed of in the Slaughter-House Cases, which, for the purposes of the case then in hand, it was not necessary to solve. But that solution is furnished in Elk v. Wilkins, where the subject received great consideration, and it was said: 'By the thirteenth

157.

amendment of the constitution, slavery was prohibited. The main object of the opening sentence of the fourteenth amendment was to settle the question, upon which there had been a difference of opinion throughout the country and in this court, as to the citizenship of free negroes (Scott v. Sandford,); and to put it beyond doubt that all persons, white or black, and whether formerly slaves or not, born or naturalized in the United States, and owing no allegiance to any alien power, should be citizens of the United States, and of the state in which they reside (Slaughter-House Cases).

'This section contemplates two sources of citizenship, and two sources only, - birth and naturalization. The persons declared to be citizens are 'all persons born or naturalized in the United States, and subject to the jurisdiction thereof.' The evident meaning of these last words is, not merely subject in some respect or degree to the jurisdiction of the United States, but completely subject to their political jurisdiction, and owing them direct and immediate allegiance. And the words relate to the time of birth in the one case, as they do to the time of naturalization in the other. Persons not thus subject to the jurisdiction of the United States at the time of birth cannot become so afterwards, except by being naturalized, either individually, as by proceedings under the naturalization acts, or collectively, as by the force of a treaty by which foreign territory is acquired.'

"To be 'completely subject' to the political jurisdiction of the United States is to be in no respect or degree subject to the political jurisdiction of any other government.

"Now, I take it that the children of aliens, whose parents have not only not renounced their allegiance to their native country, but are forbidden by its system of government, as well as by its positive laws, from doing so, and are not permitted to acquire another citizenship by the laws of the country into which they come, must necessarily remain themselves subject to the same sovereignty as their parents, and cannot, in the nature of things, be, any more than their parents, completely subject to the jurisdiction of such other country.

"Generally speaking, I understand the subjects of the emperor of China- that ancient empire, with its history of thousands of years, and its unbroken continuity in belief, traditions, and government, in spite of revolutions and changes of dynasty-to be bound to him by every conception of duty and by every principle of their religion, of which *filial piety* is the first and greatest commandment; and formerly, perhaps still, their penal laws denounced the severest penalties on those who renounced their country and allegiance, and their abettors, and, in effect, held the relatives at home of Chinese in foreign lands as hostages for their loyalty. And, whatever concession may have been made by treaty in the direction of admitting the right of expatriation in some sense, they seem in the United States to have remained pigrims and sojourners as all their fathers were. At all events, they have never been allowed by our laws to acquire our nationality, and, except in sporadic instances, do not appear ever to have desired to do so.

"The fourteenth amendment was not designed to accord citizenship to persons so situated, and to cut off the legislative power from dealing with the subject.

"The right of a nation to expel or deport foreigners who have not been naturalized or taken any steps towards becoming citizens of a country is as absolute and unqualified as the right to prohibit and prevent their entrance into the county.

"But can the persos [sic] expelled be subjected to 'cruel and unusual punishments' in the process of expulsion, as would be the case if children born to them in this country were separated from them on their departure, because citizens of the United States? *Was it intended by this amendment to tear up parental relations by the roots?*

"The fifteenth amendment provides that 'the right of citizens of the United States to vote shall not be denied or abridged by the United States or by any state on account of race, color or previous condition of servitude.' Was it intended thereby that children of aliens should, by virtue of being born in the United States, be entitled, on attaining majority, to vote, irrespective of the treaties and laws of the United States in regard to such aliens?

"In providing that persons born or naturalized in the United States, and subject to the jurisdiction thereof, are citizens, the fourteenth amendment undoubtedly had particular reference to securing citizenship to the members of the colored race, whose servile status had been obliterated by the thirteenth amendment, and who had been born in the United States, but were not, and never had been, subject to any foreign power. They were not aliens (and, even if they could be so regarded, this operated as a collective naturalization), and their political status could not be affected by any change of the laws for the naturalization of individuals.

"Nobody can deny that the question of citizenship in a nation is of the most vital importance. It is a precious heritage, as well as an inestimable acquisition; and I cannot think that any safeguard surrounding it was intended to be thrown down by the amendment.

"In suggesting some of the privileges and immunities of national citizenship in the Slaughter-House Cases, Mr. Justice Miller said: 'Another privilege of a citizen of the United States is to demand the care and protection of the federal government over his life, liberty, and property when on the high seas or within

159.

the jurisdiction of a foreign government. Of this there can be no doubt, nor that the right depends upon his character as a citizen of the United States.'

"Mr. Hall says, in his work on Foreign Jurisdiction (sections 2, 5), the principle is that 'the legal relations by which a person is encompassed in his country of birth and residence cannot be wholly put aside when he goes abroad for a time. Many of the acts which he may do outside his native state have inevitable consequences within it. He may, for many purposes, be temporarily under the control of another sovereign than his own, and he may be bound to yield to a foreign government a large measure of obedience; but his own state possesses a right to his allegiance; he is still an integral part of the national community. A state, therefore, can enact laws enjoining or forbidding acts, and defining legal relations, which apply to its subjects abroad in common with those within its dominions. It can declare under what conditions it will regard as valid acts done in foreign countries, which profess to have legal effect; it can visit others with penalties; it can estimate circumstances and facts as it chooses.'

"On the other hand, the 'duty of protection is correlative to the rights of a sovereign over his subjects. The maintenance of a bond between a state and its subjects while they are abroad implies that the former must watch over and protect them within the due limit of the rights of other states. ... It enables governments to exact reparation for oppression from which their subjects have suffered, or for injuries done to them otherwise than by process of law; and it gives the means of guarding them against the effect of unreasonable laws, of laws totally out of harmony with the nature or degree of civilization by which a foreign power affects to be characterized, and finally of an administration of the laws bad beyond a certain point. When, in these directions, a state grossly fails in its duties; when it is either incapable of ruling, or rules with patent injustice,- the right of protection emerges in the form of diplomatic remonstrance, and in extreme cases of ulterior measures. It provides a material sanction for rights; it does not offer a theoretic foundation. It does not act within a foreign territory with the consent of the sovereign; it acts against him contentiously from without.'

"The privileges or immunities which, by the second clause of the amendment, the states are forbidden to abridge, are the privileges or immunities pertaining to citizenship of the United States, but that clause also places an inhibition on the states from depriving any person of life, liberty, or property, and from denying 'to any person within its jurisdiction the equal protection of the laws'; that is, of its own laws,- the laws to which its own citizens are subjected.

"The jurisdiction of the state is necessarily local, and the limitation relates to rights primarily secured by the states, and not by the United States. Jurisdiction, as applied to the general government, embraces international relations; as applied to the state, it refers simply to its power over persons and things within its particular limits.

"These considerations lead to the conclusion that the rule in respect of citizenship of the United States *prior to the fourteenth amendment* differed from the English common-law rule in vital particulars, and, among others, in that *it did not recognize allegiance as indelible, and in that it did recognize an essential difference between birth during temporary and birth during permanent residence.* If children born in the United States were deemed presumptively and generally citizens, this was not so when they were born of aliens whose residence was merely temporary, either in fact or in point of law.

"Did the fourteenth amendment impose the original English common-law rule as a rigid rule on this country?

"Did the amendment operate to abridge the treary-making [sic] power, or the power to establish a uniform rule of naturalization?

"I insist that it cannot be maintained that this government is unable, through the action of the president, concurred in by the senate, to make a treaty with a foreign government providing that the subjects of that government, although allowed to enter the United States, shall not be made citizens thereof, and that their children shall not become such citizens by reason of being born therein.

"A treaty couched in those precise terms would not be incompatible with the fourteenth amendment, unless it be held that that amendment has abridged the treaty-making power.

"Nor would a naturalization law exceping [sic] persons of a certain race and their children be invalid, unless the amendment has abridged the power of naturalization. This cannot apply to our colored fellow citizens, who never were aliens, were never beyond the jurisdiction of the United States.

"'Born in the United States, and subject to the jurisdiction thereof,' and 'naturalized in the United States, and subject to the jurisdiction thereof,' mean born or naturalized under such circumstances as to be completely subject to that jurisdiction,-that is, as completely as citizens of the United States who are, of course, not subject to any foreign power, and can of right claim the exercise of the power of the United States on their behalf wherever they may be. When, then, children are born the United States to the subjects of a foreign power, with which it is agreed by treaty that they shall not be naturalized thereby, and as to whom our own law forbids them to be naturalized, such children are not born so subject to the jurisdiction as to become citizens, and entitled on that ground to the interposition of our government, if they happen to be found in the country of their parents' origin and allegiance, or any other.

161.

"Turning to the treaty between the United States and China, concluded July 28, 1868, the ratifications of which were exchanged November 23, 1869, and the proclamation made February 5, 8 70, [1870] we find that by its sixth article it was provided: 'Citizens of the United States visiting or residing in China shall enjoy the same privileges, immunities, or exemptions in respect of travel or residence as may there be enjoyed by the citizens or subjects of the most favored nation. And, reciprocally Chinese subjects residing in the United States, shall enjoy the same privileges, immunities, and exemptions in respect to travel or residence as may there be enjoyed by the citizens or subjects of the most favored nation. *But nothing herein contained shall be held to confer naturalization on the citizens of the United States in China, nor upon the subjects of China in the United States.'*

"It is true that in the fifth article the inherent right of man to change his home or allegiance was recognized, as well as 'the mutual advantage of the free migration and emigration of their citizens and subjects, respectively, from the one country to the other, for the purposes of curiosity, of traffic, or as permanent residents.'

"All this, however, had reference to an entirely voluntary emigration for these purposes, and did not involve an admission of change of allegiance unless both countries assented, but the contrary, according to the sixth article.

"By the convention of March 17, 1894, it was agreed 'that Chinese laborers or Chinese of any other class, either permanently or temporarily residing within the United States, shall have for the protection of their persons and property all rights that are given by the laws of the United States to citizens of the most favored nation, excepting the right to become naturalized citizens.

"These treaties show that neither government desired such change, nor assented thereto. Indeed, if the naturalization laws of the United States had provided for the naturalization of Chinese persons. China manifestly would not have been obliged to recognize that her subjects had changed their allegiance thereby. But our laws do not so provide, and, on the contrary, are in entire harmony with the treaties.

"I think it follows that the children of Chinese born in this country do not, *ipso facto*, become citizens of the United States unless the fourteenth amendment overrides both treaty and statute. Does it bear that construction; or, rather, is it not the proper construction that all persons born in the United States of parents permanently residing here, and susceptible of becoming citizens, and not prevented therefrom by treaty or statute, are citizens, and not otherwise?

162.

"But the Chinese, under their form of government, the treaties and statutes, cannot become citizens nor acquire a permanent home here, no matter what the length of their stay may be.

"In Fong Yue Ting v.U. S, it was said, in respect of the treaty of 1868: 'After some years' experience under that treaty, the government of the United States was brought to the opinion that the presence within our territory of large numbers of Chinese laborers, of a distinct race and religion, remaining strangers in the land, residing apart by themselves, tenaciously adhering to the customs and usages of their own country, unfamiliar with our institutions, and apparently incapable of assimilating with our people, might endanger good order, and be injurious to the public interests; and therefore requested and obtained form China a modification of the treaty.'

"It is not to be admitted that the children of persons so situated become citizens by the accident of birth. On the contrary, I am of opinion that the president and senate by treaty, and the congress by legislation, have the power, notwithstanding the fourteenth amendment, to prescribe that all persons of a particular race, or their children, cannot become citizens, and that it results that the consent to allow such persons to come into and reside within our geographical limits does not carry with it the imposition of citizenship upon children born to them while in this country under such consent, in spite of treaty and statute.

"*In other words, the fourteenth amendment does not exclude from citizenship by birth children born in the United States of parents permanently located therein, and who might themselves become citizens; nor, on the other hand, does it arbitrarily make citizens of children born in the United States of parents who, according to the will of their native government and of this government, are and must remain aliens.*

"Tested by this rule, *Wong Kim Ark* never became and is not a citizen of the United States, and the order of the district court should be reversed.

"I am authorized to say that Mr. Justice HARLAN concurs in this dissent."

Notwithstanding the fact that 1) the United States did *not* adopt the feudal system of England, 2) the United States did *not* adopt England's policy of forbidding expatriation, 3) The treaty of 1866 forbade citizens of China from ever becoming citizens of the United States and vice-versa, and 4) the *Slaughterhouse case* of 1872, had defined citizenship based on birth as *not* including children born of parents of foreign countries, somehow the majority of the Supreme Court in *Wong Kim Ark*, "knew better" and determined that Mr. Ark was indeed a citizen....remarkable....

163.

Eventually, to their credit, the Court recognized that *Congress, not the Court,* had unfettered power over aliens. This is exemplified by the following case.

Article I, § 8, clause 4 of the U.S. Constitution provides that Congress shall have power "to establish a uniform rule of naturalization."

Under the *Lapina* case, the authority of Congress over the admission, exclusion and deportation of aliens is plenary. Congress may exclude aliens altogether, or prescribe the terms and conditions upon which they may come into or remain in the country.

Comes now, *Lapina v. Williams*:

U.S. SUPREME COURT
LAPINA v. WILLIAMS
232 U.S. 78 (1914)

Mr. Justice Pitney delivered the opinion of the court:

"The petitioner, an unmarried woman and a native of Russia, came to the United States in the year 1897 or 1898, at the age of about twelve years, accompanied by [232 U.S. 78, 83] a man who had promised to marry her, and during the four years immediately following she practised prostitution in the city of New York, and supported her companion with the proceeds of her prostitution; she then left that city, and thereafter continuously practised prostitution in various parts of the United States, including different towns and cities in the states of Washington, Arizona, and Texas. In the month of March, 1908, she returned to Russia for the purpose of visiting her mother, intending at the same time to return to this country; she re-entered the United States at the port of New York in June, 1908, accompanied by her mother, at which time petitioner falsely represented, for the purpose of facilitating her landing, that she was Mrs. Joseph Fiore, and the wife of an American citizen; at the time of this, her second entry, she intended to continue the practice of prostitution in the United States, and almost immediately upon being admitted she engaged in that practice, and was continually engaged in it until September 21, 1909, on which date she was arrested in a house of prostitution in Phoenix, Arizona, upon a warrant of arrest duly issued by the Acting Secretary of Commerce and Labor under the provisions of the immigration act of February 20, 1907.

"Upon a hearing properly accorded to her, the foregoing facts were established and an order of deportation was made upon the ground that she was a prostitute, and was such at the time of her entry into the United States; that she entered the United States for the purpose of prostitution; and that she had been found an inmate of a house of prostitution and practising the same within three years after her entry. She obtained a writ of habeas corpus, which, after a hearing, was

164.

dismissed by the district court for the southern district of New York. Upon appeal, the circuit court of appeals affirmed the order of dismissal. The present writ of certiorari was then allowed because of the division of judicial opinion upon the question presented, which is whether the provisions of the immigration act of 1907 respecting admission and deportation apply to an alien such as the petitioner, who, having remained in this country for more than three years (in this instance for more than ten years), after first entry, and having gone abroad for a temporary purpose and with the intention of returning, again seeks and gains admittance into the United States.

"The pertinent provisions of the act of 1907 are set forth in:

Sec. 2. That the following classes of aliens shall be excluded from admission into the United States: . . . prostitutes, or women or girls coming into the United States for the purpose of prostitution, or for any other immoral purpose; . . .

Sec. 3. . . . any alien woman or girl who shall be found an inmate of a house of prostitution or practising prostitution, at any time within three years after she shall have entered the United States, shall be deemed to be unlawfully within the United States, and shall be deported as provided by sections twenty and twenty-one of this act.

Sec. 20. That any alien who shall enter the United States in violation of law, . . . shall, upon the warrant of the Secretary of Commerce and Labor, be taken into custody and deported to the country whence he came at any time within three years after the date of his entry into the United States.

Sec. 21. That in case the Secretary of Commerce and Labor shall be satisfied that an alien has been found in the United States in violation of this act, or that an alien is subject to deportation under the provisions of this act or of any law of the United States, he shall cause such alien, within the period of three years after landing or entry therein, to be taken into custody and returned to the country whence he came, as provided by section twenty of this act. . . and in which it was held that while the provisions of the act of March 3, 1891, had been construed as restricted to 'alien immigrants,' the act of 1903 had been so framed as to cover aliens, whether immigrants or not. In behalf of the petitioner it is contended that the court erred in its judgment as to the purpose of Congress in modifying the language of previous acts on adopting the revision of 1903, and that this act and the act of 1907, as well as those that preceded them, when properly construed, refer to 'alien immigrants' exclusively.

Judgment affirmed.

Now, the *Knauff* case:

165.

U.S. SUPREME COURT
KNAUFF V. SHAUGHNESSY
338 U.S. 537 (1950)

"The alien wife of a citizen who had served honorably in the armed forces of the United States during World War II sought admission to the United States. On the basis of confidential information, the disclosure of which, in his judgment, would endanger the public security, the Attorney General denied a hearing, found that her admission would be prejudicial to the interests of the United States, and ordered her excluded.

"Held: this action was authorized by the Act of June 21, 1941, 22 U.S.C. §§ 223, and the proclamations and regulations issued thereunder, notwithstanding the War Brides Act of December 28, 1945.

"(a) The admission of aliens to this country is not a right, but a privilege, which is granted only upon such terms as the United States prescribes.

"(b) The Act of June 21, 1941, did not unconstitutionally delegate legislative power to prescribe the conditions under which aliens should be excluded.

"(c) It is not within the province of any court, unless expressly authorized by law, to review the determination of the political branch of Government to exclude a given alien....

"(d) Any procedure authorized by Congress for the exclusion of aliens is due process, so far as an alien denied entry is concerned.

"(e) The regulations governing the entry of aliens into the United States during the national emergency proclaimed May 27, 1941, which were prescribed by the Secretary of State and the Attorney General pursuant to Presidential Proclamation 2523, were "reasonable" within the meaning of the Act of June 21, 1941.

"(f) Presidential Proclamation 2523 authorized the Attorney General, as well as the Secretary of State, to order the exclusion of aliens.

"(g) Petitioner, an alien, had no vested right of entry which could be the subject of a prohibition against retroactive operations of regulations affecting her status.

"(h) The national emergency proclaimed May 27, 1941, has not been terminated; a state of war still exists; and the Act of June 21, 1941, and the proclamations and regulations thereunder, are still in force.

"(i) A different result is not required by the War Brides Act, which waives some of the usual requirements for the admission of certain alien spouses only if they are "otherwise admissible under the immigration laws.

"Affirmed"

ANCHOR BABIES:

Anchor babies are defined as children born in the United States of parents, both of whom are illegal aliens.

The issue of "anchor babies" is dealt with in HR 1868 which is legislation to amend § 301 of the Immigration and Nationality Act of 1952.

Section 301:

" SEC. 301. [8 U.S.C. 1401] The following shall be nationals and citizens of the United States at birth:

"(a) a person born in the United States, and subject to the jurisdiction thereof; ...

As the cases discussed above have shown, early on, a person born here of

parents who were here illegally, was *not*.... " subject to the jurisdiction thereof"

and therefore was *not* a citizen, simply because of birth in the United States.

However, subsequent cases cast doubt on this, and Section 301 offers little help in clarifying the matter.

Now, enters HR 1868:

HR 1868, The Birthright Citizenship Act of 2009 - Amends the Immigration and Nationality Act to consider a person born in the United States "subject to the jurisdiction" of the United States for citizenship-at-birth purposes if the person is born in the United States of parents, one of whom is:

1) A U.S. citizen or national:
2) a lawful permanent resident alien whose residence is in the United States: or
3) an alien performing active service in the U.S. Armed Forces.

The noteworthy fact of this endeavor is that it is entirely up to Congress to define citizenship as it is stated in the 14th Amendment, § 1, to wit:

"All persons born or naturalized in the United States and *subject to the jurisdiction thereof*, are citizens of the United States and the state wherein they reside."

The 14th Amendment, § 5, states:

"The Congress shall have power to enforce, by appropriate legislation, the provisions of this article."

Hence, as is confirmed by the cases immediately preceding, Congress has *carte blanche* to fashion a remedy to deal with the "anchor baby"situation. It is proposed that in order to gain citizenship "by birth", as opposed to "by naturalization,"one born in the United States must have been born of parents, both of whom are citizens . . . period.

" A government big enough to give you everything you want is big enough to take everything you have."

Thomas Jefferson

CHAPTER 8

A RESOLUTION OR UNIVERSAL FORMULA

In summary, all that which has appeared in this work, thus far, is no secret to certain sectors, e.g., Hollywood, the media, and academia . The strategy was, and is, to keep the People in the state of perpetual ignorance; ignorance of the methods by which the federal government, enabled by the Supreme Court has stripped, and is stripping, the People of their constitutional rights and liberties. The Supreme Court has become what Thomas Jefferson predicted. . . .it has become an oligarchy of despots. . . .

Thus far, this work has concerned itself with the most egregious methods by which the Supreme Court has dishonored the Constitution by intentionally ignoring its text, and engaging in a virtual rewrite of this greatest of all American Documents.

Were this work to do nothing more, the most one could expect would be for the establishment to subject it to its being ignored, ridiculed or both.

However, this last chapter offers several methods by which all of the herein misconduct by the Supreme Court can be remedied, *without a constitutional amendment.*

The first of the two methods can be described as the Article III method. The second of these methods is described as the 14th Amendment, § 5 method.

The first of these methods, utilizing Article III of the U.S. Constitution, follows:

Article III, in pertinent part, states:

"§ 1. The judicial Power of the United States, shall be vested in one Supreme Court, and in such inferior courts as the Congress may from time to time ordain and establish....

"§ 2. The judicial power shall extend to all cases in law or equity arising under this Constitution, the laws of the United States ...

" 2 ...The Supreme Court shall have appellate jurisdiction, both as to law and fact, with such exceptions, and under such regulations, as the Congress shall make."

The second of these, 14th Amendment, § 5, follows:

169.

14th Amendment, § 5, states:

"The Congress shall have power to enforce, by appropriate legislation, the provisions of this article."

Hence, it is clear that, by utilizing Article III, Congress can control the Supreme Court by "excepting" and "regulating" its jurisdiction to hear cases in its appellate capacity and Congress can, in certain circumstances, indicated below, utilize § 5, to effectively "enforce" certain provisions, including the 14th Amendment "by appropriate legislation."

The Article III method was utilized in 1868 in the *Ex Parte McCardle* case, excerpts of which follows:

SUPREME COURT OF THE UNITED STATES
EX PARTE McCARDLE
74 U.S. 506 (1868)

CHIEF JUSTICE CHASE delivered the opinion of the court.

"The first question necessarily is that of jurisdiction, for if the act of March, 1868, takes away the jurisdiction defined by the act of February, 1867, it is useless, if not improper, to enter into any discussion of other questions.

"It is quite true, as was argued by the counsel for the petitioner, that the appellate jurisdiction of this court is not derived from acts of Congress. It is, strictly speaking, conferred by the Constitution. But it is conferred "with such exceptions and under such regulations as Congress shall make."

"It is unnecessary to consider whether, if Congress had made no exceptions and no regulations, this court might not have exercised general appellate jurisdiction under rules prescribed by itself. For among the earliest acts of the first Congress, at its first session, was the act of September 24th, 1789, to establish the judicial courts of the United States. That act provided for the organization of this court, and prescribed regulations for the exercise of its jurisdiction.

"The source of that jurisdiction, and the limitations of it by the Constitution and by statute, have been on several occasions subjects of consideration here. In the case of *Durousseau v. The United States* particularly, the whole matter was carefully examined, and the court held that, while 'the appellate powers of this court are not given by the judicial act, but are given by the Constitution,' they are, nevertheless, 'limited and regulated by that act, and by such other acts as have been passed on the subject.' The court said further that the judicial act was an exercise of the power given by the Constitution to Congress 'of making

170.

exceptions to the appellate jurisdiction of the Supreme Court.' 'They have described affirmatively,' said the court, its jurisdiction, and this affirmative description has been understood to imply a negation of the exercise of such appellate power as is not comprehended within it.

"The principle that the affirmation of appellate jurisdiction implies the negation of all such jurisdiction not affirmed having been thus established, it was an almost necessary consequence that acts of Congress, providing for the exercise of jurisdiction, should come to be spoken of as acts granting jurisdiction, and not as acts making exceptions to the constitutional grant of it.

"The exception to appellate jurisdiction in the case before us, however, is not an inference from the affirmation of other appellate jurisdiction. It is made in terms. The provision of the act of 1867 affirming the appellate jurisdiction of this court in cases of habeas corpus is expressly repealed. It is hardly possible to imagine a plainer instance of positive exception.

"We are not at liberty to inquire into the motives of the legislature. We can only examine into its power under the Constitution, and the power to make exceptions to the appellate jurisdiction of this court is given by express words.

"What, then, is the effect of the repealing act upon the case before us? We cannot doubt as to this. Without jurisdiction, the court cannot proceed at all in any cause. Jurisdiction is power to declare the law, and, when it ceases to exist, the only function remaining to the court is that of announcing the fact and dismissing the cause. And this is not less clear upon authority than upon principle.

"Several cases were cited by the counsel for the petitioner in support of the position that jurisdiction of this case is not affected by the repealing act. But none of them, in our judgment, affords any support to it. They are all cases of the exercise of judicial power by the legislature, or of legislative interference with courts in the exercising of continuing jurisdiction.

"On the other hand, the general rule, supported by the best elementary writers, is that, 'when an act of the legislature is repealed, it must be considered, except as to transactions past and closed, as if it never existed.' And the effect of repealing acts upon suits under acts repealed has been determined by the adjudications of this court. The subject was fully considered in *Norris v. Crecker*, and more recently in *Insurance Company v. Ritchie*. In both of these cases, it was held that no judgment could be rendered in a suit after the repeal of the act under which it was brought and prosecuted.

"It is quite clear, therefore, that this court cannot proceed to pronounce judgment in this case, for it has no longer jurisdiction of the appeal, and judicial duty is not less fitly performed by declining ungranted jurisdiction than in exercising firmly that which the Constitution and the laws confer.

171.

"Counsel seem to have supposed, if effect be given to the repealing act in question, that the whole appellate power of the court, in cases of habeas corpus, is denied. But this is an error. The act of 1868 does not except from that jurisdiction any cases but appeals from Circuit Courts under the act of 1867. It does not affect the jurisdiction which was previously exercised.

"The appeal of the petitioner in this case must be dismissed for want of jurisdiction."

Application of these two methods follows:

In Chapter 1, it was shown that the Supreme Court in 1803, in the *Marbury* case, assumed a power not granted it by the Constitution, i.e., the power to declare acts of Congress unconstitutional and therefore void, thus elevating itself to the position of superiority *vis a vis* Congress.

Resolution:
Neither the Supreme Court nor any inferior federal court ordained or established by Congress under Article III of the U.S. Constitution shall have jurisdiction to amend, rewrite or hold acts of Congress or the states in violation of the Constitution, but be limited to interpretation and application of said laws based on the actual text of said Constitution and consistent therewith. *Marbury v. Madison* and its progeny are hereby reversed and vacated.

In Chapter 2, the 1819 case of *McCulloch* was presented wherein Congress was rewarded for its reticence by the Supreme Court's granting it *carte blanche* to expand its legislative authority well beyond that which was "necessary and proper" to that which was merely "convenient" or "appropriate."

Resolution:
"Neither the Supreme Court nor any inferior federal court ordained or established by Congress under Article III of the U.S. Constitution shall have jurisdiction to hear matters involving the necessary and proper clause, i.e., Article I, § 8, clause 18, unless said clause be applied as originally intended, i.e., an implied power conferred on the Congress, without which the express powers conferred upon it, through Article I, § 8, clauses 1-17, be nugatory, i.e., inoperative. *McCulloch v .Maryland*, and its progeny are hereby reversed and vacated.

In Chapter 3, the *exclusive* method by which the Constitution was to be amended was indicated. This "proper" method has been utilized on 27 occasions. The "inappropriate" method, i.e., by the Supreme Court's rewriting the Constitution, has been utilized a total of 383 times. Between 1789 and 2002, 159 federal laws and 224 state ordinances and constitutional provisions have been declared unconstitutional.

Resolution:
Neither the Supreme Court nor any inferior federal court ordained or established by Congress under Article III of the U.S. Constitution shall have

jurisdiction to amend, rewrite or hold acts of Congress or the states in violation of the Constitution, but be limited to interpretation and application of said laws based on the actual text of said Constitution and consistent therewith. *Marbury v. Madison* and its progeny are hereby reversed and vacated.

In Chapter 4, the Commerce Clause and the Spending Clause and the Court's extreme expansion of Congress's power under these clauses was discussed.

Resolution:

Neither the Supreme Court nor any inferior federal court ordained or established by Congress under Article III of the U.S. Constitution shall have jurisdiction to hear matters involving that portion of the Commerce Clause, i.e., commerce between the states, in any matter, unless said matter involves a *bona fide* dispute or disputes between two or more states.

Neither the Supreme Court nor any inferior federal court ordained or established by Congress under Article III of the U.S. Constitution shall have jurisdiction to hear matters involving the Spending Clause in matters not within the express, limited powers conferred upon the federal government through Article I, § 8, clauses 1-18.

In Chapter 5, the Doctrine of Incorporation was shown to be a vehicle by which the Supreme Court could exert its authority beyond that of controlling Congress, and by such Court-concocted doctrine, control the states as well.

Resolution:

Article III method:

Neither the Supreme Court nor any inferior federal court ordained or established by Congress under Article III of the U.S. Constitution shall have jurisdiction to hear matters involving the 14th Amendment, Due Process clause to apply the Bill of Rights, defined as the first eight amendments to the U.S. Constitution, to the States. Said Bill of Rights, as originally intended, will henceforth apply to the federal government only.

14th Amendment, § 5 method:

Additional authority for applying such limitation to the Supreme Court exists in the 14th Amendment, § 5, which states:

"The Congress shall have power to enforce, by appropriate legislation, the provisions of this article."

Congress can legislate to the effect that the Due Process clause of the 14th Amendment shall henceforth apply the Bill of Rights to the federal government only, and *not* to the states.

In Chapter 6, the Equal Protection clause was likewise revealed as a further source of fictitious power *of* the government, *by* the government, and *for* the government.

Resolution: Article III method:

Neither the Supreme Court nor any inferior federal court ordained or established by Congress under Article III of the U.S. Constitution shall have jurisdiction to hear matters involving the 14th Amendment, Equal Protection Clause, unless one party to the matter be a slave or former slave.

14th Amendment, § 5 method:

Additional authority for applying such limitation to the Supreme Court exists in the 14th Amendment, § 5, which states:

"The Congress shall have power to enforce, by appropriate legislation, the provisions of this article."

Congress can pass legislation that states, in effect, that the 14th Amendment, Equal Protection clause shall apply as originally intended, i.e., to matters wherein at least one party is a slave or former slave.

In Chapter 7, citizenship and the problem of "anchor babies" was discussed.

Resolution:

Neither the Supreme Court nor any inferior federal court ordained or established by Congress under Article III of the U.S. Constitution shall have jurisdiction to hear matters involving U.S. citizenship by birth, unless both parents of party seeking citizenship based on birth, shall have been citizens of the United States at the time of said party's birth.

Further authority for this law is the 14th Amendment, § 5, which states:

"The Congress shall have power to enforce, by appropriate legislation, the provisions of this article." Pursuant to such power, Congress has enacted the following:

HR1868, The Birthright Citizenship Act of 2009 - Amends the Immigration and Nationality Act to consider a person born in the United States "subject to the jurisdiction" of the United States for citizenship at birth purposes if the person is born in the United States of parents, one of whom is:

1) A U.S. citizen or national:

2) a lawful permanent resident alien whose residence is in the United States: or

3) an alien performing active service in the U.S. Armed Forces.

This Work proposes that the Immigration and Nationality Act be further amended to assert that for citizenship based on birth purposes, where the child is born in the United states, both parents must be citizens of the United States at the time of the child's birth...period.

This would solve the problem presented by the so-called "anchor babies" becoming citizens by virtue of their having been born in this country of parents, neither one of whom was a citizen of this country, at the time of the child's birth.

EPILOGUE

Of course all of the above "solutions" require Congress to finally act against the Supreme Court and other federal courts to utilize the power given it through the Constitution and to thereby rein-in the federal courts and force them to apply the Constitution as originally intended and to abolish their judicial activism. *This can be done, but the People must act and demand that this be done.*

By adopting the proposed resolutions outlined herein, power is shifted back to Congress and to the states as originally intended and expressly stated in the 10th Amendment.

The 10th Amendment will at last assume its rightful position as limiting the powers of the federal government and shifting all powers, not expressly granted *to* the federal government, back *to* the states and their People, respectively. Power is also shifted *from* the federal courts back *to* Congress. *This gives Congress the power as originally intended, subject to accountability to the People.*

This requires the People to be ever-vigilant as counseled by George Washington . . . perhaps it's time we took his advice.

If the Congress fails to do that which is demanded of them herein, then we simply "throw the bastards out"... again. The People *will* prevail, perhaps without an armed revolution...

These methods, at first blush, may appear undesirable as they shift power *from* the Supreme Court *to* Congress. However, this is acceptable as it thereby shifts power *from* the Court, which is *not* accountable to the People, *to* the Congress which *is* accountable to the people.

If this be done, the Constitution will have been restored to its rightful glory and the people will again resume control of ... "a government *of* the people, *by* the people and *for* the people"... assuring that We The People ... "shall not perish from this earth."

After all, America is unique. We have had in our midst one Thomas Jefferson and his most-relevant, profound, earth-shaking words as expressed in our Declaration of Independence, to wit:

"We hold these truths to be self-evident, that all men are created equal; that they are endowed by their creator with certain unalienable rights; that among these, are life, liberty, and the pursuant of happiness.

"That, to secure these rights, governments are instituted among men, deriving their just powers from the consent of the governed; that, whenever any form of government becomes destructive of these ends, it is the right of the people to alter or to abolish it, and to institute a new government, laying its foundations on such principles, and organizing its powers in such form, as to them shall seem most likely to effect their safety and happiness ..."

175.

176.

PREAMBLE

We the people of the United States, in order to form a more perfect union, establish justice, insure domestic tranquility, provide for the common defense, promote the general welfare, and secure the blessings of liberty to ourselves and our posterity, do ordain and establish this Constitution for the United States of America.

Article I. The Legislative Branch

Section 1 - The Legislature

All legislative Powers herein granted shall be vested in a Congress of the United States, which shall consist of a Senate and House of Representatives.

Section 2 - The House

The House of Representatives shall be composed of Members chosen every second Year by the People of the several States, and the Electors in each State shall have the Qualifications requisite for Electors of the most numerous Branch of the State Legislature.

No Person shall be a Representative who shall not have attained to the Age of twenty five Years, and been seven Years a Citizen of the United States, and who shall not, when elected, be an Inhabitant of that State in which he shall be chosen.

(Representatives and direct Taxes shall be apportioned among the several States which may be included within this Union, according to their respective Numbers, which shall be determined by adding to the whole Number of free Persons, including those bound to Service for a Term of Years, and excluding Indians not taxed, three fifths of all other Persons.) (The previous sentence in parentheses was superseded by Amendment XIV, section 2.) The actual Enumeration shall be made within three Years after the first Meeting of the Congress of the United States, and within every subsequent Term of ten Years, in such Manner as they shall by Law direct. The Number of Representatives shall not exceed one for every thirty Thousand, but each State shall have at Least one Representative; and until such enumeration shall be made, the State of New Hampshire shall be entitled to chuse three, Massachusetts eight, Rhode Island and Providence Plantations one, Connecticut five, New York six, New Jersey four, Pennsylvania eight, Delaware one, Maryland six, Virginia ten, North Carolina five, South Carolina five and Georgia three.

When vacancies happen in the Representation of any State, the Executive Authority thereof shall issue Writs of Election to fill such vacancies.
The House of Representatives shall chuse their Speaker and other Officers; and shall have the sole Power of Impeachment.

Section 3 - The Senate

The Senate of the United States shall be composed of two Senators from each State, (chosen by the Legislature thereof,) (The preceding words in parentheses superseded by Amendment XVII, section 1.) for six Years; and each Senator shall have one Vote.

Immediately after they shall be assembled in Consequence of the first Election, they shall be divided as equally as may be into three Classes. The Seats of the Senators of the first Class shall be vacated at the Expiration of the second Year, of the second Class at the Expiration of the fourth Year, and of the third Class at the Expiration of the sixth Year, so that one third may be chosen every second Year; (and if Vacancies happen by Resignation, or otherwise, during the Recess of the Legislature of any State, the Executive thereof may make temporary Appointments until the next Meeting of the Legislature, which shall then fill such Vacancies.)
(The preceding words in parentheses were superseded by Amendment XVII, section 2.)

No person shall be a Senator who shall not have attained to the Age of thirty Years, and been nine Years a Citizen of the United States, and who shall not, when elected, be an Inhabitant of that State for which he shall be chosen.

The Vice President of the United States shall be President of the Senate, but shall have no Vote, unless they be equally divided.

The Senate shall chuse their other Officers, and also a President pro tempore, in the absence of the Vice President, or when he shall exercise the Office of President of the United States.

The Senate shall have the sole Power to try all Impeachments. When sitting for that Purpose, they shall be on Oath or Affirmation. When the President of the United States is tried, the Chief Justice shall preside: And no Person shall be convicted without the Concurrence of two thirds of the Members present.

Judgment in Cases of Impeachment shall not extend further than to removal from Office, and disqualification to hold and enjoy any Office of honor, Trust or Profit under the United States: but the Party convicted shall nevertheless be liable and subject to Indictment, Trial, Judgment and Punishment, according to Law.

Section 4 - The Times, Places and Manner of holding Elections for Senators and Representatives, shall be prescribed in each State by the Legislature thereof; but the Congress may at any time by Law make or alter such Regulations, except as to the Place of Chusing Senators.

The Congress shall assemble at least once in every Year, and such Meeting shall (be on the first Monday in December,) (The preceding words in parentheses were superseded by Amendment XX, section 2.) unless they shall by Law appoint a different Day.

Section 5 - Membership, Rules, Journals, Adjournment

Each House shall be the Judge of the Elections, Returns and Qualifications of its own Members, and a Majority of each shall constitute a Quorum to do Business; but a smaller number may adjourn from day to day, and may be authorized to compel the Attendance of absent Members, in such Manner, and under such Penalties as each House may provide.

Each House may determine the Rules of its Proceedings, punish its Members for disorderly Behavior, and, with the Concurrence of two-thirds, expel a Member.

Each House shall keep a Journal of its Proceedings, and from time to time publish the same, excepting such Parts as may in their Judgment require Secrecy; and the Yeas and Nays of the Members of either House on any question shall, at the Desire of one fifth of those Present, be entered on the Journal.

Neither House, during the Session of Congress, shall, without the Consent of the other, adjourn for more than three days, nor to any other Place than that in which the two Houses shall be sitting.

Section 6 - Compensation

(The Senators and Representatives shall receive a Compensation for their Services, to be ascertained by Law, and paid out of the Treasury of the United States.) (The preceding words in parentheses were modified by Amendment XXVII.) They shall in all Cases, except Treason, Felony and Breach of the Peace, be privileged from Arrest during their Attendance at the Session of their respective Houses, and in going to and returning from the same; and for any Speech or Debate in either House, they shall not be questioned in any other Place.

No Senator or Representative shall, during the Time for which he was elected, be appointed to any civil Office under the Authority of the United States which shall have been created, or the Emoluments whereof shall have been increased during such time; and no Person holding any Office under the United States, shall be a Member of either House during his Continuance in Office.

Section 7 - Revenue Bills, Legislative Process, Presidential Veto

All bills for raising Revenue shall originate in the House of Representatives; but the Senate may propose or concur with Amendments as on other Bills.

Every Bill which shall have passed the House of Representatives and the Senate, shall, before it become a Law, be presented to the President of the United States; If he approve he shall sign it, but if not he shall return it, with his Objections to that House in which it shall have originated, who shall enter the Objections at large on their Journal, and proceed to reconsider it. If after such Reconsideration two thirds of that House shall agree to pass the Bill, it shall be sent, together with the Objections, to the other House, by which it shall likewise be reconsidered, and if approved by two thirds of that House, it shall become a Law. But in all such Cases the Votes of both Houses shall be determined by Yeas and Nays, and the Names of the Persons voting for and against the Bill shall be entered on the Journal of each House respectively. If any Bill shall not be returned by the President within ten Days (Sundays excepted) after it shall have been presented to him, the Same shall be a Law, in like Manner as if he had signed it, unless the Congress by their Adjournment prevent its Return, in which Case it shall not be a Law.

Every Order, Resolution, or Vote to which the Concurrence of the Senate and House of Representatives may be necessary (except on a question of Adjournment) shall be presented to the President of the United States; and before the Same shall take Effect, shall be approved by him, or being disapproved by him, shall be repassed by two thirds of the Senate and House of Representatives, according to the Rules and Limitations prescribed in the Case of a Bill.

Section 8 - Powers of Congress

The Congress shall have Power To lay and collect Taxes, Duties, Imposts and Excises, to pay the Debts and provide for the common Defence and general Welfare of the United States; but all Duties, Imposts and Excises shall be uniform throughout the United States;

To borrow money on the credit of the United States;

To regulate Commerce with foreign Nations, and among the several States, and with the Indian Tribes;

To establish an uniform Rule of Naturalization, and uniform Laws on the subject of Bankruptcies throughout the United States;

A-4

To coin Money, regulate the Value thereof, and of foreign Coin, and fix the Standard of Weights and Measures;

To provide for the Punishment of counterfeiting the Securities and current Coin of the United States;

To establish Post Offices and Post Roads;

To promote the Progress of Science and useful Arts, by securing for limited Times to Authors and Inventors the exclusive Right to their respective Writings and Discoveries;

To constitute Tribunals inferior to the supreme Court;

To define and punish Piracies and Felonies committed on the high Seas, and Offenses against the Law of Nations;

To declare War, grant Letters of Marque and Reprisal, and make Rules concerning Captures on Land and Water;

To raise and support Armies, but no Appropriation of Money to that Use shall be for a longer Term than two Years;

To provide and maintain a Navy;

To make Rules for the Government and Regulation of the land and naval Forces;

To provide for calling forth the Militia to execute the Laws of the Union, suppress Insurrections and repel Invasions;

To provide for organizing, arming, and disciplining the Militia, and for governing such Part of them as may be employed in the Service of the United States, reserving to the States respectively, the Appointment of the Officers, and the Authority of training the Militia according to the discipline prescribed by Congress;

To exercise exclusive Legislation in all Cases whatsoever, over such District (not exceeding ten Miles square) as may, by Cession of particular States, and the acceptance of Congress, become the Seat of the Government of the United States, and to exercise like Authority over all Places purchased by the Consent of the Legislature of the State in which the Same shall be, for the Erection of Forts, Magazines, Arsenals, dock-Yards, and other needful Buildings; And

To make all Laws which shall be necessary and proper for carrying into Execution the foregoing Powers, and all other Powers vested by this Constitution in the Government of the United States, or in any Department or Officer thereof.

Section 9 - Limits on Congress

The Migration or Importation of such Persons as any of the States now existing shall think proper to admit, shall not be prohibited by the Congress prior to the Year one thousand eight hundred and eight, but a tax or duty may be imposed on such Importation, not exceeding ten dollars for each Person.

The privilege of the Writ of Habeas Corpus shall not be suspended, unless when in Cases of Rebellion or Invasion the public Safety may require it.

No Bill of Attainder or ex post facto Law shall be passed.

(No capitation, or other direct, Tax shall be laid, unless in Proportion to the Census or Enumeration herein before directed to be taken.) (Section in parentheses modified by Amendment XVI.)

No Tax or Duty shall be laid on Articles exported from any State.

No Preference shall be given by any Regulation of Commerce or Revenue to the Ports of one State over those of another: nor shall Vessels bound to, or from, one State, be obliged to enter, clear, or pay Duties in another.

No Money shall be drawn from the Treasury, but in Consequence of Appropriations made by Law; and a regular Statement and Account of the Receipts and Expenditures of all public Money shall be published from time to time.

No Title of Nobility shall be granted by the United States: And no Person holding any Office of Profit or Trust under them, shall, without the Consent of the Congress, accept of any present, Emolument, Office, or Title, of any kind whatever, from any King, Prince or foreign State.

Section 10 - Powers prohibited of States

No State shall enter into any Treaty, Alliance, or Confederation; grant Letters of Marque and Reprisal; coin Money; emit Bills of Credit; make any Thing but gold and silver Coin a Tender in Payment of Debts; pass any Bill of Attainder, ex post facto Law, or Law impairing the Obligation of Contracts, or grant any Title of Nobility.

No State shall, without the Consent of the Congress, lay any Imposts or Duties on Imports or Exports, except what may be absolutely necessary for executing it's inspection Laws: and the net Produce of all Duties and Imposts, laid by any State on Imports or Exports, shall be for the Use of the Treasury of the United States; and all such Laws shall be subject to the Revision and Controul of the Congress.

No State shall, without the Consent of Congress, lay any duty of Tonnage, keep Troops, or Ships of War in time of Peace, enter into any Agreement or Compact with another State, or with a foreign Power, or engage in War, unless actually invaded, or in such imminent Danger as will not admit of delay.

Article II. - The Executive Branch

Section 1 - The President

The executive Power shall be vested in a President of the United States of America. He shall hold his Office during the Term of four Years, and, together with the Vice-President chosen for the same Term, be elected, as follows:

Each State shall appoint, in such Manner as the Legislature thereof may direct, a Number of Electors, equal to the whole Number of Senators and Representatives to which the State may be entitled in the Congress: but no Senator or Representative, or Person holding an Office of Trust or Profit under the United States, shall be appointed an Elector.

(The Electors shall meet in their respective States, and vote by Ballot for two persons, of whom one at least shall not lie an Inhabitant of the same State with themselves. And they shall make a List of all the Persons voted for, and of the Number of Votes for each; which List they shall sign and certify, and transmit sealed to the Seat of the Government of the United States, directed to the President of the Senate. The President of the Senate shall, in the Presence of the Senate and House of Representatives, open all the Certificates, and the Votes shall then be counted. The Person having the greatest Number of Votes shall be the President, if such Number be a Majority of the whole Number of Electors appointed; and if there be more than one who have such Majority, and have an equal Number of Votes, then the House of Representatives shall immediately chuse by Ballot one of them for President; and if no Person have a Majority, then from the five highest on the List the said House shall in like Manner chuse the President. But in chusing the President, the Votes shall be taken by States, the Representation from each State having one Vote; a quorum for this Purpose shall consist of a Member or Members from two-thirds of the States, and a Majority of all the States shall be necessary to a Choice. In every Case, after the Choice of the President, the Person having the greatest Number of Votes of the Electors shall be the Vice President. But if there should remain two or more who have equal Votes, the Senate shall chuse from them by Ballot the Vice-President.) (This clause in parentheses was superseded by Amendment XII.)

The Congress may determine the Time of chusing the Electors, and the Day on which they shall give their Votes; which Day shall be the same throughout the United States.

No person except a natural born Citizen, or a Citizen of the United States, at the time of the Adoption of this Constitution, shall be eligible to the Office of

President; neither shall any Person be eligible to that Office who shall not have attained to the Age of thirty-five Years, and been fourteen Years a Resident within the United States.

(In Case of the Removal of the President from Office, or of his Death, Resignation, or Inability to discharge the Powers and Duties of the said Office, the same shall devolve on the Vice President, and the Congress may by Law provide for the Case of Removal, Death, Resignation or Inability, both of the President and Vice President, declaring what Officer shall then act as President, and such Officer shall act accordingly, until the Disability be removed, or a President shall be elected.) (This clause in parentheses has been modified by Amendments XX and XXV.)

The President shall, at stated Times, receive for his Services, a Compensation, which shall neither be increased nor diminished during the Period for which he shall have been elected, and he shall not receive within that Period any other Emolument from the United States, or any of them.

Before he enter on the Execution of his Office, he shall take the following Oath or Affirmation:

"I do solemnly swear (or affirm) that I will faithfully execute the Office of President of the United States, and will to the best of my Ability, preserve, protect and defend the Constitution of the United States."

Section 2 - Civilian Power over Military, Cabinet, Pardon Power, Appointments

The President shall be Commander in Chief of the Army and Navy of the United States, and of the Militia of the several States, when called into the actual Service of the United States; he may require the Opinion, in writing, of the principal Officer in each of the executive Departments, upon any subject relating to the Duties of their respective Offices, and he shall have Power to Grant Reprieves and Pardons for Offenses against the United States, except in Cases of Impeachment.

He shall have Power, by and with the Advice and Consent of the Senate, to make Treaties, provided two thirds of the Senators present concur; and he shall nominate, and by and with the Advice and Consent of the Senate, shall appoint Ambassadors, other public Ministers and Consuls, Judges of the supreme Court, and all other Officers of the United States, whose Appointments are not herein otherwise provided for, and which shall be established by Law: but the Congress may by Law vest the Appointment of such inferior Officers, as they think proper, in the President alone, in the Courts of Law, or in the Heads of Departments.

The President shall have Power to fill up all Vacancies that may happen during the Recess of the Senate, by granting Commissions which shall expire at the End of their next Session.

Section 3 - State of the Union, Convening Congress

He shall from time to time give to the Congress Information of the State of the Union, and recommend to their Consideration such Measures as he shall judge necessary and expedient; he may, on extraordinary Occasions, convene both Houses, or either of them, and in Case of Disagreement between them, with Respect to the Time of Adjournment, he may adjourn them to such Time as he shall think proper; he shall receive Ambassadors and other public Ministers; he shall take Care that the Laws be faithfully executed, and shall Commission all the Officers of the United States.

Section 4 - Disqualification

The President, Vice President and all civil Officers of the United States, shall be removed from Office on Impeachment for, and Conviction of, Treason, Bribery, or other high Crimes and Misdemeanors.

Article III. - The Judicial Branch

Section 1 - Judicial powers

The judicial Power of the United States, shall be vested in one supreme Court, and in such inferior Courts as the Congress may from time to time ordain and establish. The Judges, both of the supreme and inferior Courts, shall hold their Offices during good Behavior, and shall, at stated Times, receive for their Services a Compensation which shall not be diminished during their Continuance in Office.

Section 2 - Trial by Jury, Original Jurisdiction, Jury Trials

(The judicial Power shall extend to all Cases, in Law and Equity, arising under this Constitution, the Laws of the United States, and Treaties made, or which shall be made, under their Authority; to all Cases affecting Ambassadors, other public Ministers and Consuls; to all Cases of admiralty and maritime Jurisdiction; to Controversies to which the United States shall be a Party; to Controversies between two or more States; between a State and Citizens of another State; between Citizens of different States; between Citizens of the same State claiming Lands under Grants of different States, and between a State, or the Citizens thereof, and foreign States, Citizens or Subjects.) (This section in parentheses is modified by Amendment XI.)

In all Cases affecting Ambassadors, other public Ministers and Consuls, and those in which a State shall be Party, the supreme Court shall have original Jurisdiction. In all the other Cases before mentioned, the supreme Court shall have appellate Jurisdiction, both as to Law and Fact, with such Exceptions, and under such Regulations as the Congress shall make.

The Trial of all Crimes, except in Cases of Impeachment, shall be by Jury; and such Trial shall be held in the State where the said Crimes shall have been committed; but when not committed within any State, the Trial shall be at such Place or Places as the Congress may by Law have directed.

Section 3 - Treason

Treason against the United States, shall consist only in levying War against them, or in adhering to their Enemies, giving them Aid and Comfort. No Person shall be convicted of Treason unless on the Testimony of two Witnesses to the same overt Act, or on Confession in open Court.

The Congress shall have power to declare the Punishment of Treason, but no Attainder of Treason shall work Corruption of Blood, or Forfeiture except during the Life of the Person attainted.

Article IV. - The States

Section 1 - Each State to Honor all others

Full Faith and Credit shall be given in each State to the public Acts, Records, and judicial Proceedings of every other State. And the Congress may by general Laws prescribe the Manner in which such Acts, Records and Proceedings shall be proved, and the Effect thereof.

Section 2 - State citizens, Extradition

The Citizens of each State shall be entitled to all Privileges and Immunities of Citizens in the several States.

A Person charged in any State with Treason, Felony, or other Crime, who shall flee from Justice, and be found in another State, shall on demand of the executive Authority of the State from which he fled, be delivered up, to be removed to the State having Jurisdiction of the Crime.

(No Person held to Service or Labour in one State, under the Laws thereof, escaping into another, shall, in Consequence of any Law or Regulation therein, be discharged from such Service or Labour, But shall be delivered up on Claim of the Party to whom such Service or Labour may be due.) (This clause in parentheses is superseded by Amendment XIII.)

Section 3 - New States

New States may be admitted by the Congress into this Union; but no new States shall be formed or erected within the Jurisdiction of any other State; nor any State be formed by the Junction of two or more States, or parts of States, without the Consent of the Legislatures of the States concerned as well as of the Congress.

The Congress shall have Power to dispose of and make all needful Rules and Regulations respecting the Territory or other Property belonging to the United States; and nothing in this Constitution shall be so construed as to Prejudice any Claims of the United States, or of any particular State.

Section 4 - Republican government

The United States shall guarantee to every State in this Union a Republican Form of Government, and shall protect each of them against Invasion; and on Application of the Legislature, or of the Executive (when the Legislature cannot be convened) against domestic Violence.

Article V. - Amendments

The Congress, whenever two thirds of both Houses shall deem it necessary, shall propose Amendments to this Constitution, or, on the Application of the Legislatures of two thirds of the several States, shall call a Convention for proposing Amendments, which, in either Case, shall be valid to all Intents and Purposes, as part of this Constitution, when ratified by the Legislatures of three fourths of the several States, or by Conventions in three fourths thereof, as the one or the other Mode of Ratification may be proposed by the Congress; Provided that no Amendment which may be made prior to the Year One thousand eight hundred and eight shall in any Manner affect the first and fourth Clauses in the Ninth Section of the first Article; and that no State, without its Consent, shall be deprived of its equal Suffrage in the Senate.

Article VI. - The United States

All Debts contracted and Engagements entered into, before the Adoption of this Constitution, shall be as valid against the United States under this Constitution, as under the Confederation.

This Constitution, and the Laws of the United States which shall be made in Pursuance thereof; and all Treaties made, or which shall be made, under the Authority of the United States, shall be the supreme Law of the Land; and the Judges in every State shall be bound thereby, any Thing in the Constitution or Laws of any State to the Contrary notwithstanding.

The Senators and Representatives before mentioned, and the Members of the several State Legislatures, and all executive and judicial Officers, both of the United States and of the several States, shall be bound by Oath or Affirmation, to support this Constitution; but no religious Test shall ever be required as a Qualification to any Office or public Trust under the United States.

Article VII. - Ratification Documents

The Ratification of the Conventions of nine States, shall be sufficient for the Establishment of this Constitution between the States so ratifying the Same.

Done in Convention by the Unanimous Consent of the States present the Seventeenth Day of September in the Year of our Lord one thousand seven hundred and Eighty seven and of the Independence of the United States of America the Twelfth. In Witness whereof We have hereunto subscribed our Names.

Go Washington - President and deputy from Virginia

New Hampshire - John Langdon, Nicholas Gilman

Massachusetts - Nathaniel Gorham, Rufus King

Connecticut - Wm Saml Johnson, Roger Sherman

New York - Alexander Hamilton

New Jersey - Wil Livingston, David Brearley, Wm Paterson, Jona. Dayton

Pensylvania - B Franklin, Thomas Mifflin, Robt Morris, Geo. Clymer, Thos FitzSimons, Jared Ingersoll, James Wilson, Gouv Morris

Delaware - Geo. Read, Gunning Bedford jun, John Dickinson, Richard Bassett, Jaco. Broom

Maryland - James McHenry, Dan of St Tho Jenifer, Danl Carroll

Virginia - John Blair, James Madison Jr.

North Carolina - Wm Blount, Richd Dobbs Spaight, Hu Williamson

South Carolina - J. Rutledge, Charles Cotesworth Pinckney, Charles Pinckney, Pierce Butler

Georgia - William Few, Abr Baldwin

Attest: William Jackson, Secretary

The Amendments

The following are the Amendments to the Constitution. The first eight, often ten, Amendments, are commonly known as the Bill of Rights.

Amendment I - Freedom of Religion, Press, Expression. Ratified 12/15/1791.

Congress shall make no law respecting an establishment of religion, or prohibiting the free exercise thereof; or abridging the freedom of speech, or of the press; or the right of the people peaceably to assemble, and to petition the Government for a redress of grievances.

Amendment II - Right to bear arms. Ratified 12/15/1791.

A well regulated Militia, being necessary to the security of a free State, the right of the people to keep and bear Arms, shall not be infringed.

Amendment III - Quartering of soldiers. Ratified 12/15/1791.

No Soldier shall, in time of peace be quartered in any house, without the consent of the Owner, nor in time of war, but in a manner to be prescribed by law.

Amendment IV - Search and seizure. Ratified 12/15/1791.

The right of the people to be secure in their persons, houses, papers, and effects, against unreasonable searches and seizures, shall not be violated, and no Warrants shall issue, but upon probable cause, supported by Oath or affirmation, and particularly describing the place to be searched, and the persons or things to be seized.

Amendment V - Trial and Punishment, Compensation for Takings. Ratified 12/15/1791.

No person shall be held to answer for a capital, or otherwise infamous crime, unless on a presentment or indictment of a Grand Jury, except in cases arising in the land or naval forces, or in the Militia, when in actual service in time of War or public danger; nor shall any person be subject for the same offense to be twice put in jeopardy of life or limb; nor shall be compelled in any criminal case to be a witness against himself, nor be deprived of life, liberty, or property, without due process of law; nor shall private property be taken for public use, without just compensation.

Amendment VI - Right to speedy trial, confrontation of witnesses. Ratified 12/15/1791.
In all criminal prosecutions, the accused shall enjoy the right to a speedy and public trial, by an impartial jury of the State and district wherein the crime shall have been committed, which district shall have been previously ascertained by

law, and to be informed of the nature and cause of the accusation; to be confronted with the witnesses against him; to have compulsory process for obtaining witnesses in his favor, and to have the Assistance of Counsel for his defence.

Amendment VII - Trial by jury in civil cases. Ratified 12/15/1791.

In Suits at common law, where the value in controversy shall exceed twenty dollars, the right of trial by jury shall be preserved, and no fact tried by a jury, shall be otherwise re-examined in any Court of the United States, than according to the rules of the common law.

Amendment VIII - Cruel and Unusual punishment. Ratified 12/15/1791.

Excessive bail shall not be required, nor excessive fines imposed, nor cruel and unusual punishments inflicted.

Amendment IX - Construction of Constitution. Ratified 12/15/1791.

The enumeration in the Constitution, of certain rights, shall not be construed to deny or disparage others retained by the people.

Amendment X - Powers of the States and People. Ratified 12/15/1791.

The powers not delegated to the United States by the Constitution, nor prohibited by it to the States, are reserved to the States respectively, or to the people.

Amendment XI - Judicial Limits. Ratified 2/7/1795.

The Judicial power of the United States shall not be construed to extend to any suit in law or equity, commenced or prosecuted against one of the United States by Citizens of another State, or by Citizens or Subjects of any Foreign State.

Amendment XII - Choosing the President, Vice- President. Ratified 6/15/1804. The Electoral College

The Electors shall meet in their respective states, and vote by ballot for President and Vice-President, one of whom, at least, shall not be an inhabitant of the same state with themselves; they shall name in their ballots the person voted for as President, and in distinct ballots the person voted for as Vice-President, and they shall make distinct lists of all persons voted for as President, and of all persons voted for as Vice-President and of the number of votes for each, which lists they shall sign and certify, and transmit sealed to the seat of the government of the United States, directed to the President of the Senate;

The President of the Senate shall, in the presence of the Senate and House of Representatives, open all the certificates and the votes shall then be counted;

The person having the greatest Number of votes for President, shall be the President, if such number be a majority of the whole number of Electors appointed; and if no person have such majority, then from the persons having the highest numbers not exceeding three on the list of those voted for as President, the House of Representatives shall choose immediately, by ballot, the President. But in choosing the President, the votes shall be taken by states, the representation from each state having one vote; a quorum for this purpose shall consist of a member or members from two-thirds of the states, and a majority of all the states shall be necessary to a choice. And if the House of Representatives shall not choose a President whenever the right of choice shall devolve upon them, before the fourth day of March next following, then the Vice-President shall act as President, as in the case of the death or other constitutional disability of the President.

The person having the greatest number of votes as Vice-President, shall be the Vice-President, if such number be a majority of the whole number of Electors appointed, and if no person have a majority, then from the two highest numbers on the list, the Senate shall choose the Vice-President; a quorum for the purpose shall consist of two-thirds of the whole number of Senators, and a majority of the whole number shall be necessary to a choice. But no person constitutionally ineligible to the office of President shall be eligible to that of Vice-President of the United States.

Amendment XIII - Slavery Abolished. Ratified 12/6/1865.

1. Neither slavery nor involuntary servitude, except as a punishment for crime whereof the party shall have been duly convicted, shall exist within the United States, or any place subject to their jurisdiction.

2. Congress shall have power to enforce this article by appropriate legislation.

Amendment XIV - Citizenship rights. Ratified 7/9/1868.

1. All persons born or naturalized in the United States, and subject to the jurisdiction thereof, are citizens of the United States and of the State wherein they reside. No State shall make or enforce any law which shall abridge the privileges or immunities of citizens of the United States; nor shall any State deprive any person of life, liberty, or property, without due process of law; nor deny to any person within its jurisdiction the equal protection of the laws.

2. Representatives shall be apportioned among the several States according to their respective numbers, counting the whole number of persons in each State, excluding Indians not taxed. But when the right to vote at any election for the choice of electors for President and Vice-President of the United States,

Representatives in Congress, the Executive and Judicial officers of a State, or the members of the Legislature thereof, is denied to any of the male inhabitants of such State, being twenty-one years of age, and citizens of the United States, or in any way abridged, except for participation in rebellion, or other crime, the basis of representation therein shall be reduced in the proportion which the number of such male citizens shall bear to the whole number of male citizens twenty-one years of age in such State.

3. No person shall be a Senator or Representative in Congress, or elector of President and Vice-President, or hold any office, civil or military, under the United States, or under any State, who, having previously taken an oath, as a member of Congress, or as an officer of the United States, or as a member of any State legislature, or as an executive or judicial officer of any State, to support the Constitution of the United States, shall have engaged in insurrection or rebellion against the same, or given aid or comfort to the enemies thereof. But Congress may by a vote of two-thirds of each House, remove such disability.

4. The validity of the public debt of the United States, authorized by law, including debts incurred for payment of pensions and bounties for services in suppressing insurrection or rebellion, shall not be questioned. But neither the United States nor any State shall assume or pay any debt or obligation incurred in aid of insurrection or rebellion against the United States, or any claim for the loss or emancipation of any slave; but all such debts, obligations and claims shall be held illegal and void.

5. The Congress shall have power to enforce, by appropriate legislation, the provisions of this article.

Amendment XV - Race no bar to vote. Ratified 2/3/1870.

1. The right of citizens of the United States to vote shall not be denied or abridged by the United States or by any State on account of race, color, or previous condition of servitude.

2. The Congress shall have power to enforce this article by appropriate legislation.

Amendment XVI - Income taxes authorized. Ratified 2/3/1913.
The Congress shall have power to lay and collect taxes on incomes, from whatever source derived, without apportionment among the several States, and without regard to any census or enumeration.

Amendment XVII - Senators elected by popular vote. Ratified 4/8/1913. History

The Senate of the United States shall be composed of two Senators from each State, elected by the people thereof, for six years; and each Senator shall have one vote. The electors in each State shall have the qualifications requisite for electors of the most numerous branch of the State legislatures.

When vacancies happen in the representation of any State in the Senate, the executive authority of such State shall issue writs of election to fill such vacancies: Provided, That the legislature of any State may empower the executive thereof to make temporary appointments until the people fill the vacancies by election as the legislature may direct.

This amendment shall not be so construed as to affect the election or term of any Senator chosen before it becomes valid as part of the Constitution.

Amendment XVIII - Liquor abolished. Ratified 1/16/1919. Repealed by Amendment XXI, 12/5/1933.

1. After one year from the ratification of this article the manufacture, sale, or transportation of intoxicating liquors within, the importation thereof into, or the exportation thereof from the United States and all territory subject to the jurisdiction thereof for beverage purposes is hereby prohibited.

2. The Congress and the several States shall have concurrent power to enforce this article by appropriate legislation.

3. This article shall be inoperative unless it shall have been ratified as an amendment to the Constitution by the legislatures of the several States, as provided in the Constitution, within seven years from the date of the submission hereof to the States by the Congress.

Amendment XIX - Women's suffrage. Ratified 8/18/1920.

The right of citizens of the United States to vote shall not be denied or abridged by the United States or by any State on account of sex.

Congress shall have power to enforce this article by appropriate legislation.

Amendment XX - Presidential, Congressional terms. Ratified 1/23/1933.

1. The terms of the President and Vice President shall end at noon on the 20th day of January, and the terms of Senators and Representatives at noon on the 3d day of January, of the years in which such terms would have ended if this article had not been ratified; and the terms of their successors shall then begin.

2. The Congress shall assemble at least once in every year, and such meeting shall begin at noon on the 3d day of January, unless they shall by law appoint a different day.

3. If, at the time fixed for the beginning of the term of the President, the President elect shall have died, the Vice President elect shall become President.

If a President shall not have been chosen before the time fixed for the beginning of his term, or if the President elect shall have failed to qualify, then the Vice President elect shall act as President until a President shall have qualified; and the Congress may by law provide for the case wherein neither a President elect nor a Vice President elect shall have qualified, declaring who shall then act as President, or the manner in which one who is to act shall be selected, and such person shall act accordingly until a President or Vice President shall have qualified.

4. The Congress may by law provide for the case of the death of any of the persons from whom the House of Representatives may choose a President whenever the right of choice shall have devolved upon them, and for the case of the death of any of the persons from whom the Senate may choose a Vice President whenever the right of choice shall have devolved upon them.

5. Sections 1 and 2 shall take effect on the 15th day of October following the ratification of this article.

6. This article shall be inoperative unless it shall have been ratified as an amendment to the Constitution by the legislatures of three-fourths of the several States within seven years from the date of its submission.

Amendment XXI - Amendment XVIII repealed. Ratified 12/5/1933.

1. The eighteenth article of amendment to the Constitution of the United States is hereby repealed.

2. The transportation or importation into any State, Territory, or possession of the United States for delivery or use therein of intoxicating liquors, in violation of the laws thereof, is hereby prohibited.

3. The article shall be inoperative unless it shall have been ratified as an amendment to the Constitution by conventions in the several States, as provided in the Constitution, within seven years from the date of the submission hereof to the States by the Congress.

Amendment XXII - Presidential term limits. Ratified 2/27/1951.

1. No person shall be elected to the office of the President more than twice, and no person who has held the office of President, or acted as President, for more than two years of a term to which some other person was elected President shall be elected to the office of the President more than once. But this Article shall not apply to any person holding the office of President, when this Article was proposed by the Congress, and shall not prevent any person who may be holding the office of President, or acting as President, during the term within which this

Article becomes operative from holding the office of President or acting as President during the remainder of such term.

2. This article shall be inoperative unless it shall have been ratified as an amendment to the Constitution by the legislatures of three-fourths of the several States within seven years from the date of its submission to the States by the Congress.

Amendment XXIII - Presidential vote for District of Columbia. Ratified 3/29/1961.

1. The District constituting the seat of Government of the United States shall appoint in such manner as the Congress may direct: A number of electors of President and Vice President equal to the whole number of Senators and Representatives in Congress to which the District would be entitled if it were a State, but in no event more than the least populous State; they shall be in addition to those appointed by the States, but they shall be considered, for the purposes of the election of President and Vice President, to be electors appointed by a State; and they shall meet in the District and perform such duties as provided by the twelfth article of amendment.

2. The Congress shall have power to enforce this article by appropriate legislation.

Amendment XXIV - Poll tax barred. Ratified 1/23/1964.

1. The right of citizens of the United States to vote in any primary or other election for President or Vice President, for electors for President or Vice President, or for Senator or Representative in Congress, shall not be denied or abridged by the United States or any State by reason of failure to pay any poll tax or other tax.

2. The Congress shall have power to enforce this article by appropriate legislation.

Amendment XXV - Presidential disability and succession. Ratified 2/10/1967.

1. In case of the removal of the President from office or of his death or resignation, the Vice President shall become President.

2. Whenever there is a vacancy in the office of the Vice President, the President shall nominate a Vice President who shall take office upon confirmation by a majority vote of both Houses of Congress.

3. Whenever the President transmits to the President pro tempore of the Senate and the Speaker of the House of Representatives his written declaration that he is unable to discharge the powers and duties of his office, and until he transmits to

them a written declaration to the contrary, such powers and duties shall be discharged by the Vice President as Acting President.

4. Whenever the Vice President and a majority of either the principal officers of the executive departments or of such other body as Congress may by law provide, transmit to the President pro tempore of the Senate and the Speaker of the House of Representatives their written declaration that the President is unable to discharge the powers and duties of his office, the Vice President shall immediately assume the powers and duties of the office as Acting President.

Thereafter, when the President transmits to the President pro tempore of the Senate and the Speaker of the House of Representatives his written declaration that no inability exists, he shall resume the powers and duties of his office unless the Vice President and a majority of either the principal officers of the executive department or of such other body as Congress may by law provide, transmit within four days to the President pro tempore of the Senate and the Speaker of the House of Representatives their written declaration that the President is unable to discharge the powers and duties of his office. Thereupon Congress shall decide the issue, assembling within forty eight hours for that purpose if not in session. If the Congress, within twenty one days after receipt of the latter written declaration, or, if Congress is not in session, within twenty one days after Congress is required to assemble, determines by two thirds vote of both Houses that the President is unable to discharge the powers and duties of his office, the Vice President shall continue to discharge the same as Acting President; otherwise, the President shall resume the powers and duties of his office.

Amendment XXVI - Voting age set to 18 years. Ratified 7/1/1971.

1. The right of citizens of the United States, who are eighteen years of age or older, to vote shall not be denied or abridged by the United States or by any State on account of age.

2. The Congress shall have power to enforce this article by appropriate legislation.
Amendment XXVII - Congressional pay increases. Ratified 5/7/1992.

No law, varying the compensation for the services of the Senators and Representatives, shall take effect, until an election of Representatives shall have intervened.

INDEX TO CONSTITUTION AND AMENDMENTS

www.ingramcontent.com/pod-product-compliance
Lightning Source LLC
Chambersburg PA
CBHW060018210326
41520CB00009B/925